From the Big Bang to Biology:
where is God?

Graham Swinerd and John Bryant

Copyright © 2020 GG Swinerd and JA Bryant.

All rights reserved.

ISBN: 9798682034901

Published by **Kindle Direct Publishing.**

Cover design by Graham Swinerd.

Attributions for cover: front cover – the original galaxy image (NGC 6814) by ESA/Hubble with acknowledgement to Judy Schmitt (Geckzilla), and the DNA strand courtesy of the National Human Genome Research Institute; back cover image has been released into the public domain by pexels.com.

All quotations from Scripture are taken from THE HOLY BIBLE, NEW INTERNATIONAL VERSION®, NIV® Copyright © 1973, 1978, 1984, 2011 by Biblica, Inc.™ Used by permission. All rights reserved worldwide.

Figures with non-photographic images without a credit have been created by the authors.

The author of the Nitrogen Cycle diagram (Figure 8.1) is Johann Dréo. This image is licensed under the Creative Commons Attribution-Share Alike 3.0 Unported license. No changes have been made to the original image.

Dedication.

To our grandchildren
Fred and Thomas Swinerd,
Joseph and Daniel Bryant,
Finlay and Amélie Bryant.
They are a joy and a blessing.
Theirs is the future.

Contents.

	Foreword.	i
	Preface.	v
1	Where are we Today – and how did we get here?	1
2	The Science Delusion.	13
3	God, the Big Bang and the Universe.	43
4	A Cosmos fine-tuned for Life.	81
5	Life in the Goldilocks Zone.	109
6	What makes us Human?	145
7	The Big Bang, Biology and the Bible.	161
8	In the Balance.	175
9	Epilogue.	205
	Glossary.	223
	Index.	231

Acknowledgements.

Now that this book is finished there are many people we wish to acknowledge, and to whom we wish to say 'thank you', starting with our wives, Marje Bryant and Marion Swinerd. They have been constant in their support and patience throughout the long process.

Graham also wishes to express his gratitude to his now-deceased parents, Fred and Amy, who had to make great sacrifices to allow him to become the first family member to attend university, and to pursue his love of science. His journey of science (and faith) would not have happened without their unconditional love and support.

John is equally grateful for helpful discussions with friends and colleagues in Christians in Science, The Faraday Institute, God and the Big Bang and in the LASAR project.

We are also indebted to the Christian communities at Lee Abbey, Devon and Scargill House, North Yorkshire, not only for inviting us to lead conferences but also for their support and encouragement as we wrote this book of the conference.

Finally, we are very grateful for the thorough 'sub-editing' job performed by Dr Clare Jefferis, that resulted in a significantly enhanced final text, and the technical assistance of Marion Swinerd in producing a print-ready version.

From the Big Bang to Biology – where is God?

Foreword.

The appearance of a new book seeking to draw together understanding and insights from the scientific endeavour with those from the realm of Christian faith may cause some to ask whether this is desirable or wanted. This reaction might come from avowed atheists or those who have simply accepted a conflict between science and faith as an irreconcilable given. However, it may also be felt by those who have already recognised that the disciplines of theology and science are not always to be regarded as rivals engaged in a game in which one wins at the expense of the other.

For the latter group, the fact that so many scientists from across the breadth of scientific disciplines – from molecular biology and genetics to cosmology and particle physics – do not have difficulty in holding these in harmony with their religious conviction is eloquent testimony. That said, within the various streams which recognise and accept the place of the biblical writings and the creedal statements foundational to the Christian faith, it cannot be said there is a uniformity of attitude towards the sciences across them, let alone the individuals within each tributary.

As some readers might be aware, and to which the authors refer themselves, the Belgian astrophysicist, Georges Lemaître, who formulated the Big Bang theory, was also a Priest in the Roman Catholic tradition of Christianity. When asked about possible tensions between being a scientist and a priest, Lemaître famously observed there were two paths to truth and he had chosen both of them.

For the scientist who is also a practising Christian, choosing to walk two paths is not about compartmentalisation but integration, and allowing the insights from one to illuminate the other. The ever-present question for a scientist and Christian – as it will be for those of other religious convictions – will be how their work and its account of reality interplays with the practice and understanding of their faith. Those who find themselves making a genuinely fresh discovery – perhaps seeing something no one has ever found before – will naturally find themselves expressing this in the light of the relationship they have with God. It may be awe, it may be concern, depending on the finding, but the paths to truth will be travelled together and held in a union which may be marked by praise and amazement or invite profound, and perhaps challenging, reflection.

In our churches we do not seem to be at our best in nurturing the vocation to serve and honour God through being a scientist. Those in certain disciplines do feature in our church intercessions but rarely, if ever, astrophysicists and geologists, for example. As my Christian faith was renewed and deepened in my twenties, so was a sense of vocation to serve God and society as a research scientist in the field of immunology, studying for a PhD and later holding a lectureship at a medical and dental school, and engaging in a variety of different research interests and projects.

One of the most memorable moments in relation to this vocation occurred when my wife and I moved house and were seeking to join a local church. Arriving on a Sunday morning at one which had been commended, we found the service was a relatively informal one intended for all ages. The person giving the talk on the bible reading and service theme, we later discovered, was a regular member of the congregation who taught biology at a nearby secondary school. The theme of her talk was the Church as the body of Christ and she started by projecting on a screen an outline of a person from the chest upwards. She then drew a very small circle within the outline of the head and asked if anyone knew what this 'pea-sized' part of the body might be. I whispered to my wife – the pituitary gland – which turned out to be correct. The speaker then went on to share how important this apparently insignificant part of the body was for our health and wellbeing. The talk skilfully engaged, and informed adults and children alike with a combination of science and biblical teaching which simply and powerfully drew together those worlds. As a scientist engaged in medical research it felt like I belonged and would be supported.

I tell these stories in the hope that this book will be a

comprehensive source of understanding, insight, stories, analogies and fresh thoughts on the rich relationship between Christian faith and the scientific endeavour. I trust the lived experience and approach of its authors will remind readers who are church ministers, or part of the leadership team of a church, to regularly affirm the vocation of Christians engaged in science, technology and research. Taking or making opportunity for them to speak about the interplay between their faith and work dispels the sense of being in a profession which can feel at the margins of church life and understanding. When done well, this not only builds holistic bridges, it so often clears the way for those who have seen science and faith as rivals to explore the faith and come to embrace it for themselves.

Lee Swindon

The Right Revd Dr Lee Rayfield is the Bishop of Swindon.

Bishop Lee is a member of the Society of Ordained Scientists, a Holy Order offering to God in their ordained roles across the work of science and technology in the exploration and stewardship of creation. The Order expresses the commitment of the Church to the scientific and technological enterprise, and concern for its impact on the world.

From the Big Bang to Biology – where is God?

Preface.

"Spending your life in understanding and appreciating a little more of God's created order and, for some, applying that understanding to help others, is a great privilege."
Denis Alexander[1]

"Science is not threatened by God; it is enhanced. God is certainly not threatened by science; He made it all possible."
Francis Collins[2]

John and Graham write ...

We live in extraordinary times. Science and technology advance exponentially, providing huge benefits in the way we live, including global communications, ease of transportation, the internet and advances in health care and agriculture. Our knowledge of the world and of the Universe in which we live has progressed remarkably, largely because of rapid advances in the development of techniques and methods used to observe the way nature works.

A revolution in physics began in 1905 when Albert Einstein's insights about space and time swept away the classical, Newtonian view of the world. In the last century, advances in physics have led us to 'standard models' of particle physics (the very small) and of the Universe (the very large). Our knowledge remains incomplete, and it is likely that these models will change as new discoveries are made. However, physicists continue to strive to achieve a 'theory of everything' that will unify all the diverse aspects of the laws of nature.

Similarly, extraordinary progress has been made in understanding the science of life. Mendel's discovery of genes and of inheritance patterns, published in 1866, was rediscovered by three different scientists in 1900. The existence of specific physical entities that could be passed on from generation to generation enhanced hugely our understanding of natural selection and evolution and had clear applications in many other areas of biology. The demonstration in 1944 that genes are made of DNA and the elucidation of its double helical structure (published in 1953) kick-started the revolution in our understanding of genes and the way they work, a revolution that shows no sign of slackening in pace in the early decades of the 21st century.

Despite these remarkable developments, we are also aware that the energy-hungry, technological culture that has arisen as a result of our application of advances in science comes with many problems – these being significant enough to demand urgent resolution in the face of the threat of irreparable damage to Earth's biosphere. In that sense, science has two faces but nevertheless is widely held in high esteem. One consequence of this is that 'the average man in the street' thinks that science is all-conquering in understanding the world and the Universe in which we live. As we will explore in what follows, it is a very common mindset to believe that science has effectively solved all the mysteries of life, the Universe and everything, and only loose ends remain that need to be tidied. However, if you take the time to investigate this belief, it is very far from the truth. There are also many big questions, some of which are actually scientific questions, that science is unable to answer. But further, there are questions that are fundamentally to do with matters of meaning and purpose, which science is ill-equipped to address. As human beings, these other questions are of great importance to us rather than the dry 'analytical truths' derived by scientific method (the latter described perhaps most coldly of all by Ludwig Wittgenstein: "The world is the totality of facts, not of things.").

These big questions that lie outside the realm of science lead to the suggestion that there are effectively two worldviews, two

Preface

ways of looking at existence, one stemming from science and the other from philosophy/theology. Can a satisfying synthesis of these two major worldviews be achieved? Can they learn from each other? Or has science made God irrelevant? Is it possible to be a scientist with a faith in God, or is the notion of God an archaic legacy of a distant and superstitious past? It is the answers to questions such as these that have inspired us – moved us 'to put pen to paper' in producing this book.

This project has grown out of a series of one-week conferences we have jointly led at Lee Abbey on the North Devon coast and Scargill House located in the Yorkshire Dales. Both venues accommodate Christian communities which operate a conference and holiday centre. The first of our conferences took place at Lee Abbey under the banner of 'God, the Big Bang and Biology' in March 2015 (although John had led/co-led several science-faith conferences at Lee Abbey before that date), and we have run them on a regular basis since.

The structure of this book expands on the content of these conference weeks. A brief introductory view of the science and faith debate, and its evolution over time, is presented in Chapter 1. Chapter 2 takes a look at scientific method, and the importance of recognising its limitations. Chapters 3 and 4 examine the physics of the cosmos, firstly looking at the concordance of the Big Bang theory with the Genesis account in the Bible; then moving on to the revelation that the structure and laws that govern the Universe are strongly bio-friendly. The latter aspect had surprising consequences for one of us, and the story of how this played out is described in Chapter 4. Chapters 5 and 6 discuss the biology of our planet from the origin of life right through to the arrival of humans and our growing awareness of God the creator. In Chapter 7 we talk about the relationship between the scientific understanding of creation and the Biblical accounts thereof while Chapter 8 discusses the amazing 'balance of nature' and the damage being done to it by humankind. In the final chapter, we attempt to bring it all together to show that science and faith are complementary in understanding what we see around us and that a satisfying harmony can be achieved.

It is also worth mentioning that in co-authoring this book, it has been difficult to produce a text in which our contributions are seamlessly and beautifully merged to produce an integrated whole. Hence we have indicated who has authored each of the chapters, or parts thereof. There are effectively two reasons for this. Firstly, we wished to express personal experiences, views and anecdotes, so that 'first person' narration was unavoidable. Secondly, we each have a lifetime's experience of our own individual area of expertise – physics for Graham and biology for John. Hopefully that means we complement each other perfectly!

Please note that occasionally you will come across terminology in the text displayed in bold font. This indicates that a definition may be found in the Glossary. Also, where references or additional explanation of the text are deemed appropriate, endnotes are included at the end of each chapter.

Before we get into the main text to consider the relationship between science and faith in contemporary society, it might be helpful to say something about who we are, and what makes us tick.

Something about the authors

John writes ...

I grew up on a council estate in Croydon on the southern edge of London, UK. In strict sociological terms we were a working-class family but that term hides the attitudes and aspirations that my parents, Joe and Pat held. Although they had left school in their mid-teens and had not had opportunities to continue their education, both could see the value in continued schooling and so my brother and I were very much supported and encouraged in our schoolwork (and for me, later on, in my university career). My parents both found time to read and were interested in current affairs, in the natural world and in sport (I'll refrain from extolling the virtues of Crystal Palace Football Club or Surrey County Cricket Club!). Further, they were both Christians who brought a straightforward faith to everything they did, in work, in social interactions, and in family life. Inevitably I absorbed their attitudes and their faith and gradually took on that faith for myself. Consequently, I have been a Christian for long time.

As well as my faith being initiated in that council prefab in

Croydon, so was my interest in science. The borough of Croydon is on the southern edge of the London conurbation and our estate was on the south-eastern edge of Croydon, adjacent to London's greenbelt. Further, since we had no car until I was well into my teenage years, we did a lot of walking. Within minutes of leaving our front door we could be in partly managed, partly wild parkland which quickly led on to both farmland and to properly wild woodland and downs. The areas near our estate were considered safe and thus it was quite normal for small groups of children – friendship groups from primary school – to wander and play there without adult supervision. It was an ideal environment in which to encounter nature, in which to go pond-dipping, to find caterpillars, butterflies, moths and to see birds (in addition to climbing trees, damming streams, making dens, and playing football and cricket).

My primary school also had a major formative role in my early scientific development (although we obviously did not call it that). 'Nature study' was an important part of the primary school curriculum and we were encouraged to engage with nature in different ways. I can remember two teachers in particular who were very enthusiastic about the natural world and who, to us pupils, seemed very knowledgeable. They were always ready to encourage those of who were especially interested and to this day I remain grateful for that encouragement. And on a wider note, I also remain grateful that two teachers in particular suggested that some of us were able enough to go to university – not that we had much idea of what that meant – our knowledge of university life was limited to the annual Cambridge-Oxford Boat Race!

So, by the time I went to secondary school I was hooked: I had a very keen interest in, perhaps even a passion for, the natural world and, at the level that a pre-teen boy would understand the concept, a knowledge that it was created by God. At secondary school my knowledge grew as we studied biology in a more scientific way and as we also studied other sciences, especially chemistry and physics and the physical aspects of geography. Further, it was a real eye-opener to discover that one could have a career in biology so that by my mid-teens I was convinced that I wanted to be a scientist. The curate (assistant minister) at the local church suggested to me that society needed more scientists who were Christians. This was one of the factors that led me to think then – and to still think now – that working in science was my Christian vocation. This led on to A-levels in the sciences, to studying Natural Sciences at Cambridge and then doing a PhD in Plant Biochemistry.

It was during my degree course that I became very interested in the sub-cellular and molecular aspects of biology and especially in the 'molecule of life', DNA. So, although I have retained my love of nature, of the environment and of wild places, DNA and genes have been the focus of my research throughout my career, starting with my PhD project. It has been a real privilege to discover some of the awesomely beautiful and complex biochemical and genetic mechanisms by which DNA works. The double helix is a brilliant structure for enabling DNA to carry and pass on genetic information and for facilitating the use of that information in the minute-by-minute workings of cells. DNA leads me to worship!

I am also very committed to share my passion for biology, especially molecular biology, with others. My career has progressed almost entirely within the UK university system (albeit with international research collaborations in several countries) and it has been a privilege to teach and to interact with many generations of undergraduate students and to supervise about 35 PhD students at the start of their scientific careers.

Further, my research and teaching interests have led to other things. Our growing ability to manipulate genes right down to the basic molecular structure of DNA has raised ethical concerns. As a scientist working in this area I have thought it my responsibility not only to act ethically but also to enable others to understand and think about the ethical issues arising from modern science. I am equally as enthusiastic about communicating in the bioethics arena as I am about science communication.

Throughout my career, even going back to those teenage years, I have never experienced a clash between being a scientist and being a person of faith. I have never taken a '**God of the Gaps**' position (that is, ascribing to God those aspects of our universe which science has not yet 'unpicked') and so our increasing scientific knowledge is a matter for thanksgiving, not for concern that it undermines faith. Some people suggested that my acceptance of evolution was at odds with the Bible but I reasoned

Preface

that the Bible was not a scientific textbook, consisting as it does of literature written in a pre-scientific age. However, in 21st century Britain we increasingly hear that science and faith are not compatible or that science has done away with the need for God. We examine this attitude in more detail in Chapters 1 and 2. Here, I just want to say that it both angers me (in the right sort of way!) and inspires me to go out to contradict these erroneous views; I will do so whenever I am given the opportunity. I am as enthusiastic about this as I am about the other aspects of science communication I mentioned earlier.

My enthusiasm for communicating science and bioethics has led me to write books. My enthusiasm to communicate the compatibility of science and faith leads me to co-author this book with my friend and fellow-communicator, Graham Swinerd.

Graham writes ...

Born in 1950 in East Kent, UK, I was brought up in what was then considered to be a 'Christian country', but not in a Christian family. What I mean is that my loving family had no explicit faith in a God, so that church attendance, or any other manifestation of worship, played no part in my upbringing. However, like a lot of kids I did go to church occasionally and was taught RE (Religious Education) in school – which was all Christian-based in the 1950s, unlike today. Consequently, I heard all the usual Christian 'stories' of the nativity, the crucifixion and resurrection many, many times throughout my young life. It now seems extraordinary to me that, despite this, I had no appreciation or understanding of the profound meaning of these events that took place in a land so far away in both space and time.

Another facet of the young Swinerd was a deep interest in all things scientific, and in particular the sciences of astronomy and astrophysics, although the latter word was not part of my vocabulary then. I recall that this was awakened by Mrs Christian, my first primary school teacher. From my perspective as a very young boy, I remember her as a rather kind-hearted old lady – I'm always astonished that I have any such recollection as it is such a long time ago! It was she that planted the first seeds of interest in astronomy, which was then underlined by a school trip to the

London Planetarium. At the time, I remember not knowing what a planetarium was, but once there, and having seen the 'show', I was hooked.

I have spent most of my life subsequently looking up into the sky at the beautiful manifestations of what I now consider to be God's Universe. I suppose I have a rather unusual perspective on life here on planet Earth – most people share the geocentric view that the only things that happen in the Universe of interest and importance occur here on Earth, whereas in reality the arena of human affairs is a very small two-dimensional surface, containing a small planet in what is an unimaginably large Universe. To quote Douglas Adams[3], 'the Universe is big'. Current scientific orthodoxy suggests that the visible Universe is around 90 **billion** light years[4] 'across', containing something like 10^{22} (that's 1 with 22 zeros behind it) stars. Someone with time on their hands guesstimated that this is more than the number grains of sand on planet Earth! Although it is difficult to have a personal mental grasp of what these numbers mean, nevertheless they certainly put the affairs of 'man' into perspective. So why is it that I believe that God is so intimately interested in little old me? – a potent question that I will leave hanging in the air for now.

My childhood interest in science was a powerful driver in terms of educational development and career ambitions. Most adolescents have childhood heroes from among the ranks of musical, film or sporting stars, but believe it or not the hero of the rather strange young Swinerd was Albert Einstein (with the moon-walking Apollo astronauts coming a close second). To me the intellectual achievement of Albert was massive, and my teenage years were spent attempting to accumulate sufficient mathematical skills in order to 'just understand' what he had told us about the Universe. After a PhD in Einstein's gravity (the 'general theory of relativity'), I was fortunate enough to spend a fulfilling career as a space scientist and engineer in both industry and academia.

During a few years working at (what was then) British Aerospace Space Systems, I was lucky enough to work on a number of satellite projects. This was followed by an extended period at the University of Southampton, UK, before my retirement in 2010. The latter involved me in teaching and research on a variety of space science and space engineering topics, which you can read about elsewhere[5]. My teaching activity included organising and presenting courses for the European Space Agency, principally at their technical HQ in Noordwijk, The Netherlands. This vocation led to me being labelled inevitably, if rather inaccurately, as a 'rocket scientist'!

However, during these busy years at the university, something rather extraordinary (and surprising!) happened in November 2001, when I came to faith in the Christian God. How this came to be is very much related to the issue of science and faith, and I wish to explain my testimony as part of this text. Before this extraordinary event, I would have described myself as a tolerant **agnostic**, firmly entrenched in the notion that science had explained everything to the extent that any form of god was irrelevant (I considered atheism at the time, but have always thought that it is untenable, as it is just as difficult to be sure that God doesn't exist, as it is to prove He does). The event has also stimulated my desire to co-author this book with John – to produce something which may be of help to anyone else who finds themselves in a similar place that I was prior to 2001. During this early part of my life, I would say that another personal characteristic was a deficit of 'spirituality'. However much I wanted to experience the 'unexplained', all I ever saw were things that could be accounted for by the laws of the physical world.

This little bit of background by no means paints a complete picture, but it does give some insights into some of the characteristics that have shaped my life over the years. And those that I have chosen to reveal are, I think, relevant to the understanding of what has happened to me since the autumn of 2001. Life has been transformed – and I want to write this book to express my desire to stand up and be counted.

Graham Swinerd, Southampton
John Bryant, Exeter
November 2020

Preface endnotes:

[1] Denis Alexander, Is There Purpose in Biology?, Lion Books, 2018, p. 249.
[2] Francis Collins, The Language of God, Pocket Books, 2007, p. 233.
[3] Douglas Adams, The Hitchhiker's Guide to the Galaxy, Pan Books, 1979.
[4] A light year is a unit of distance. It is the distance travelled by light during the period of one year, propagating at a speed of 300,000 km/sec. This is approximately 9.5×10^{12} km (or 95 with 11 zeros).
[5] Graham Swinerd, How Spacecraft Fly – spaceflight without formulae, Copernicus Books (Springer), 2008.
Peter Fortescue, Graham Swinerd & John Stark (editors), Spacecraft Systems Engineering (4th Edition), John Wiley & Sons, 2011.

1 Where are we today – and how did we get here?

"Science and religion are two windows that people look through, trying to understand the big Universe outside, trying to understand why we are here. The two windows give different views, but both look out at the same Universe. ... neither is complete. Both leave out essential features of the real world. And both are worthy of respect."
Freeman Dyson[1]

"There are more things in heaven and earth, Horatio, Than are dreamt of in your philosophy."
William Shakespeare[2]

John writes ...

1.1 Introduction – a short story.

A few years ago, I was on a crowded train travelling between London and Exeter and found a seat at a table with two BBC engineers. They were on their way to Glastonbury, part of the team that was setting up for the broadcasts from the music festival. I was actually on my way home from Cambridge where I had been speaking at a conference in the general area of science and religious faith. On learning this, the two engineers were incredulous – surely science and faith were incompatible? Had not

1

science done away with the possibility that there is a God? Needless to say, lively discussion ensued until the BBC men left the train. This brief encounter illustrates the view that science has put paid to religion, a view based on two background assumptions. The first is that there is no credible evidence for the existence of God and the second is that only the methods of science give us reliable information about the world. The second assumption places science on a pedestal; it regards science as the only valid way of approaching an understanding of existence. This view is known as **scientism**. We discuss it more extensively in Chapter 2. Here, I just want to point out that science itself cannot make the claim that there are no other ways of knowing; such a claim would be unscientific. Science has its limits.

1.2 Prevailing views and persistent myths.

The view, scientism, is widespread in the UK, in several other European countries and to a lesser extent, in parts of the USA. It comes in various guises, including those mentioned above, but the clear underlying theme is that in this scientific age, religion is irrelevant and that belief in God is 'unscientific.' In the UK, those who present this view the most vigorously often also present the idea that for centuries, the church (or religion) suppressed scientific investigation and that, in the **Enlightenment**, religious superstition gave way to a view of the world based on human intellect or 'reason'. This then allowed science to flourish.

With this in mind, I invite you to join me in a brief but not too onerous ramble through history. I will come back to the Enlightenment shortly but in the meantime I want to discuss briefly the idea that in earlier centuries, religion suppressed science. This myth has been well and truly dispelled by authors such as Allan Chapman[3], James Hannam[4] and David Bentley Hart[5]. These authors present the evidence at much greater length than I have space for here. I simply want to draw attention to Muslim scholars, especially in mathematics, and to the contributions of Christian scholars, many of whom had a specific role in the church itself, in mathematics, physics, astronomy and natural history. The latter were exemplified by the work of St.

Hildegard of Bingen (1098-1179). These pre-Enlightenment scholars had long ago done away with the notion that the Earth is flat and were beginning to describe the movements of planets and other celestial bodies. The work of the Bishop of Lincoln, Robert Grosseteste (1175-1253) on astronomy and on light (including rainbows) was truly remarkable. His work in some ways predicted the Big Bang theory of the origin of the Universe; he has been described as the real founder of the tradition of scientific thought in medieval Oxford and, in some ways, of the modern English intellectual tradition. Indeed, it is the view of the writers mentioned above, and of physicist Tom McLeish[6] that the work of these medieval 'natural philosophers' made possible the research carried out by Galileo, Newton and others.

Further to this, some authors, including David Bentley Hart[5], believe that it was the growth of Christendom that allowed science to flourish because the God we worship is a God of order, not of chaos (using 'chaos' in its non-scientific sense). This leads to the idea that the Creation is predictable and measurable, enabling us to investigate ordered processes as we seek to understand how the Universe/world works. It is said therefore that the Universe is 'non-capricious' in the sense that, provided we repeat our observations, measurements and experiments carefully, we will obtain results that are repeatable[7].

However, despite this rosy picture, I need to add that there is a more negative episode in the overall story and that concerns Galileo (1564-1642). He is the example nearly always given by those who claim that 'the Church' suppressed science and thus it deserves our attention. Galileo's problems started in 1610 when he published the results of observations made with his telescope. These observations confirmed what had been proposed by Copernicus 65 years earlier, namely that planets, including the Earth, revolve round the Sun[8]. This is known as **heliocentrism** and on hearing of Galileo's work, the Roman Catholic Church formally declared that it contradicted the Bible and was therefore heresy. The Bible was interpreted as showing that the Sun rotates round the Earth and thus any opposing view ran contrary to Scripture. Galileo was eventually placed under house arrest in

1633 for holding and publishing heretical views; he died, still under house arrest, in 1642[9]. However, this episode has to be regarded as somewhat of an anomaly because in the previous century, Copernicus had published his ideas about a heliocentric planetary system without apparently attracting opposition. It seems that the Galileo episode alerted the Church to the work of Copernicus and for a few years, his book, *On the Revolutions of the Celestial Spheres (De revolutionibus orbium coelestium)*, was, like those of Galileo, also banned.

Figure 1.1 The statue of Nicolaus Copernicus outside the Polish Academy of Sciences in Warsaw. Credit: John Bryant.

I should stress that both Copernicus and Galileo were Christian believers and did not perceive that their work undermined faith in any way. Indeed, Copernicus (Figure 1.1) was emphatic in declaring that investigation of the workings of the Universe was an act of worship:

> "To know the mighty works of God, to comprehend His wisdom and majesty and power; to appreciate, in degree, the wonderful workings of His laws, surely all this must be a pleasing and acceptable mode of worship to the Most High, to whom ignorance cannot be more grateful than knowledge."

Whilst the Roman Catholic Church does not emerge well from this episode we should also look at what was happening elsewhere in Europe. Luther had published his theses in 1517, an event that is regarded as initiating the Protestant Reformation across much of Europe. In Britain, the Reformation was partly political, based on Henry VIII's disagreements with the Pope and leading, in 1534, to an Act of Parliament in which the authority of 'the Bishop of Rome' was rejected. Thus, in many countries, the authority of the Roman Catholic Church was in decline by the time Galileo's problems with Rome were beginning (1633). In the field of science, still known then as 'natural philosophy', Francis Bacon (1561-1626) set out in a formal manner the way that science should work. He is often called the Father of Modern Science but in view of the natural philosophy of previous centuries we need to downplay that title. Western science did not start with Bacon, but his work was nevertheless very important. He gave science a framework for its investigations, a contribution that is often referred to as the Baconian or Scientific Revolution. Further, in the context of the science-religion debate, Bacon was a devout Christian who stated that "God has, in fact, written two books, not just one...", suggesting that the Creation itself was the other of God's books. So, it is apparent that the emerging Protestant church did not seem to have the problems with science that were apparent, at least temporarily, in the Roman Catholic Church.

1.3 So, what did happen in the Enlightenment?

Mention of Francis Bacon brings us conveniently to the Enlightenment itself. The definition and dating of this period depend upon which viewpoint we take. French philosophers and historians tend to restrict the dating of the Enlightenment to the period between 1715 and 1789 (the start of the French Revolution). Those with a wider European perspective tend to place the start of the Enlightenment at around 1620, coinciding with the scientific revolution, and then continuing until the late 18th century. So, was the Enlightenment a period when 'religious superstition' gave way to 'reason' as has been stated by some 20th and 21st century atheists? Certainly, the authority of the Church (mainly meaning the Roman Catholic Church) and of monarchies were challenged, but at the same time Enlightenment ideas included religious tolerance, alongside individual liberties and the exercise of human reason.

Nevertheless, the idea that religious faith is not rational is somewhat pervasive in today's society (as evidenced by my story at the opening of this chapter) and we need to address this, starting by looking again at the Enlightenment itself. It is certainly true that some Enlightenment thinkers were atheists, such as the philosopher David Hume, while others, such as the social reformer Thomas Paine, criticised or even ridiculed organised religion while retaining some sort of belief in a deity. However, many others were Christians, including natural philosophers/scientists such as Francis Bacon, Robert Boyle, Isaac Newton, Johannes Kepler, John Ray, Stephen Hales, Antoine Lavoisier and Carl Linnaeus.

1.4 Moving on.

As the post-Enlightenment, early-Modern period progressed, overt atheism became more widespread and church-going started to decline. Thus, by the mid-19th century it was certainly acceptable in wider society to declare that one had no belief in God. Nevertheless, many intellectuals of the 19th century, including numerous scientists, were Christians. Even Charles Darwin, although unable to believe in a personal loving God after the death of one of his daughters, was never an atheist (see Chapter 7). Further, the occurrence in the 20th century of two World Wars caused many people to lose their faith. They could not see how a God of love could 'allow' so much suffering, even though the ultimate cause of war is actually human wrong-doing. Nevertheless, in the late 1940s and through the 1950s, going to church (and for children, Sunday School) was very much part of the weekly routine for many people. This was also an era of emerging technologies when the applications of science started to become widely embedded in our daily lives. This has continued at an increasing pace up to the present day, very much as predicted in a speech in October 1963 by the then Prime Minister of the UK, Harold Wilson. He spoke of Britain being 'forged in the white heat of technological revolution.' Increasingly then, science and technology, including medicine, were seen as solving our problems and enhancing our life-styles. We were masters and mistresses of our own destiny.

The late 1960s saw the arrival of what has been called a counter-culture, largely but not exclusively amongst young people. There were protests, some quite violent, at universities in Europe, including the UK, in which students demanded more say in the governance of their educational institutions. Social norms were challenged, often associated with use of drugs such as cannabis. In the USA, and to some extent in other countries, there were increasingly vocal protests against the continuing war in Vietnam. Much of the music enjoyed by young people focussed on alternative life-styles or protest. The challenges to social norms included challenges to established religion and there was a further decline in church attendance among young people.

At this point we need to consider another philosophical and sociological trend: **post-modernism**. This emerged in the 1970s and has only recently started to fade away. Relevant here is that in post-modernism there are no universal truths, no 'meta-narratives' or over-arching stories that give us a 'handle' on existence. Our understanding of existence at any one moment is said to be a social construct rather than reflecting objective truth. Indeed, any claim of objective truth was regarded as false. One of post-modernism's slogans was 'All things are relative.' (this is of course a self-defeating slogan, as is pointed out by non-post-modern philosophers and sociologists. If everything is relative, that includes the slogan). We can see immediately that this is a threat to both science and religious belief. In science, experience demonstrates that a properly designed experiment, with tightly controlled conditions, will give similar results independently of where it is carried out and by whom. If this were not so, science could not progress because there would be no firm basis from which to move forward. In our religious faith we hold that there are deeper truths which do actually give a picture of an over-arching grand narrative. Part of that grand narrative, that the amazing Universe in which we live is the work of a creator God, is the subject of this book.

In wider society, the most obvious symptom of post-modernism is the idea that on any given subject, any one view is as valid as any other. In the UK, in several other European countries and (to a lesser extent) in the USA, such views have permeated the media for over thirty years. They were certainly held, at least implicitly, by the average man-in-the-street, even though most had never actually heard of post-modernism. Today, in the early decades of the 21st century, post-modernism has faded away. Nevertheless it remains in what the American commentator Tom Nichols called 'The Death of Expertise'. He does not mean that there are no experts, but that expertise is no longer respected or even acknowledged. The UK newspaper columnist Lucy Mangan wrote: "Being an expert is a tricky business these days ... What was once respected – the careful, deliberate acquisition of knowledge – is now an affront"[10], while the UK physicist and TV presenter Brian Cox said 'anti-expertise' is the "road back to the cave" [11]. And if post-modernism is the 'road back to the cave' in respect of science and technology, it is also the road to belief in nothing (or anything that takes your fancy) in respect of religious faith.

1.5 Science and faith in the 21st century.

As mentioned already, science in general has made and continues to make huge advances since the beginning of the 20th century. In industrialised nations, the applications of science in medicine, agriculture, engineering, technology and travel (to name but a few) are embedded in society at large and into our daily lives. Over this same period, religious belief is declining. In many European countries, only a small minority of the population participate regularly in religious services, whether Christian, Jewish or Muslim. In a recent survey[12] in the UK, 35 - 39% (depending on how the question was presented) of adults said that they believed in God and a further 12% indicated a belief in some sort of higher spiritual being or power (the equivalent combined figure in the USA was 90%). However, only 18% attend a 'religious service' once a month or more.

Can we then attribute the general decline in religious observance or belief to the growth of science and technology? In other words, has science 'done away' with God? In general, that view comes from outside the scientific community. Only a minority of scientists believe that science and faith are in conflict, although this minority, exemplified in the UK by Richard

Dawkins, is often very vocal in presenting this view. However, as pointed out by many scientists, including some who are atheists, science can never disprove the existence of God; religious faith and science are entirely compatible. In the 120 years since the start of the 20th century there have been many scientists who are as well-known for their religious faith as for their science. I will just mention three, but there are hundreds more[13]. My first example is Georges Lemaître, a Roman Catholic priest and professor of physics who originated the Big Bang theory (see section 3.4). Secondly, there is Ghillean Prance, an expert on plant evolution and ecology and Director of the Royal Botanic Gardens, Kew, UK, and thirdly, Francis Collins, known for his role in discovery of the cystic fibrosis gene, who became Director of the US sector of the Human Genome Project (and who is now the Director of the USA's National Institutes of Health). Nevertheless, in the UK, the percentage of scientists who believe in God is about half that of the general population. However, the percentage of scientists who *attend church* regularly is more than twice that of the general population. This suggests that scientists with a belief in God are much more likely to be active in expressing that belief. Further, in all the mainstream churches, significant numbers of scientists are now serving as church ministers, again indicating an active belief in God, rather just than a passive assent.

1.6 Science – asking questions and answering some of them.

At this point it is helpful to focus on science itself – what it is and what it does; this discussion is continued in the next chapter. Although the word *science* simply means *knowledge*, science itself is more than that. This is because it includes the means of obtaining that knowledge. However, we need to recognise that the extent of knowledge that science gives us is limited. The methods of science do not give us direct access to all knowledge, for example knowledge about non-material aspects of existence such as spirituality or consciousness.

Science is firmly based on human curiosity about the Universe – we have questions and we want to know the answers. We can envisage that in the earliest phases of existence of humankind, curiosity led to useful knowledge, for example, what could be eaten, which animals were dangerous and so on. It is also clear that in the ensuing 250,000 years, knowledge about the world became more and more detailed (at least by the standards of the time), especially after the foundation of agriculture about 12,000 years ago and the subsequent development of human settlements. In the third millennium BC (4,000 to 5,000 years before the present day), the builders of Stonehenge knew about the seasonal variations in day-length, the variation in the position of the Sun in the sky and in its elevation above the horizon (unfortunately that culture left no written records so we cannot look at their notes!).

In the same period, the Egyptians were able to align the pyramids north-south by using the positions of stars. They were also aware of seasonal variations in the flow of the Nile and indeed, predictions of flow in any one year were used in estimating how much tax to impose. Moving on again, the Greek culture that flourished for several hundred years before the birth of Jesus Christ (and for about a century afterwards) is well known for philosophy and arts but it was also a culture in which mathematics and science, especially physics and astronomy, flourished. For example, the Greek mathematician Eratosthenes of Cyrene suggested in the 3rd century BC, that the Earth was spherical, and devised and executed an accurate method to measure its diameter.

It is not my intention here to spell out the scientific activities that prevailed in subsequent phases of the history of the western world. I just want to emphasise that curiosity about how the world works is one aspect of the human psyche and has been exercised in different ways over the millennia. Today, scientific research is embedded into the functioning of industrialised nations and of groups of nations cooperating in large projects. The domain of science covers everything from the smallest elementary particles to the vastness of the Universe. In formal terms, research proceeds by the use of the **empirical** methods of science: observation, measurement and experimentation. However, science is not quite as mechanical as this. To these empirical methods we need to add intuition, **serendipity**, guesswork and, dare I say it, luck. Within the sciences, there is a good deal of variation in the way the three empirical methods predominate. Indeed, there are some areas of science which are not open to direct experimentation, while there are others in which experimentation and/or measurement can only reveal repeatable patterns and not precise numbers. Let me illustrate what I mean. If we measure the physical properties of, let's say, an element, we will always arrive at the same numbers, provided we have done the work properly and used the same processes each time. Now consider a biological system. We can for example, describe a biochemical reaction in precise chemical terms and present its physical properties (such as energy exchange) in precise values. However, measuring the rate at which the reaction occurs under real conditions is a different matter. In an example from my research, the rate at which a particular gene is expressed (that is, the rate at which the gene 'works') always increases before a cell starts to copy its DNA in preparation for cell division. However, actual rates and the timing of the peak of activity are not precisely reproducible from experiment to experiment, even if we use a uniform culture of lab-grown cells. What is reproducible is the pattern – there is always an approximately n-fold increase in rate approximately x hours before the start of DNA replication. Furthermore, we find that as we go up through the levels of biological complexity (that is, from gene to cell to organism to ecosystem), the ability to put precise numbers on the patterns we see declines even though the patterns themselves are clearly recognisable and reproducible.

This book is the work of a physical scientist and a biological scientist and this means that different angles may be presented on how science progresses. Nevertheless, we are in total agreement that science is good at what it sets out to do – that is, to answer questions as to how the Universe works at all levels. Many of the answers are truly amazing and inspire in us a sense of awe and wonder. However, there are questions that science has not been able to answer. Some of these are certainly within the realm of science but we have no means of answering them. Examples include 'How did life originate?' and 'What is consciousness and how does it arise from brain activity?' But there are also bigger questions that lie outside the capabilities of science to answer: 'Why is there something rather than nothing?', 'Is there a creator/mind behind the laws of nature and hence behind the Universe itself?', 'Has the evolution of the planet and life thereon been guided or is it all random?' 'Does life have a meaning or a purpose?' and so on. Thus, science, however brilliant it is (and it is brilliant), has its limits These limits are discussed by my co-author in the next chapter.

Chapter 1 endnotes:

[1] Freeman Dyson, Progress in Religion – his acceptance speech for the Templeton Prize, Washington National Cathedral, 9 May 2000.
[2] Hamlet, Act 1, Scene 5.
[3] Allan Chapman, Slaying the Dragons, Lion Hudson, 2013.
[4] James Hannam, God's Philosophers, Icon Books, 2010.
[5] David Bentley Hart, Atheist Delusions, Yale University Press, 2009.
[6] Tom McLeish, Faith and Wisdom in Science, Oxford University Press, 2014.
[7] I acknowledge that at the very small scale of sub-atomic particles, deterministic behaviour gives way to probabilistic behaviour, as described in quantum theory.
[8] Actually, as long ago as the 3rd century BC, the Greek mathematician Aristarchus of Samos had presented a similar model for planetary movements.
[9] I note in passing that Galileo was not tortured during interrogation, neither did he go to prison (except for one day). The torture and prison stories, although untrue, have become established amongst those who believe that science and religion are in conflict.
[10] The Guardian Weekend, 5 April 2014.
https://www.theguardian.com/lifeandstyle/2014/apr/05/doctor-dont-want-my-opinion-lucy-mangan.
[11] The Guardian, 2 July 2016 https://www.theguardian.com/tv-and-radio/2016/jul/02/professor-brian-cox-interview-forces-of-nature.
[12] British Social Attitudes Survey 2018: Religion.
https://bsa.natcen.ac.uk/media/39293/1_bsa36_religion.pdf.
[13] A long, but still only partial list is given here:
https://en.wikipedia.org/wiki/List_of_Christians_in_science_and_technology.

2 The Science Delusion.

"It would be possible to describe everything scientifically, but it would make no sense; it would be without meaning, as if you described a Beethoven symphony as a variation of wave pressure."
Albert Einstein[1]

"The conflicts only arise if you try to make religion into a science or if you try to make science into a religion." Freeman Dyson[2]

Graham writes ...

2.1 Introduction.

Before I begin, I must acknowledge Rupert Sheldrake, from whom I appropriated the title of this Chapter. Sheldrake's book *The Science Delusion*[3] examines what he refers to as the ten dogmas of modern science, which he argues impose unnecessary limitations on science, diminishing its domain of investigation. Although I did not agree with some of what he has to say, nevertheless I thought the book title a good phrase to describe my mindset concerning science prior to my coming to faith.

Despite this chapter title, I love science. I cannot remember a time when this was not true – I have spent my career as a scientist and engineer, and since retirement I have delighted in attempting to keep track of developments in physics and cosmology. The scientific worldview is immensely powerful and influential in our culture, because the sciences have been so successful. Our lives have changed beyond imagination during my lifetime, mostly for the better, as developments in technology and medicine, for example, have grown exponentially. Scientific investigation of our Universe has stretched and overwhelmed our imagination as improvements in observational technology have allowed us to glimpse its complexity and beauty – from the weirdness of the **quantum** world to the vastness of the visible Universe populated by 100s of billions of galaxies. How can I not love science! My co-author John, shares this same awe and inspiration when considering the beautiful and complex mechanisms involved in the workings of genes or the amazing ways in which those genes are regulated during the course of development from a single cell.

However, to introduce a note of caution – despite the global success of the scientific enterprise it is necessary to appreciate its limitations, and in this chapter I want to explore this a little. In his 1935 book *Religion and Science*[4], Bertrand Russell declares: "Whatever knowledge is attainable, must be attained by scientific methods; and what science cannot discover, mankind cannot know". One can easily provide examples which counter the logic of the latter part of this statement, but this aside, I think we understand what he was trying to say. Following on from this, it is valid to ask: is this excessive belief in the power of scientific methodology (scientism) warranted? Can science be all-powerful in addressing the ultimate questions of meaning and purpose which are so important to each of us? Alister McGrath expresses this sentiment very well:

> "Scientists are human beings. Because they are scientists, they have highly developed ideas about how the Universe works. Because they are human beings, they also have views on the deeper questions such as, amongst many other things, the meaning of their own individual existence and how to live a good life. But what happens if science cannot answer these deeper questions? In the end, most scientists end up believing rather a lot of things that lie beyond the scope of scientific method. These are things that really matter to us – not the shallow truths of reason, but the deep existential truths about who we are and why we are here." [5]

2.2 The Science Delusion.

As mentioned earlier, when I came to faith so late in life it was a huge surprise to everyone, especially me! A year to the day later I was confirmed into the Anglican Church, although I have to say that I'm not much of one for denominations. During this journey, many people commented about how God approaches each person in a way that 'speaks to them'. In my case, remarkably, God used the barrier – science – to turn me round. I will tell the story of how this happened in Chapter 4, but for now I would like to say a little about my attitude to science (and religion) prior to my 'turn around'.

I have adopted the phrase 'the science delusion' as a concise way of expressing what seems to be a widely-held belief that:

- Science explains everything (and consequently leaves no room for God);
- Science can ultimately produce a 'Theory of Everything' that will give us an ultimate understanding of the physical Universe (and maybe even of the issues of meaning and purpose).

My own attitude towards science in my pre-Christianity years was along similar lines, especially the first bullet point. I would say that I was either too arrogant or, more probably, too lazy to actually look at the evidence for this *belief*. At the time it seemed a self-evident truth, no doubt reinforced by similar sentiments propagated by popular media. Regarding the second bullet point, I do not think I gave much thought then to the notion of a Theory of Everything, but if one were to come along it seemed to me common sense to suppose that it would address the physics, but not the philosophical/theological/moral questions concerned with the meaning of life. I think you would have to be pretty dogmatic to suppose that scientific truth is the only truth (**logical positivism**), and I did not have any such axe to grind. However, I did have a rather severe case of the 'the science delusion', that created a significant personal barrier to the notion that there may be a spiritual dimension to the Universe, as well as the physical one.

The 'new atheists'

Logical positivism emerged in the 1920s and 30s principally in Europe, but then was largely discredited. However, with the rise of the so-called new atheists, it is now making a come-back. The general philosophy of this group seems to be along the lines of science and faith are incompatible, and you *do* have to choose. In other words, you cannot hold a faith, while being a scientist, or indeed the other way around. The significant number of scientists that are Christians today provides clear evidence that this view is mistaken. This science *or* faith stance is something that we will attempt to counter in this book. It has been observed that a more appropriate label for the new atheists would be anti-theists, as their philosophy is not simply a passive unbelief in God or gods, but rather a more belligerent desire to rid the world of the scourge (in their eyes) of any form of religion. However, the influence of this relative minority would be sorely stretched to sway the more than eight-in-ten people worldwide that profess a religious faith of some kind.

In the UK, Richard Dawkins is usually cited as a leader of this particular group, and it seems to be mandatory to mention his name when considering the interface of science and religion. I hope to confine Richard to this small section in my writings, as I want this text to be mostly about God, and His creation. But I have no doubt that he is very worthy of a mention, as he has done a great deal to provoke discussion of the science and faith issue in recent times. Of his many literary offerings, one stands out as making waves, and a great many sales – over 3 million copies of the English version of *The God Delusion*[6] have been sold. However, this 'atheistic manifesto' could be considered to have given atheism a bad name in academic circles. Dawkins makes clear at the outset in his original preface that his principal aim in writing is to de-convert people with a religious faith, and so realistically the prospect of a balanced, objective and well-argued text is unlikely. Moreover, I do not think the book has reached Dawkins' intended audience. When speaking to predominantly Christian groups about the science and faith debate, I have asked many people if they have read *The God Delusion*, and literally only a handful have responded positively over the years.

It is some time now since I read the book but one lingering memory of the style of writing is the overt rudeness and ridicule directed towards people who profess a faith – a strategy unlikely to win converts to Dawkins' cause. Another is the cynical confusion between God and religion – religion is *what we do* in the name of God, and I'm sure that God looks down on much of it with the same dismay, shock and sadness that we all experience. Many pages of *The God Delusion* are devoted to the tragedy of man's inhumanity to man in the name of God, as an argument for the condemnation of God himself. It is the work of man – our religious differences – that cause such conflict, the terrible evidence for which is displayed most evenings in the daily news broadcasts.

As a result of *The God Delusion*, Richard Dawkins has received a good deal of hate mail, much of it from people professing a Christian faith. He makes no attempt to conceal this, having published videos of himself online reading some of the more 'entertaining' contributions! I think a more appropriate Christian response would be prayer for Dawkins – he deserves respect even if you do not agree with his views, and I sincerely wish for a 'turn around' for him too.

Anyway, let's move on and have a look at how science works, what it does, and what it does not do.

2.3 How science works.

Many of the pioneering scientists were Christians – Robert Grosseteste (1175-1253), Nicolaus Copernicus (1473-1543), Johannes Kepler (1571-1630), Galileo Galilei (1564-1642), René Descartes (1596-1650), Isaac Newton (1642-1727), Robert Boyle (1627-1691) and Michael Faraday (1791-1867), to name but a few. Albert Einstein (1879-1955), in my view the most eminent scientist of the twentieth century, was raised a Jew, but ultimately never came to believe in a personal God. During his lifetime he had a keen interest in religion, and spoke and wrote much about it. Despite this, however, there remains no consensus among biographers about what he believed, most likely because his declarations evolved throughout his lifetime. Throughout his later years, however, he persisted in referring to a 'greater spirit' as 'the Old One', which guided the created order and also influenced the way that he thought about his science. Speaking figuratively, he personified this deity when he said "I want to know how God created this world. I am not interested in this or that phenomenon, in the spectrum of this or that element. I want to know His thoughts. The rest are details"[7].

Indeed, the faith of many pioneering scientists in a Creator God who fashioned an ordered world (Universe) was a firm foundation upon which to build a scientific worldview, and to attempt to "think God's thoughts after Him"[8]. A Christian belief was therefore a powerful and natural philosophical framework within which to nurture the development of science.

Order in the world

In our day-to-day lives it is apparent that we live in a structured, ordered world. When we do something – like kick a ball or perform a somersault – the outcome of our actions remains the same (given the same starting conditions). You almost certainly have not given any thought to this notion, because since childhood we take such things for granted. When scientists say the world (Universe) is ordered, they mean that it is governed by rules, which we call the 'laws of nature' (throughout this section I tend to use the words 'world' and 'Universe' interchangeably). The progress of science relies on the principle that the world is structured in this way. This belief is the scientist's step of faith. If it were otherwise, we would very likely not be here to contemplate it, as the resulting universe would be a chaotic turmoil, inhospitable to life. It need not necessarily be like this, but it is certainly to our advantage that it is. Why does the world exhibit such structure and order, to allow us to reach some understanding of physical reality?

Scientists and philosophers have commented on this apparent order in nature, for example, the Christian **apologist** C. S. Lewis observed: "We are not reading rationality into an irrational

Universe but responding to a rationality with which the Universe has always been saturated"[9]. In other words, we are responding to the Universe as it actually is, full of rationality (or order), which allows the process of scientific method to operate and make progress. Albert Einstein expressed his incredulity at this aspect of the natural world: "The eternal mystery of the world [Universe] is its comprehensibility ... The fact that it is comprehensible is a miracle"[10].

In the 1660s, Sir Isaac Newton was the first to truly witness the power and elegance of mathematics in describing the motion of the planets about the Sun. We can only imagine his excitement and inspiration at this insight, that no doubt reinforced his unswerving belief in a creator God, and motivated his famous quote: "Whence arises all that order and beauty in the world [Universe]?"

The methodology of science

Isaac Newton can be considered to be the father of modern science not only because of his major contributions to many areas of scientific activity (including mathematics, dynamics, gravitation, theoretical astronomy, optics and light), but also because he was the first to adopt a modern methodology of scientific investigation. Although I'm sure he was not conscious of following any such method at the time, nevertheless the process by which he developed the contributions to mathematics and dynamics that led to his great work *Principia* [11] echoes that which we use today. In this section, I will discuss in general terms this formal process, and I will use Newton's work on gravitation, and its application to understanding planetary motion, as an example to illuminate the discussion.

Newton was born on Christmas Day 1642, and his mission to understand the world began at Trinity College, Cambridge, UK at the age of 18. However, in the summer of 1665, the university was shut down by an outbreak of plague and Newton returned to his birthplace, the village of Woolsthorpe in Lincolnshire. It was during the following two years that he had a remarkably productive period, when his main focus was on gravity. Science today has so far identified four fundamental forces in nature (see later), and gravity was obviously the first to be identified; ironically it turns out to be the most difficult to unify with the rest of modern physics as it is currently formulated. However, returning to Newton in Woolsthorpe, his quest to understand gravitation was said to have been initiated by a falling apple striking him on the head (a story that is most likely apocryphal), which motivated questions about the nature of gravity.

Whilst we cannot be certain what aroused his curiosity, his remarkable endeavours during these two years can be summarised as follows. Firstly, Newton devised his law of gravitation and his laws of motion – for those who are interested, these are stated in the Text Box 2.1 (it would be helpful to understand the text box information, but a detailed grasp of the mathematics is not necessary to progress through the text). Combining these laws, he was able to formulate the equations that govern the motion of the planets around the Sun. However, he quickly realised that these equations could not be solved by the mathematical methods then available. To remove this obstacle, he invented a new branch of mathematics which we now call calculus. All of these achievements have had a lasting influence upon science and engineering to the present day, and any one of them would be considered to be a major intellectual achievement. For them all to have come from one individual in such a short period of time is remarkable. When asked how he discovered the law of gravity, Newton simply replied "By thinking about it all the time".

Coming back to our discussion of scientific methodology, we can summarise a formal process step by step. However, it should also be emphasised that science does not always proceed in this way.

1. Note an attribute of the physical world that is not understood.
Clearly, this leads to questions, for which we seek answers.

The most obvious question for Newton was 'why do objects fall to Earth?' or more precisely, 'why do objects fall towards the centre of the Earth?' There were obviously deeper questions that could be posed. For example, the body of the moon appeared to be suspended in the sky – why did that not share the same fate as

---

Text Box 2.1: Newton's Laws.

Newton's Law of Universal Gravitation.

The force of gravity between two bodies is directly proportional to the product of their masses, and inversely proportional to the square of their distance apart.

Expressed in terms of mathematics, the magnitude of the gravitational force $F_{gravity}$ between two masses m_1 and m_2, that are a distance r apart, is given by

$$F_{gravity} = G \frac{m_1 m_2}{r^2}, \qquad (2.1)$$

where G is simply a number which determines the strength of the force of gravity (referred to as Newton's constant)

Newton's Laws of Motion.

Newton 1 – A body will continue in a state of rest, or of uniform motion in a straight line, unless compelled to change this state by forces acting upon it.
Newton 2 – The rate of change of momentum of a body is proportional to the force acting upon it, and is in the same direction as the force.
Newton 3 – To every action there is an equal and opposite reaction.

---

the apple, and fall to Earth? Was there a common link between these happenings that provided clues about how gravity works?

2. Formulate a hypothesis.

A hypothesis is a supposition, or proposed explanation, which is made on the basis of limited evidence, as a starting point for further investigation.

Newton's hypothesis was that gravity was a 'force field'

between two objects by virtue of their masses. In general terms, the mass of an object is a measure of the amount of matter in contains (the basic unit of measurement of mass is the kilogram). Further he also thought it reasonable to suggest that the magnitude of the gravitational force between two masses would be affected by their distance apart. So close objects would experience a relatively strong force, which would diminish as they moved apart.

3. Construct a theory.

In the physical sciences, moving beyond the hypothesis usually entails constructing a theory, which is most often couched in the language of mathematics.

If we look again at the Text Box 2.1, we can see that the law of gravitation is almost an equation anyway, but expressed in words. I have also included the equation, as I feel confident that it is straight forward enough to allow explanation in simple terms. The top line of the equation is the 'product of their masses' referred to in the statement of the law, so we can see that if we have two very large masses – say, two planets or two stars – then the resulting force of gravity between them will be very large indeed. Consequently, gravity turns out to be the principal force that governs the dynamics of the Universe on the largest scales. On the other hand, if the masses are small – say, two people – then the product is correspondingly small. In fact, gravity is by far the weakest fundamental force yet discovered (that is, G is a very small number) so that the force of gravity between two people is tiny[12]. If it were otherwise, a walk down the High Street would be very different proposition!

The way the force varies with distance is given by the bottom line of the equation, and this is usually referred to as an inverse square law. This defines how the force of gravity diminishes as the masses move apart. If you envisage two objects a particular distance apart, then the force of gravity between them will have a specific magnitude. However, if you double the distance, the inverse square law says that the force is one quarter of what it was before. To get this, take 2 for 'double the distance', square it to give 4, and then take the inverse to give ¼. By the same logic, 3 times the distance will give $1/9^{th}$ the force, and 10 times the distance will give $1/100^{th}$ the force, and so on.

4. Apply the theory.

Clearly, the main motivation in developing a theory is its application to those mysterious attributes of the real world mentioned earlier in step 1.

For Newton, the application of his universal law of gravitation to celestial bodies – the motion of the moon around the Earth and the motion of the planets around the Sun – allowed him to open a door to the huge topic of the theory of orbital motion that had never been opened before.

However, a law defining the gravitational force, in itself, is insufficient to examine this application. To do this we need an understanding of how forces influence the motion of objects, and this is indeed what Newton created in stating his laws of motion – once again, see Text Box 2.1. These laws are stated in words here, but again it is important to realise that they have their most powerful expression when written in mathematical form. In Newton's time, they revolutionised science, and remarkably still dominate engineering science today. So, for example, when I worked in the space industry in the 1980s as part of a team designing and building satellites, our theoretical tools were Newtonian. Similarly, today's engineers still use these laws when designing buildings, bridges, cars, aeroplanes, and indeed space vehicles – what an amazing legacy!

5. Gather evidence.

The ultimate test of a theory is how closely it fits with reality. To ascertain this, we need to gather evidence, in the form of observations or data derived from experiments. There may already be a body of evidence, which provoked the questions mentioned in step 1 above.

For Newton, much of the drudgery of gathering evidence had been done by Johannes Kepler and Tycho Brahe[13]. Kepler's first two laws of planetary motion were published in 1609, and the third in 1619 – just 23 years before Newton was born. These were expressed mathematically but derived empirically, based on

Tycho Brahe's catalogue of observed planetary positions. In summary, Kepler's 1st law states that planets move on elliptical orbits, the 2nd that planets move more quickly when close to the Sun, and more slowly when further away, and the 3rd that the time it takes for a planet to orbit the Sun depends on the size of its orbit. When Newton applied his laws of gravity and motion to the planets, Kepler's laws were revealed, hence providing a theoretical foundation to understanding planetary motion. In terms of 17th century science, Newton's achievement was astonishing. The power in his triumph lay principally in the unification of a number of physical phenomena – in this case, the fall of an apple, the motion of the moon and the dynamics of the Solar System – in one all-encompassing theory. This pursuit of unification in physics persists up to the present time, and remains a main driver in modern day research into the very large (gravity) and the very small (quantum physics).

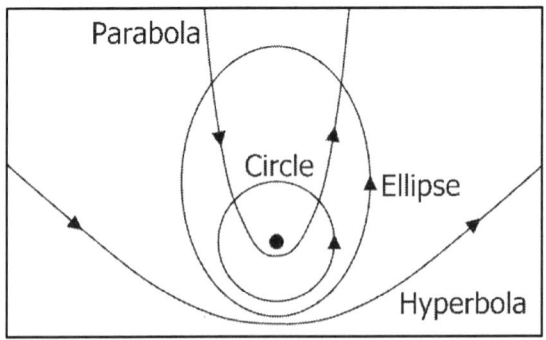

Figure 2.1. In Newton's day, circular and elliptical orbits were known, but parabolic and hyperbolic trajectories were discovered as predictions of his theory of gravitation.

6. *Does the theory lead to predictions?*

The power of a theory is enhanced if it not only fits with existing observational data, but also predicts phenomena as yet unseen.

Having acquired a mathematical model of planetary motion, Newton was now able to 'work the equations' to investigate what other attributes of orbits might be revealed by the theory. Having found Kepler's results in his mathematics, he went on to uncover others forms of trajectories that objects can travel in a gravity field. For, example, an object moving around the Sun is not confined to circular and elliptical orbits. He also found parabolic[14] and hyperbolic trajectories[15] – see Figure 2.1.

There are many other such instances throughout history when a working of the mathematics of a theory has led to a prediction of an unexpected phenomenon, which has then been found in the real world – so strengthening confidence in the theory itself.

7. Publication.

While this may not be a formal step in the methodology of science, nevertheless it is a vital process in communicating progress – what's the point of doing something if you're not going to tell others about it?

In the modern-day scientific community, 'publish or perish' is the mantra. However, in Newton's time, this was not so. The final chapter in the story of his achievement is surprising. Having 'solved the Solar System' in the way that we have described, he then failed to tell anyone. Meanwhile, unknown to Newton, contemporary scientists – mainly Robert Hooke and Edmund Halley – were struggling with the problem of planetary motion. Finally, in 1684, Halley visited Newton in Cambridge, hoping to gain some insight into the puzzle. When Halley posed the question about gravitational trajectories about the Sun, Newton revealed that he had already solved the problem, but ... had misplaced it! Ultimately, it was Halley that encouraged Newton to write his landmark work, the *Principia*, which required two years of hard work to complete. In this rather tortuous manner, Isaac Newton was finally recognised as one of the greatest scientific thinkers of all time.

Another interesting consequence of the scientific method is that *theories cannot be proven to be true,* but only modified or falsified. As we saw above, the only way to test a theory is by comparing its results with the real world. So, if the theory passes this test then confidence in the theory is strengthened. On the other hand, if theory and reality do not agree, then the theory is falsified, and the scientists are back to the drawing board – modifying the original theory or devising a new one which addresses the weaknesses. Consequently, and rather alarmingly, it is possible to claim that, *in principle*, there is no such thing as scientific truth. Although this can be regarded as a consequence of the scientific method, it would be foolish to suppose that this undermines the power and efficacy of science in exploring the Universe. It is also worth emphasising that the process of falsification is not straightforward, and requires a degree of judgement to be exercised. One good example of this is the discovery, in the 19th century, that the orbit of Uranus deviated from its predicted path as determined by Newton's law of gravitation. Could this spell the end of Newton's theory, or was there another explanation? In fact, the anomaly was found to be due to the perturbing effect of a yet-undiscovered planet. Indeed, by the ingenious application of Newton's theory, the French mathematician Urbain Le Verrier provided positional information which led to the telescopic discovery of Neptune in 1846. Hence, a potential falsification was transformed into a triumph for Newton. John Polkinghorne makes the point that falsifiability is irrelevant for a wide spectrum of 'core' scientific knowledge: "… surely, in actual fact, we have learned some things scientifically that we are never going to have to revise. Atoms have come to stay, and so has the helical structure of DNA."[16]

Newton's law of gravity survived every test thrown at it for over 150 years, but thereafter small discrepancies between the theory and observations began to show, for example in the rate of movement of the perihelion (point of closest approach to the Sun) of the elliptical orbit of Mercury[17]. In November 1915 Einstein published a new theory of gravity (called the general theory of relativity, of which more in Chapter 3). Although his motivation for doing this was not to address the weaknesses in Newton's theory, nevertheless these failings posed opportunities to test the new theory, and Einstein's theory won where Newton's was found wanting.

At the time of writing Einstein's gravity has reigned successfully for just over 100 years. It is worth clarifying that Newton's simpler theory works well and is still used by scientists and engineers within the domain of the Solar System where speeds are low (relative to the speed of light) and gravity field strengths are small. However, as we look out into the wider Universe at exotic objects – like **neutron stars** and **black holes** – then we see more extreme conditions. Einstein's gravity has successfully survived the more stringent tests arising from these objects, but its status is the same as Newton's gravity; there will likely be a test that Einstein's theory fails, and it too will be superseded. As Einstein himself said "No amount of experimentation can ever prove me right; a single experiment can prove me wrong".

To conclude this section, we return to Rupert Sheldrake's book *The Science Delusion*. One of the issues that he discusses is how, in recent times, the scientific worldview has adopted an (almost mandatory) emphasis on the philosophy of materialism. This is not the sort of materialism to do with a craving for consumer goods, but rather the assumption that reality is material or physical, and that everything – including thought, feelings, will and mind/consciousness – will be ultimately be explained solely in terms of physical matter and physical energy. Sheldrake argues that this assumption has hardened into a dogma, which effectively places limits on science's domain of investigation. So deeply entrenched is this notion that contemporary scientists are required to be materialists in order have credibility in the science community. The so-called new atheists have gleefully seized on the assumption of materialism, and have hardened it into a kind of anti-faith ideology with which to beat the faith community. However, if you believe what Scriptures say about God, that 'God is spirit'[18], then the 'hypothesis of God' becomes by definition outside the realms of scientific process or thought. As a consequence, the materialist brand of science can contribute nothing to the question of the existence or non-existence of God.

2.4 The laws of nature.

Put simply, the laws of nature describe how the physical content – matter and energy (stuff!) – of the Universe behaves under the influence of the fundamental forces of nature. Currently, science has discovered four such forces:

- *The gravitational force* – a long-range attractive force between objects by virtue of their mass (as discussed above).
- *The electromagnetic force* – a long-range force which governs the interaction between electrically charged particles. In the 19th century, Michael Faraday discovered that electric currents (i.e. moving electrical charges) produce magnetic fields, and dynamic magnetic fields induce electric currents. Consequently, the two phenomena, electricity and magnetism, are considered to be two sides of the same coin.
- *The strong nuclear force* – a very short-range force that acts between sub-atomic particles of matter. It binds **quarks** together in clusters to form the more-familiar subatomic particles, such as protons and neutrons. It also holds together the atomic nucleus, and plays an essential part in the process of creating elements in the nuclear furnaces of stars.
- *The weak nuclear force* – a very short-range force that governs the process of **radioactive decay**. It too plays an important role in nuclear fusion, the process that powers the stars.

However, in discussing the 'laws of nature', we must be very careful to distinguish them from the 'laws of science'.

The laws of nature are the powerful agency that governs the physical Universe. The laws are active in that they evolve the state of the Universe in time. For example, the law of nature governing gravity is the powerful mechanism that produces the huge force acting upon our planet, that keeps the Earth in orbit around the Sun (rather than the equation in Text Box 2.1, which is a law of science). Their influence is universal, but they themselves are not made of matter or energy. What then can the current materialistic brand of science say about them?

Since I was a small babe in arms, the laws of nature have exercised their influence over me – a great deal of my early learning, as my neural net was making connections as I discovered the world around me, was focused on the way that the laws worked. In fact, my survival depended upon a good working knowledge of the law of gravity, in particular. This is part of the problem. The laws of nature are so inculcated in infant humans, that it is difficult to step back and ask – how do they exercise such a powerful influence over everything, but without being in any way physically tangible, other than by means of that influence? I have to say that I cannot conceive of how they work.

As I write, I'm beginning to feel that there might be more questions than answers in this section, as I am seriously stumped to know very much about the laws of nature, other than that they exist and govern everything. Where do the laws or nature come from? Who, or what, is the law giver? It's fair to say that no one knows, and these questions are not currently addressed by science – because they are difficult, and scientists are rightly baffled. For example, the American theoretical physicist Lee Smolin comments on one perplexing aspect of nature's laws:

> "Even more puzzling are questions about timeless laws [of nature]: If laws are timeless, then what were they doing before there was a Universe for them to govern? Clearly the answer is that there *was* no time before the Universe, which means that the laws must be a deeper aspect of the [Universe] than time."[19]

We will discuss the Big Bang theory of the origin of the Universe in more detail in Chapter 3, but I think that most people know that it claims that the Universe was formed about 14 billion years ago in a violent expansion of a tiny nugget of space and time. Currently we do not have a scientific theory to describe the instant of creation at time zero, but amazingly we do know that at the shortest measurable time thereafter (10^{-43} seconds, a period of time that makes the blink of an eye seem like an eternity) the laws of nature were already imprinted upon the fabric of the cosmos. Subsequently, the behaviour of matter and energy has been governed very precisely and powerfully by these laws, and that has enabled the development of galaxies, stars, solar systems, planets and ultimately us.

What then are the 'laws of science', as opposed to the 'laws of nature'? In this case we *do* know where they came from, which is probably their major distinguishing feature. The laws of science are what we do in trying to describe the laws of nature. For example, Newton's equation for the law of universal gravitation (equation (2.1) above) is an attempt to express in mathematics how gravity works. It is, of course, simply an equation (a law of science), rather than the powerful agency that enacts gravity in the real world (a law of nature). Stephen Hawking expressed very well this distinction between science and nature when discussing a possible theory of everything:

> "Even if there is only one possible unified theory, *it is just a set of rules and equations*. What is it that breathes fire into the equations and makes a universe for them to describe?"[20] (my italics)

The equations are a law of science, whereas the 'fire' is the powerful agency that enacts what we call a law of nature.

Having appreciated the clear distinction, an obvious question might be – how can we have any comprehension of the laws of nature? Even Einstein said that he thought this comprehensibility was miraculous. Curiously, as we have seen, this understanding is usually through the medium of mathematics. Abstract mathematical theories that were originally developed without any practical application in mind later turn out to be powerful predictive physical models of reality. We have got so used to this that we easily forget that this is strange.[21] This observation of the intelligibility of the Universe rests well within a theistic framework. If we are God's creation, and we bear His image, then we too should expect to share in His creativity. We should expect God to appeal to our rational faculties, and for there to be some resonance between His mind and ours.

Soon after I came to faith I began to explore scripture, which was very unfamiliar to me at the time. In this process, I was quite excited to come across a passage in the book of Proverbs which was essentially an alternate creation account. Then, as now, I was not expecting the Bible to be a science text book, but this passage from the book of Proverbs struck a chord. I would suggest you read the whole passage, but the following paraphrase gives something of the essence:

The Lord brought me forth as the first of his works, ... I was formed long ages ago, at the very beginning, when the world came to be. When there were no watery depths, I was given birth, when there were no springs overflowing with water; ... I was there when he set the heavens in place, ... Then I was constantly at his side. I was filled with delight day after day, rejoicing always in his presence, ... [22]

In this passage, 'wisdom' is personified, and speaks of her origin, her active operations, the part she played in the creation of the Universe and her relationship to God. This is essentially a Biblical account of the creation of the Universe, but further, it expresses the notion that part of this entailed the creation of the laws of nature. The beauty, complexity and elegance of the laws as revealed by science would indeed require a great deal of wisdom on the part of a Creator, who in the beginning 'spoke them into being'! However, theology does not have all the answers. Can the same be said of science?

2.5 Does science explain everything?

After this introduction to the so-called scientific method, and to the ordered Universe in which we live that allows this method to operate and progress, we can now return to some of the issues considered at the opening of this chapter; specifically the notion that, despite the power and authority of science in our culture, nevertheless it has limitations. Science has a clearly defined domain of investigation, which does not include two of the things that are really important to us as human beings: meaning and purpose.

What science does

Once an authoritative scientific theory is established, it can reliably describe how something happens, by evolving a physical process (the 'state of the system') in time, from a given set of initial conditions to an accurate prediction of the future state of the process. Science is good at the mechanistic aspects of how a physical process works; how a physical process evolves in time. I am not omitting the discussion of biological processes – clearly the complex behaviour of biological systems too depends on the way that matter works at a physical level.

An exciting example from contemporary physics involves the application of Newton's gravity (with Einsteinian corrections) to an astrophysical problem, which has had a profound impact on our understanding of galaxies. At a distance of about 26,000 light years away in the centre of our galaxy is a very bright and very compact radio source which has the rather unimaginative label 'Sagittarius A*' (known as Sag A*). In recent times, observational technologies have improved amazingly to allow the observation of how the neighbouring stars move around this object. The observed positions and velocities of a particular star allow its orbit to be determined, by the application of the theory of gravity. Two main aspects of the mysterious central object were discovered. Firstly, the determined orbits of a number of surrounding stars allowed the mass of Sag A* to be estimated – and this turns out to be an astonishing 4 million times the mass of our own Sun. Secondly, the point of closest approach of each star (on its elliptical orbit) to the central object define a maximum volume within which Sag A* is confined. This volume was found to be extremely compact. Indeed, the only conclusion that can be drawn from this combination of characteristics is that Sag A* is a super-massive black hole. In this case, Einstein's theory of gravity confirms unambiguously that such a massive object confined to such a compact volume can only be a black hole. Subsequent observation of other galaxies suggests that super-massive black holes are ubiquitous within the hubs of galaxies throughout the Universe.

This discovery of Sag A* illustrates how physics can be used to describe a complex system, and in that process, provide a deep understanding of some aspect of the physical world. In other situations, however, physical science describes, but often does not provide understanding of an object or process. In biology, observation often starts the investigative process, and, in some instances, investigation may consist of nothing more complex than systematised observations. Furthermore observation, even when followed by experiment, may often not lead to a full understanding of a biological process.

However, it is the realm of the physical sciences that brings into sharp focus issues with our understanding of the nature of reality. It does depend upon your definition of 'understanding'. To see this, let's adopt a rather straight-forward definition. We could say that we understand something when we can reduce it to intuitive (common sense?) concepts. If we adopt a definition such as this – which we often do in everyday situations – we have a fundamental problem. That is, the nature of reality revealed by science does not often lend itself to common sense. The 'new' theories of relativity and **quantum mechanics** (QM), developed during the early part of the 20th century, reveal many counter-intuitive aspects of the world.

To give one illustration, we can ask the simple question 'what is an electron?', which is an issue within the domain of QM. This theory was developed in the 1920s, principally by Erwin Schrödinger and Werner Heisenberg, to describe the physics of the very small – atoms and subatomic particles. One principal characteristic of the theory is that it overturns the deterministic character of Newton's laws, and introduces uncertainty into reality at the microscale. For example, if you wish to know the position of a particle, the theory tells us that it could be literally anywhere, and provides a probability density that indicates where the particle is most likely to be found.

Coming back to our question, the common definition of an electron is that it is a tiny fundamental particle of matter, with a negative electrical charge, which orbits the nucleus of atoms. If we were to ask a Nobel Prize-winning physicist 'what is an electron?', then they would be unable to offer a definitive answer. This is because sometimes the electron (or indeed any other subatomic particle) displays the characteristics of a wave and sometimes that of a particle. Many of the founders of the theory of QM spent much time trying to understand this schizophrenic character of matter, but to no avail. The 'scientific explanation' is that the electron is said to exhibit the attribute of 'wave-particle duality'. Some kind of clarity of how wave-particle duality may be interpreted is acquired by looking more deeply at the mathematical details of the theory, but in terms of an intuitive understanding there is no consensus. As Paul Davies, physicist and science writer, says: "It is impossible to visualise a wave-particle, so don't try"[23]. The point I am making here is that physics does not provide an understanding of the underlying nature of the electron, but rather introduces a mysterious label – wave-particle duality – as a substitute. More generally, nearly one hundred years on from the origins of QM there is still controversy about how the theory should be interpreted.

Heisenberg quantified the notion of uncertainty in the microworld with his uncertainty principle, which, for example, states that the precise position and momentum of a particle cannot be known simultaneously (momentum is defined as the product of mass and velocity of the particle). In other words – and more loosely – if you know where it is, you have no idea how fast it is moving, and if you know how fast it is moving then you don't know where it is. This is a fundamental feature of reality, due to the attribute of wave-particle duality. Einstein, who was influential in establishing the foundations of the quantum revolution, could not accept the theory and rejected it in his later years. This was primarily because he expected there to be an underlying deterministic reality in the microworld that QM did not provide. In response to this, he commented "Quantum mechanics ... delivers much, but [it] does not really bring us any closer to the secrets of the Old One. I, at any rate, am convinced that *He* does not play dice." [24]

Contemporary physicists are pragmatic beings that accept the success of QM in predicting the outcome of experiments, while not paying too much attention to its foundational issues. However, American theoretical physicist Lee Smolin has drawn attention to this matter, by recognising the need to "resolve the problems in the foundations of quantum mechanics, either by making sense of the theory as it stands or by inventing a new theory that does make sense."[25] Although few physicists work on this venture, its importance cannot be underestimated. The task that occupies the vast majority of contemporary researchers is the quest to find a Theory of Everything. This is understood to be the process of unifying the theories of the very big (Einstein's gravity) with the

The Science Delusion

very small (quantum mechanics), and this is compromised if QM turns out to be an incomplete description of reality.

Nevertheless, having said all this, it is also the case that there is a booming, global electronics industry. This underlines the nature of scientific method – on the one hand, we have no real idea what an electron is, but, on the other, we can describe with great accuracy *how* it behaves, so allowing the engineering of a plethora of electronic equipment and devices. Despite the apparent weirdness of quantum mechanics, it has to be said that the numerical accuracy of its predictions surpasses all other theories. This is what science does very well, across the whole spectrum of technical specialisms, but what are its limitations?

What science does not do
I have always believed that science will never be equipped to address the issues of meaning and purpose – even if a so-called Theory of Everything is found. Since coming to faith, I think I have become more aware that the so-called ultimate questions are beyond the grasp of science. The scientific method discussed earlier is a potent form of rational enquiry, but we must let science be science. In other words, we must guard against over-extending the use of its methodology to domains where its application is inappropriate.

As a generalisation, we could characterise the ultimate questions as *why?* questions, as opposed to the mechanistic *how?* questions discussed in the last section. Clearly, this *how?/why?* approach is not rigorous, but as a working proposition it may be helpful. Common examples of questions outside the remit of scientific enquiry are things like:

- Why are we here?
- Why is there so much suffering in the world?
- Why is something considered right or wrong?
- Why did we go to the moon?

Okay, the last of these questions is perhaps not often posed as a relevant example, but it is a useful one because it can be asked in two ways – 'how did we go to the moon?' and 'why did we go to the moon?' – which leads to very different answers. The *how* question can be addressed by the methods of scientific enquiry. The orbits and trajectories required can be defined quantitatively by Newton's gravity, and the requirements for the software and hardware systems needed to do the job can be derived in every detail. However, the *why* question is beyond the remit of scientific method. It also depends on who you ask. For example, at the time when the Apollo moon landings occurred (1969-1972), I would probably have said, with my young idealistic view of the world, that it was done with the best of intentions in the name scientific enquiry. However, with the benefit of hindsight, and instilled perhaps with a degree of cynicism that comes with age, I now can appreciate that the primary reason for doing it was probably for the Capitalist West to demonstrate its superiority over Communism.

Can we have a 'Theory of Everything'?
In 2014 the film *The Theory of Everything*[26] was released, which was a dramatization of the early life of the theoretical physicist Stephen Hawking. Inevitably the drama focusses mainly on his relationship with his first wife Jane Wilde, and the ensuing impact of Stephen's tragic diagnosis, at age 21, of motor neurone disease. As an aside, the glibbest moment of the film comes early on, when Stephen and Jane are in the first moments of their opening conversation. Stephen tells her that he studies cosmology and adds that it is a kind of religion for intelligent atheists – a conversation that is most likely fictional! At that time, Hawking was struggling with the search for meaning and almost certainly would not have considered himself to be an atheist. Indeed, God figures frequently in his early writings, but something like atheism seems to have emerged gradually as he aged.

Viewers of the film could be forgiven for believing that Stephen had actually developed a Theory of Everything (TOE) during his lifetime, but of course, the search for such a thing continues unabated. But what does a TOE actually mean? As mentioned briefly above, the physics community's major challenge currently is producing a TOE that will unify the very large (planets, stars, galaxies, Universe – Einstein's theory of gravity) with the very small (the subatomic world – the theory of QM). This can be referred to as the problem of **quantum gravity**. This problem has been around for a long time. The two major pillars of modern physics, Einstein's theory of gravity (the general theory of relativity) and quantum mechanics, were developed alongside each other during the very productive first 30 years or so of the 20th century. Within their own domains, both of these theories have been remarkably successful. That is, Einstein's gravity has been applied to innumerable exotic phenomena associated with very massive bodies, such as neutron stars, black holes and even the Universe as a whole, and after about 100 years has yet to fail the crucial test of comparison with reality. Similarly, quantum mechanics has given an excellent account of itself when applied to the microworld of molecules, atoms and subatomic matter.

So why is it important to develop a unified theory that encompasses both? Science now finds itself in a place where the domains of these theories intersect. That is, when we try to understand what happens at the centre of a black hole, or at the instant the Big Bang occurred that brought our Universe into existence, we find that our current theories break down. Instead of giving sensible quantitative results, we find infinities. In both of these examples, we are trying to understand the physics of something which is both very tiny and very massive. As far as I am aware, nature does not do infinities, but our current laws of science certainly do. Consequently, the need for a unified theory of quantum gravity, or a TOE.

This problem of unification has been with us since the 1930s, and although there are some relatively recent theories that attempt to resolve the issue, it remains intractable. Clearly, we await a new Einstein to show us how to complete the revolution in science that began with general relativity and QM. This is a fascinating story, and there is a wealth of excellent popular science texts written by practitioners for the lay reader for those wishing to take it further.[27] One of these is Stephen Hawking's best seller *A Brief History of Time*[28]. In the final paragraph of his conclusion he talks of finding a TOE:

"However, if we do discover a complete theory, it should in time be understandable in broad principle by everyone, not just a few scientists. Then we shall all, philosophers, scientists and just ordinary people, be able to take part in the discussion of the question of why it is that we and the Universe exist. If we find the answer to that, it would be the ultimate triumph of human reason – for then we would know the mind of God."

Great prose, but I think it unlikely that 'ordinary people' would either understand it or discuss it. This is not meant as a slight on the intellect of ordinary people, but rather a comment on the nature of current research avenues to quantum gravity. For example, one candidate – **String Theory** requires the Universe to have ten spatial dimensions, rather than the three with which we are familiar! This is viable within the framework of a complex mathematical theory, but it's unlikely to inflame conversation over the breakfast table, or further our intuitive understanding of physical reality. Furthermore, there is no attempt in the current search for a TOE to include issues of meaning and purpose. The much-sought-after TOE may exist, but sadly the questions of *why* we and the Universe exist will remain firmly beyond the grasp of science. While science can benefit aspects of our lives, nevertheless we still need to find peace, wellbeing, love and purpose. Science is not the route to this.

When I attended a recent talk on issues of science and faith, the speaker used a striking metaphor, comprising an image of an avenue of street lighting on a dark, murky night. In the same way, the light of scientific revelation shines brightly, and illuminates a great deal of the 'landscape of reality', the Universe in which we live. But there are undeniably things which the scientific method cannot illuminate – for which science is an inappropriate tool. While searching the web, I came across a quote by George Ellis, a Professor of Applied Mathematics at the University of Cape Town, in the journal *Nature* which summarises this very well:

"A simple statement of fact: there is no physics theory that explains the nature of, or even the existence of, football matches, teapots, or jumbo-jet aircraft. The human mind is physically based, but there is no hope whatever of predicting the behaviour it controls from the underlying physical laws. Even if we had a satisfactory fundamental physics 'theory of everything', this situation would remain unchanged: physics would still fail to explain the outcomes of human purpose, and so would provide an incomplete description of the real world around us." [29]

2.6 Concluding remarks.

After all the discussion above, concerning the shortcomings of science to address all of reality, I think I should remind the reader that this book is *pro-science*, and that I love science!

I also appreciate that this discourse on the interaction between science and faith has been written in a very personal and pragmatic manner, prioritising the reader's comprehension over rigor. For readers wishing to have a more academic, yet concise discussion of the issues, I would recommend one of John Polkinghorne's texts.[30]

Finally, the biggest Science Delusion of all is that science already knows all the answers – the notion that the details still need to be worked out but, supposedly, the fundamental questions are settled. There are a great many topics – big questions – which are within the domain of scientific investigation that currently evade resolution. And these are not small matters, as mentioned briefly in Chapter 1. They are huge issues of fundamental importance, for example:

- The origin of the Universe
- The origin of the laws of nature
- The origin of life
- The origin and mechanism of mind/consciousness (the human brain) ...

to mention but a few. It is not my intention therefore to say 'God did it' when science falls short – there will be no God of the Gaps in these pages. I repeat my belief that science is simply God's revelation in nature, and that God is sovereign over all of His creation. How I got to this point, I will explain later.

One last thought – when I talk interminably about the scientific stuff, please keep in mind the author of this Creation. When you consider the elegance and power of His laws of nature, and the beauty of His design, give Him the credit. Allow yourself to be awed, and praise God!

Chapter 2 endnotes:

[1] Quoted in Max Born, Physics In My Generation, Springer Science+Business Media, 1969.
[2] Freeman Dyson – Science and Religion, Interview with Sam Schweber, July 2016: https://www.youtube.com/watch?v=xwoVrSICaTA. Dyson sums up nicely the clash between fundamentalists on both sides of the science and faith debate (see quote at the opening of this chapter).
[3] Rupert Sheldrake, The Science Delusion, Coronet (Hodder & Stoughton), 2012.
[4] Bertrand Russell, Religion and Science, Oxford University Press, 1935, p. 243.
[5] Alister McGrath, Inventing the Universe, Hodder & Stoughton, 2015, p. 143.
[6] Richard Dawkins, The God Delusion, Black Swan, 2006.
[7] Albert Einstein and Alice Calaprice (Editor), The Expanded Quotable Einstein, Princeton University Press, 2000, p. 202.
[8] Attributed to Johannes Kepler.
[9] C. S. Lewis, Christian Reflections, Grand Rapids (Eerdmans), 1967, p. 65.
[10] Albert Einstein, Physics and Reality, Journal of the Franklin Institute (1936), Vol. 221, Issue 3, pp. 349-382.
[11] Newton's epic Philosophiæ Naturalis Principia Mathematica was published 5 July 1687. Over time, this brought Isaac Newton international fame. For brevity's sake the title is often shortened to 'Principia', which, incidentally, is the name given to UK astronaut Tim Peake's Space Station mission Dec. 2015 – June 2016. The work comprises three parts, in which he lays out in mathematics his account of universal gravitation and his laws of motion.
[12] For those with a technical background, the force of gravity between two people, each with a mass of 70 kg, spaced 1 metre apart is of the order of one-tenth of a μNewton (3 x 10^{-7} N).
[13] Tycho Brahe was a Danish nobleman who spent much of his time and resources developing precision instruments housed in an observatory on an island off the coast of Denmark. Brahe compiled what was then the most complete and accurate catalogue of planetary position measurements.
[14] A parabolic trajectory is the path of an object that falls from a great distance, with initially zero speed, towards the Sun (for example). As it

reaches the vicinity of the Sun, gravity sling-shots the object around the far side of the Sun so that the object travels back in the direction from whence it came.

[15] An example of a hyperbolic trajectory relevant to spacecraft mission design is the path of a spacecraft 'swinging-by' a planet, a manoeuvre that has been done many times in recent astronautical history. The interest of the modern-day spacecraft mission analyst in such a manoeuvre is that, if performed correctly, it can increase the spacecraft's speed relative to the Sun without using rocket fuel.

[16] John Polkinhorne, Science & Theology: an introduction, SPCK/Fortress Press, 1998, p. 14.

[17] The movement (or 'precession') of the perihelion of Mercury. There are Newtonian effects which cause this movement, but Newton's gravity underestimated the effect. This anomaly was first discovered in 1859 by Urbain Le Verrier, a French mathematician and celestial mechanics specialist. Although the magnitude of the discrepancy was tiny, it was nevertheless considered too large to be disregarded as observational error. When Einstein's new theory accounted for the anomaly precisely, it was for him a eureka moment of 'joyous excitement'.

[18] The Holy Bible (NIV): John's Gospel, Chapter 4, verse 24.

[19] Lee Smolin, Time Reborn, Penguin Books, 2013, p. 74.

[20] Stephen Hawking, A Brief History of Time, Bantam Press, 1990, p. 174.

[21] Alister McGrath, Inventing the Universe, Hodder & Stoughton, 2015, p. 76.

[22] The Holy Bible (NIV): The book of Proverbs, Chapter 8, verses 22-30.

[23] Paul Davies, Superforce: the Search for a Grand Unified Theory of Nature, Simon & Schuster, 1984, p. 24.

[24] From a letter, written in German, in December 1926 to his friend and theoretical physicist Max Born.

[25] Lee Smolin, The Trouble with Physics, Penguin Books, 2006, p. 8.

[26] The Theory of Everything, Universal Pictures, 2014.

[27] Brian Greene, The Elegant Universe, Vintage Books, 2000.
Brian Greene, The Fabric of the Cosmos, Penguin Books, 2004.
Lee Smolin, Three Roads to Quantum Gravity, Basic Books, 2001.
Lee Smolin, The Trouble with Physics, Penguin Books, 2006.

[28] Stephen Hawking, A Brief History of Time, Bantam Press, 1990, p. 175.

[28] George F. R. Ellis, Physics, complexity and causality, Nature (2005), Vol. 435, p. 743.

[30] For example, John Polkinghorne, Science & Theology: an introduction, SPCK/Fortress Press, 1998.

From the Big Bang to Biology – where is God?

3 God, the Big Bang and the Universe.

"The epic of cosmic evolution had begun, a hierarchy in the condensation of matter from the gas of the Big Bang – clusters of galaxies, galaxies, stars, planets and, eventually, life and an intelligence able to understand a little of the elegant process responsible for its origin." Carl Sagan[1]

"Where Einstein really affects the Bible is the fact that general relativity is the organizing principle for the Big Bang." Neil deGrasse Tyson[2]

Graham writes ...

3.1 Introduction.
In this chapter, I consider the current scientific orthodoxy concerning the origin and fate of the Universe. Amazing progress has been made in the last four or five decades or so, largely due to advances in the engineering of observational technology. Coincidentally, it is about four decades since I completed my PhD in cosmology – at which time the study of the Universe was very much a theoretical enterprise. We have now arrived at a plausible and coherent picture of how the Universe began; how it will evolve; and what its ultimate fate will be, based on a foundation of observational data.

This stunning achievement has, however, been accompanied by something of a celebratory mood in the scientific ranks, and we should introduce a note of caution. Parallels can be drawn between the present day and the beginning of the last century. At that time, Newtonian physics had reigned for 200 years or so, and the general mood was one of having wrapped-up physics. In April 1900, British physicist William Thomson (Lord Kelvin) presented a talk at the Royal Institution, London, entitled '19th-Century Clouds over the Dynamical Theory of Heat and Light', and famously declared that physics was over. However, Lord Kelvin's 'clouds' turned out to be the clues that led to the development of quantum mechanics and relativity theory. So, as was said in Chapter 2, we have to be aware that theories come and go, and maybe the current orthodoxy will be overturned in due time.

At this point, I should alert readers that this chapter is quite long and 'science-y'. It is perhaps a challenging read, but I hope that the content is accessible. My aim is to try to share some of the awe-inspiring attributes of the science that, to my mind, reveal the creative hand of God. With limited space I can only touch on the most prominent discoveries about the origin and ultimate fate of the Universe, for example:

- the extraordinary revelation that space and time are dynamic, and participate in the physics of gravitation,
- the evidence for the existence of a creation event, the Big Bang, at the beginning of our Universe,
- the mechanism of the Bang that initiated the cosmic expansion, and
- the discovery of dark matter and dark energy, and how they affect the long-term fate of the cosmos.

In Chapters 5 and 8, my co-author John talks about the beauty, diversity and interdependencies of life on this planet, and how that speaks to him about God's power and creativity in creation. In the same way, as we explore the physics of cosmology in this chapter and the next, what science says about the underlying nature of reality is truly inspiring. There is a parallel process of the diversity and inter-connectiveness of natural law that has driven the

God, the Big Bang and the Universe

Universe from the initial creation event to the diverse and beautiful cosmos we see today. If you too hold a faith, it is my hope that you will share my sense of awe at what the science is telling us about God and His creation.

3.2 The beginning according to Genesis.

Although the majority of what follows in this Chapter focusses on the scientific account, I want to consider briefly the scriptural account of creation in the first two chapters of Genesis.

The first time I recall this having any impact upon me was on Christmas Eve 1968. In what was then the most watched television broadcast, the crew of Apollo 8 took turns to read the first 10 verses of Genesis Chapter 1 from lunar orbit. The world seemed to be buzzing with excitement as three brave souls – Frank Borman, Jim Lovell and William Anders – ventured beyond the gravity field of cradle Earth. Amid the busyness of the 'high-tech' adventure, those ancient scriptural words seemed so appropriate at such a moment in history. As I recall the event now, the hairs on the back of my neck stand up! As an interesting aside, an atheist Madalyn Murray O'Hair sued the US government over violations of the first amendment by the reading of Genesis on a government-sponsored mission. The case was ultimately dismissed by the US Supreme Court due to a lack of jurisdiction!

According to Jewish tradition, Genesis was the first of five books (the Pentateuch) thought to have been written by Moses, who lived around 1400 BC[3]. This appears to estimate when the creation account in Genesis 1 and 2 was written, but Bible scholars disagree about when precisely Moses lived, and indeed about his authorship of the text at all. However, setting these controversies aside, these two chapters provide the scriptural account of the origins of the Universe, the world, and life, and have themselves generated their own controversies and debate over many centuries. Indeed, many authors have taken up the challenge of interpreting the message of the Genesis creation account[4]. Can I suggest you familiarise (or refamiliarise) yourself with Genesis Chapters 1 and 2 before reading on?

When reading this text we need to be mindful of the cultural and social setting of the times in which it was written – clearly it was not intended to be a science textbook. As Galileo said around four centuries ago 'The Bible shows the way to go to heaven, not the way the heavens go'! The story of creation told by Scripture is obviously different from that told by science. The truths expressed in Genesis are more to do with recounting for the Jewish people, at that time, the origin and destiny of the world and humankind in light of their belief in God. The theological message of these opening chapters of Genesis is clear – that there is one God who is eternal and the creator of all things. That He is outside and distinct from His creation, that He creates by 'His word', that He has a goal in creation (that is, us), and that He has a personal interest in each one of us. For a more detailed outworking of the theological message of Genesis 1, I would direct the reader to Chapter 5 of Lennox[4].

There is insufficient room here to unpack the creation account in all its details, and many books have been written in attempting to do this. Aside from the theological message, how well does the scriptural account perform in describing the sequence of the physical and biological aspects of creation? Overall, to me as a physicist, it does not accord well with the scientific account. For example, the occurrence of 'first light' and the formation of the Sun and moon are placed after that of the Earth – and to a biologist the account has only the vaguest parallels with evolution (John will develop this story in Chapter 5).

However, the principal physical message of Genesis is that there was a creation event that brought the Universe into being. It was only during the early years of the twentieth century that science began to uncover evidence that such a creation event may have occurred. Prior to this, the prevailing view was that the Universe was eternal, having no beginning or end, and consequently the theological and scientific accounts were in conflict. I would like to tell the story of how this conflict was resolved in what follows, but first there a few technical preliminaries which need to be introduced to aid in the understanding of the remainder of this chapter.

3.3 Some groundwork.

Dealing with big and small numbers
In the discussion of the physical attributes of the Universe, we come across a lot of very large and very small numbers. To avoid writing strings of zeros in expressing these, scientists adopt a short hand system, involving powers of ten. This system is explained in Text Box 3.1 It would be helpful, but not essential, to understand the additional information in the text boxes throughout.

Text Box 3.1: Preliminaries.

An abbreviated system for expressing large and small numbers – to get the idea, consider the following sequence,

$$\frac{1}{1000} = \frac{1}{10 \times 10 \times 10} = \frac{1}{10^3} = 10^{-3} = 0.001,$$

which demonstrates that one thousandth can be expressed as 10^{-3}. Note that the number after the minus sign indicates how many digits there are after the decimal point. By the same argument we can see that, say, one millionth (0.000001) can be written in shorthand as 10^{-6}. For big numbers, by similar logic, we can see that 1,000 can be expressed as 10^3, and 1,000,000 is given by 10^6. Finally, this shorthand can also be used to express numbers that are not just powers of ten; for example,

$27,000,000 = 2.7 \times 10 \times 10^6 = 2.7 \times 10^7$, and

$0.000035 = 3.5 \times 0.00001 = 3.5 \times 10^{-5}$.

What is a light year?
There is a common misconception that this is a unit of time, whereas it is actually a measure of distance. Due to the huge distances involved in describing the Universe, a sensible unit of measuring distance is required, and one commonly used by

astronomers is the light year. This is the distance travelled by light in the period of one year. Given that light propagates at a speed of 300,000 km per second (186,000 miles per second), a light year is a very long way! To work out how far this is, we take light speed in km/sec (miles/sec) and multiply it by the number of seconds in one hour (3,600), then by the number of hours in a day (24) and then finally by the number of days in a year (365). This turns out to be about 9,461,000,000,000 km (5,866,000,000,000 miles). So, one light year is 9.461×10^{12} km (5.866×10^{12} miles), or approximately 9,500,000,000,000 km (5,900,000,000,000 miles). This is used by astronomers as a kind of measure, or ruler, to quantify cosmic distances. For example, the nearest star (apart from the Sun) is about 4 light years distant, the disk of our home galaxy the Milky Way is around 100,000 light years across, and the distance to the neighbouring Andromeda galaxy is approximately two and a half million light years.

Time travel!

As a consequence of the finite speed of light, when you look up into the night sky you are seeing everything as it was, so effectively you are time-travelling into the past. Given that moonlight takes about 1.3 seconds to reach us, then (if we had a big enough telescope) we would see events on the moon as they occurred 1.3 seconds ago. Events seen on the Sun's surface took place around 8 minutes prior to current time, and events in the Andromeda galaxy about 2 ½ million years ago. This attribute of being able to study the past history of the Universe is very helpful to astronomers. For example, if we observe the characteristics and distribution of galaxies billions of light years away, then this gives information about their historical attributes, and about the way the Universe has evolved over time.

Einstein's gravity theory tells us that time travel into the future is also possible, but a little more difficult, since it involves orbiting a black hole (as fans of the film *Interstellar*[5] will know), but that's a different story.

Space-time

The world of contemporary physics is a four-dimensional one, comprising the three spatial dimensions and one time dimension. Any event can be defined by four numbers, three giving the event's location and one giving the time at which it took place (see Figure 3.1). We use this convention often, without thinking about it – for example "meet me at the pub at 7 o'clock" implicitly entails knowledge of the pub's location (three spatial coordinates), and of the time of the meeting. In this way, the interrelationship of physical events can be captured by a complex web of points in a 4D space that physicists call 'space-time'.

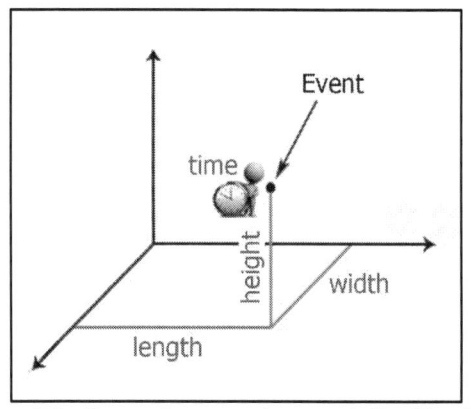

Figure 3.1 Events in space-time are defined by three spatial coordinates, and one of time.

In other words, space-time is the arena within which physics happens. Although Newton never coined the phrase 'space-time', nevertheless he used it simply as an invariant backdrop – a convenient way to describe and quantify events and motions in space and time. For him, this framework in space and time was fixed and absolute. As we will see later, Einstein showed us that space-time itself is flexible and dynamic, participating in the physics of motion and gravitation.

The equivalence of mass and energy

In developing his theories of relativity, Einstein discovered a relationship between the mass of an object and its energy. This is defined by his simple, iconic equation $E = mc^2$ – see Text Box 3.2. This principle of the equivalence of mass and energy creeps into

---

Text Box 3.2: Preliminaries.

The equivalence of mass and energy – Einstein's equation relating mass and energy is,

$$E = mc^2, \qquad (3.1)$$

where E is energy (Joules), m is mass (kilograms) and c is the speed of light (metres/second).

As a consequence of this, when scientists specify the mass of a sub-atomic particle they talk about its 'rest mass' – in other words the mass of the particle when it is at rest.

If the particle is accelerated to high speed its energy increases and consequently so does its mass.

Given that $c = 300{,}000{,}000$ m/s is such a large number, this implies that there is a very large amount of energy in a small amount of mass. A quick calculation shows that the amount of energy associated with 1 kg of mass is 9×10^{16} J.

To sustain the Sun's radiant energy output, the nuclear reactions in its core convert approximately 4 ¼ million tonnes of its mass into energy each second.

The destruction of the city of Hiroshima, Japan in August 1945 by an atomic weapon involved the conversion of 0.7 grams of mass into energy.

---

the discussion in several ways. One consequence of this is to do with the physical sources of the gravitational field. For Newton, the source of gravity was simply mass. However, in Einstein's theory, gravity is not only produced by mass, but also by energy (as we will see later, pressure is also a source of Einsteinian gravity). For example, the energy of electromagnetic radiation was so significant in the early Universe that the dynamics of the expansion of the Universe was dominated by radiation, rather than by matter, for the first thousand years or so after the Big Bang.

The Large Hadron Collider (LHC) at CERN (Conseil Européen pour la Recherche Nucléaire) is a particle accelerator, which is currently the most energetic machine of its kind in the world. It is famous principally for the discovery of the **Higgs Boson** in 2012 (see section 3.6). The principle of operation of a particle accelerator is simple in concept, but difficult in the engineering. Streams of hadrons, which are particles such as protons and their **antiparticle**, are accelerated to near the speed of light and then impacted head-on to produce hugely energetic collision events. The equivalence of mass and energy means that matter particles can be created in these collisions from the abundant energy available, with the species of particles produced differing from those originally used in the impact. In this way, the scientists can hope to find something new in the debris from these collisions, such as the Higgs Boson, in the endeavour to understand the subatomic world. The collisional impacts in the LHC again speak of the strangeness of this quantum world. For a macroscopic analogy of these events, imagine the head-on impact of two cars, and finding that the resulting debris consists of a collection of motorcycles, trucks and buses!

Effectively, the LHC is simulating the environment that existed in the early Universe. At the time of writing (2019), the maximum energy achieved at CERN is equivalent to a time about 10^{-14} seconds after the Big Bang. Each collision occurring in the LHC emulates what was happening then. It is remarkable to think that nowhere else in the known Universe are such energies occurring naturally. Einstein's equation provides the mechanism for the transformation of this huge energy in the early Universe into mass – that is, matter particles – so creating the familiar particles (protons, neutrons, electrons) which ultimately came to make up stars, planets and people.

3.4 How did we get to the Big Bang?

As already mentioned, since the beginning of recorded history, people have speculated about the origins and fate of the Universe. Over time this has developed into a branch of science we now call cosmology. Until the 20th century, these speculations were the domain of theologians and philosophers, as there was no observational evidence to form the basis of a scientific theory, or an opinion. However, in the last century two major experimental discoveries were made which have placed cosmology on a sound scientific footing – the expansion of the Universe and the cosmic microwave background. This section looks at these remarkable developments, which brings an alignment of the Biblical and scientific views of creation.

The general theory of relativity – Einstein's theory of gravity

Prior to the 20th century, the Universe was considered to be eternal, static and unchanging as there was no scientific evidence to suggest otherwise[6]. If we imagine ourselves as ancient humans, looking up at the night sky with unaided eyes, then the visible Universe would provide a calming impression of ageless invariability. So how did this change?

As with so many aspects of the revolution in physics that occurred in the early decades of the 20th century, the story starts with Albert Einstein, and his radical new theory of gravitation. This was developed during the period 1907 to 1915, when Einstein wrestled with the physics and, in particular, the mathematics required to create his theory. Although he considered his own mathematical skills to be poor, the mathematics required to describe his theory of gravity were so complex that it was claimed that few scientists in the world actually understood it when first published. Fortunately, the basics of his theory can be explained in relatively straightforward terms.

Einstein's major contribution in formulating his theory was in revolutionising our ideas about space and time. His picture of the way planets move around the Sun was very different to Newton's. In Einstein's theory, the 4D world of space-time is not just a background reference system, but rather a dynamic entity, determining the way things move in a gravity field. The foundation of his theory is the principle that massive objects, like the Sun, distort the geometry of the space-time surrounding them. This is the celebrated 'warped space', which has become so 'familiar' to us all, from the genre of popular science fiction.

However, although we have heard a lot about it in sci-fi stories, an intuitive appreciation of what a 'curved four-dimensional space-time continuum' means is still difficult to comprehend, even for those equipped to cope with the mathematics! Einstein's basic idea of motion in a gravity field is that objects move in such a way as to take a path which gives the shortest distance between two points in the curved geometry.

The resulting orbital trajectories are effectively those found by Kepler and Newton. Figure 3.2 shows a depiction of the inner Solar System, superimposed upon a 2D representation of the space-time curvature produced by the Sun. The reader might ask why Einstein's very complex theory of gravity is needed, when Newton does a perfectly good job already. The answer is that Einstein's theory goes further, and predicts additional effects which are particularly conspicuous in very intense gravitational fields. Another feature of the theory is that it affects the way light propagates. In our everyday experience, a beam of light is perhaps the best way of defining a straight line. However, in the warped space surrounding the Sun, the path of the light is deflected (very slightly) in response to the curvature of space-time.

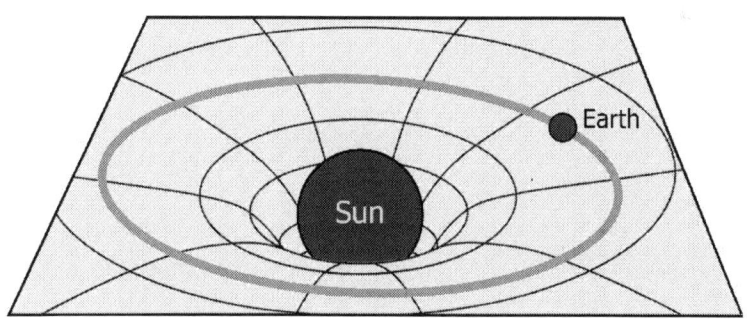

Figure 3.2 Planetary orbits in Einstein's gravity theory.

Figure 3.3 shows this effect, but with the amount of the deflection exaggerated for the sake of clarity. The bending of light by the Sun was confirmed by a team led by Arthur Eddington in 1919, using photographic plates taken during a total eclipse on the island of Principe (off the west coast of Africa)[7]. When Einstein received news that his prediction of the magnitude of the deflection was correct, he was unmoved and simply commented "but I knew the theory was correct"[8]. In general, Einstein had great humility, and this obviously sounds uncharacteristically arrogant. For him, the beauty and elegance of the theory was such that he just knew it to be correct. It was the media publication of the success in predicting the deflection of light that made Einstein an international celebrity.

It is also worth emphasising that when space-time is curved by the presence of a massive object, not only are the spatial dimensions curved, but the time dimension is as well – in other words we are presented with the bizarre notion that clocks run at different rates depending on how close they are to the object! This too has been confirmed experimentally, and has an important influence on, for example, the accuracy of satellite navigation systems[9].

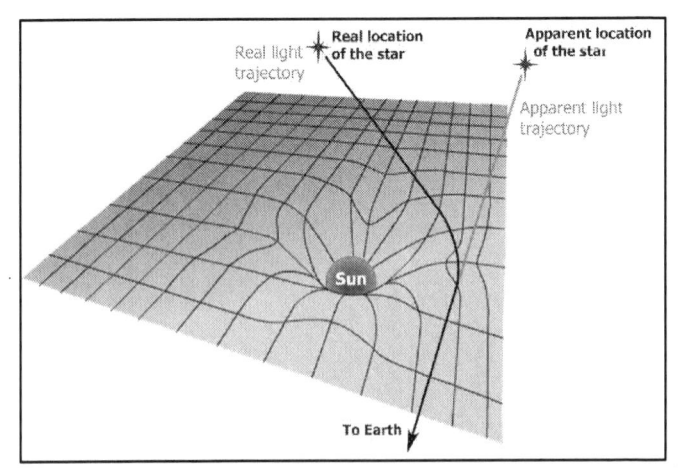

Figure 3.3 The deflection of light in a curved space-time. Credit: Artwork by Luis Maria Benitez (Public Domain).

A good analogy to get a feel for how the theory works involves a trampoline with a bed comprising a smooth rubber membrane, a jar of marbles and a heavy bowling ball. If you imagine placing the bowling ball on the bed of the trampoline, then clearly the weight of the ball will produce an indentation, a curvature, in the 2D surface of the bed. If we then place the marbles on the membrane and roll them with a variety of speeds and directions on the surface, then the marbles will appear to be attracted to the bowling ball, some rolling down the slope in the bed to impact the central ball, others appearing to 'orbit' it. Such a thought-experiment would be even better if we can imagine turning off the friction between the marbles and the surface, so that the resulting orbital motion would continue indefinitely. However, like all analogies, this one has its limitations – things become a little more difficult to imagine when we crank up the dimensions from a 2D spatial surface to 4D space-time![10] In summary, to describe how the theory works one could say that *matter (e.g. the Sun) tells space-time how to curve, and the curvature of space-time tells matter how to move.*[11] For readers interested in more technical details, see Text Box 3.3.

At this point, you may be wondering why you have been treated to an introduction to this rather esoteric theory? Firstly, Einstein's gravity theory turns out to be key in understanding the creation of the Universe as we will see in the next section. Also it may be good to pause for a moment and contemplate what the theory is telling us about the nature of space and time, and the surprising role they play in how gravity works.

On 25 November 1915, Einstein published the gravitational field equations of general relativity (equation (3.2) in Text Box 3.3), which opened a new chapter in theoretical physics which continues to this day. Soon after publication, Einstein himself was interested to know what his theory said about the Universe as a whole. However, he was surprised to find that his theory predicted a dynamic Universe, either contracting or expanding. The prevailing prejudice that the Universe was eternal and static had such a powerful influence on his thinking that he modified his field equations to produce static solutions. To do this he introduced a 'fudge factor' into the equations, which he referred to as the cosmological constant, usually denoted by an upper-case Greek letter lambda Λ – see equation (3.3) in Text Box 3.3. Effectively, this was a repulsive gravity term, for which there was no known physical mechanism, that countered the effect of the customary attractive gravity field, so allowing static solutions.

Other researchers at the time also seized the opportunity to apply Einstein's new theory to the Universe as a whole. The first noteworthy contributions came from Alexander Friedmann, a

---

Text Box 3.3: Einstein's field equations.

The equations defining Einstein's theory of gravity are extremely complex, comprising a set of non-linear, partial differential equations. As a consequence, there are relatively few analytic solutions, so scientists resort to solving them using a computer.

The simplest, symbolic form of the equations can be expressed as

$$G_{\mu\nu} = \frac{8\pi G}{c^4} T_{\mu\nu}. \qquad (3.2)$$

The RHS of the above equation represents the distribution of the physical sources of the gravitational field (mass, energy and pressure), and the LHS side embodies the geometry (curvature) of space-time produced by the sources. In a particular case, the physical sources (the RHS) are usually specified, and the equations are solved to determine the resulting geometry of space-time, and then the geometry is used to determine trajectories in a gravity field.

Einstein introduced an additional term into his original formulation, referred to as the cosmological constant Λ to ensure a static Universe. This form of the equations can be expressed as

$$G_{\mu\nu} + \Lambda g_{\mu\nu} = \frac{8\pi}{c^4} T_{\mu\nu}. \qquad (3.3)$$

Non-technical folk can regard these equations as symbolic relationships, that is (geometry) = (sources of gravity).

Russian mathematical physicist, who produced solutions to Einstein's original equations during the period 1922-1924[12]. These, too, described a dynamic – expanding or contracting –

Universe, which Einstein strongly opposed in favour of his static solution. Then in 1927[13] a landmark contribution was produced by a Belgian priest and professor of physics, Georges Lemaître, again working with Einstein's original field equations. Lemaître's paper described an expanding Universe, originating from a dense initial state that he referred to as the 'primeval atom'. As a consequence, he went on to propose that the recessional speed of the far galaxies (called 'nebulae' at that time) would be proportional to their distance – effectively a statement of what has become known as the Hubble-Lemaître Law[14]. Lemaître met Einstein for the first time in October 1927 at the 5th Solvay Conference of Physics in Brussels, Belgium. Commenting on his 1927 paper, Einstein complimented Lemaître on the rigour of his mathematics, but added, rather harshly, "from the point of view of physics this seems to me abominable". However, Lemaître must be credited with the first description of a Universe very similar to that adopted by contemporary cosmologists. Einstein, on the other hand, remained entrenched in his view that the Universe was static – prejudice is a powerful thing.

To break the cosmological deadlock, some experimental evidence was required at this moment in history. This came in the form of the publication in 1929 of astronomical observations performed by Edwin Hubble, after whom the celebrated space telescope is named. At that time Hubble was working with the Mount Wilson 100 inch aperture telescope in the mountains above Los Angeles, USA. In this paper[15], he described an observed relationship between the distance of galaxies from Earth and their speeds. This showed that the further away a galaxy is, the more its light shifts towards the red end of the spectrum[16]. This indicated that the far galaxies are all moving away from the Earth, and astronomers interpreted this as evidence that the Universe is expanding[17].

Measuring the recessional speed of galaxies is relatively straightforward. Hubble measured the spectrum of distant galaxies and used the Doppler effect to estimate their speed. We are familiar with the Doppler effect when we hear the passing of an emergency vehicle. As the vehicle approaches, the siren has a high pitch (higher frequency, shorter wavelength), and as it passes and recedes from us the pitch lowers (lower frequency, longer wavelength). This effect on the propagation of sound has its parallel when thinking about the light from distant galaxies. If they are approaching, then the light is shifted toward the blue end of the spectrum (shorter wavelength), and if receding it is shifted toward the red end of the spectrum (longer wavelength). Hubble found all of the distant galaxies to be red-shifted, and was able to estimate their recessional speed.

Finding the distance to distant galaxies is altogether more difficult. Hubble used a particular type of variable star – called a Cepheid variable – to estimate the distance to near-by galaxies, such as the Andromeda galaxy. These stars change brightness in a predictable way, and the period of this variability is directly related to their absolute brightness. Hubble painstakingly searched for Cepheid variables in these neighbouring galaxies, and then used them as 'standard candles' to estimate their distance. For more distant galaxies, he determined their distance based on the assumption that the brightest star in each galaxy had about the same absolute brightness. In this way, the Hubble-Lemaître Law was established experimentally – that galaxies are moving away from us at a speed proportional to their distance. In terms of the numbers, very roughly galaxies around 100 million light years distance are found to be receding at about 4.5 million mph, those at 200 million light years at twice this speed – approximately 9 million mph – and so on.

So why does this empirical law imply an expanding Universe? To see this, consider Figure 3.4 which shows three galaxies, A, B and C, where A is our home galaxy, the Milky Way (these can be aligned in any direction). At time 'time 1' they are equidistant from each other, one unit of distance apart. If the Universe is expanding, at some later time 'time 2' the Universe will have doubled in size, and then the three galaxies are still equidistant, but are now 2 units of distance apart. Note that in the intervening time, galaxy B has had to move one unit of distance, whereas galaxy C has had to move two units of distance. Hence, in the expanding Universe the more distant galaxy is receding more rapidly, which is precisely what Hubble found experimentally.

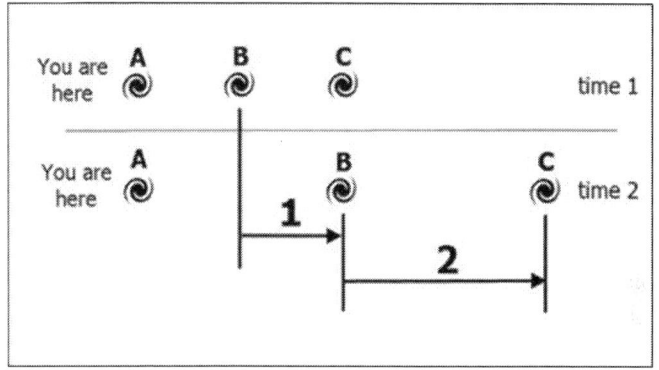

Figure 3.4 The Hubble-Lemaître Law in an expanding Universe.

So, it was Hubble's discovery that galaxies were rushing away from us that finally convinced Einstein to abandon his static Universe solution, and accept that the Universe was expanding. As a consequence, Einstein modified his theory again, reverting to his original field equations (equation (3.2) in Text Box 3.3), and abandoning his 'fudge factor' Λ. Later he is said to have admitted that the introduction of the cosmological constant was his "biggest blunder". No doubt, if he had only believed his theory when he did his initial studies, he could have predicted that the Universe was expanding – which arguably would have been the greatest theoretical prediction of all time. However, as we will see later, the cosmological constant is not dead – it has recently made a comeback to help explain the recent discovery that the expansion of the Universe is accelerating.

The Steady State theory

The discovery of the expansion of the Universe was influential in confirming the notion that there was a creation event in the distant past. The logic seems inescapable that if the motions of all the galaxies are time-reversed, then all the matter and energy in the cosmos would accumulate into an initially hot, dense 'fireball', an event which we now call the Big Bang (BB). However, many scientists were perturbed by this view of a Universe that had an origin in time. Apart from the obvious parallel with the scriptural description of creation, which was a deterrent to some, it was also unattractive because it required speculation about cosmic origins, and the out-working of the physical detail required to describe such a genesis event.

In response to this impasse, Fred Hoyle, Hermann Bondi and Thomas Gold proposed the Steady State (SS) theory in 1948. The primary attributes of a SS Universe are that it is both eternal and dynamic. The theory conjectured that the Universe is always expanding but maintains a constant average density, matter being continuously created to form new stars and galaxies as space-time expands. During the 1950s and 1960s, I followed the lively debate — which I recall — between the supporters of the two theories. However, over time experimental evidence accumulated, in particular the discovery of the cosmic microwave background radiation, which sounded the death knell of the SS theory.

The 'afterglow' of the Big Bang

If indeed the Big Bang happened, then it would seem reasonable to suppose that such a hugely energetic event would leave some evidence. Two American physicists Ralph Alpher and Robert Herman, published a theoretical prediction[18] in 1948 of the expected characteristics of such evidence. To understand the nature of this 'smoking gun', we need to look at what the BB theory says about the universal origin in a little more detail.

According to the BB, when the Universe began it was filled with a dense and very hot soup of free particles — mostly protons, neutrons and electrons — and electromagnetic (EM) radiation. Since the EM radiation and the free electrons were constantly interacting with each other, the radiation was unable to propagate freely so the Universe was effectively opaque. As the Universe continued to expand and cool, its temperature decreased to a critical level (of about 3000°C) at around 380,000 years after the Bang, when the free electrons and free protons were able to combine to form neutral hydrogen. At this epoch, the fog cleared and the EM radiation was released to propagate unhindered throughout the Universe. Over the subsequent billions of years, the Universe expanded by a factor of around 1000, and this expansion stretched the radiation to a wavelength of about 2 mm in a region of the EM spectrum that we now call microwaves. So, if the BB happened, there would be an expectation that a low-energy field of microwave radiation would pervade the cosmos, and manifest itself as a tell-tale radio signal uniformly spread across the sky. It is this signal – the afterglow of the BB – that we now call the cosmic microwave background (CMB).

Figure 3.5 The Holmdel horn antenna at the Bell Telephone Laboratories in New Jersey, USA. Credit: NASA.

Although Alpher and Herman made their prediction in 1948, it took a further 16 years for experimentalists to catch up with the theoreticians. The discovery of the CMB was made serendipitously by two radio astronomers, Arno Penzias and Robert Wilson in 1964. They were then working with a 15 metre (50 foot) horn antenna (Figure 3.5) which was originally designed for satellite communication experiments. At that time satellite communications comprised bouncing radio signals off large Echo balloon satellites. They had built a particularly sensitive radio receiver, and their intention was to use the antenna for the purposes of radio astronomy. However, while preparing the system they found a weak but steady unexplained noise in their receiver which was evenly spread over the sky, and was present day and night. After exhausting all possible sources of extraneous noise in their instrument, they finally concluded that the source of the signal was extra-terrestrial. The final piece of the jigsaw fell into place when a friend of Penzias informed him of published literature about the possibility of finding the relic radiation from the BB. Penzias and Wilson began to realise the cosmological significance of their endeavours, and the story of the discovery of CMB concluded in 1978 when they received the Nobel Prize for Physics.

The principal evidence for the BB theory

The current theory that the Universe originated in a BB event around 14 billion years ago is built upon an edifice of experimental data, but, in my view, there are four main pillars upon which the theory rests. These are summarised as:

1. *The recession of the distant galaxies indicates an expanding universe.*

A reversal in time of this outward motion would imply the coming together of all matter and energy in the Universe into an extremely hot, dense initial state.

2. *The cosmic microwave background radiation.*

The CMB has now been studied in huge detail by a succession of satellite missions, and the more we discover, the more our confidence in the BB theory is strengthened.

3. *The abundances of the elements in the Universe.*

Nuclear physics can be applied to determine which elements – and their relative abundances – would be produced if a hot BB is assumed to have occurred. This process is referred to as primordial nucleosynthesis, and this is what Alpher and Herman were attempting to flesh-out in their 1948 paper. Further work was done in the 1950s and 1960s to gain an understanding of this process. Remarkably, the generation of elements in the BB was all over in a matter of minutes.[19] Directly after nucleosynthesis, the Universe is predicted to comprise around 76% hydrogen and 24% helium, with a smattering of lithium, which is in very good agreement with observations. This result, however, raises the question of where the heavier elements came from, such as those vital for life (carbon, nitrogen, oxygen, and so on), an issue that we will return to in Chapter 4.

4. The evolution of the Universe over time.

In the late 1950s, a group of astronomers led by Martin Ryle at Cambridge University, UK, embarked on a study of distant galaxies using the relatively new technique of radio astronomy. By looking at objects at varying distances, they could sample populations at different epochs in the past history of the Universe (recall the discussion about 'time travel' in the section 3.3). Their main focus was to study **quasars** (quasi-stellar objects), which are compact but strong emitters of radio waves. The radio astronomers set out to determine where these objects were located. If they could demonstrate that they were all at great distance then it would show that they were more common in the distant past, so strengthening the notion that the Universe was evolving. This scenario of a changing Universe would favour the BB theory, and weaken the SS theory. Although initial results were ambiguous, eventually Ryle's group was able to demonstrate that their results supported the BB theory. This was not welcome news for Fred Hoyle, the originator of the SS theory, who was also working at Cambridge, and a bitter and public row ensued. Although Hoyle lost the BB/SS debate, his resistance to the BB theory played an important role in encouraging astronomers to test the theory.

As the evidence accumulated in favour of the BB theory, Arno Penzias, co-discoverer of the CMB, was moved to comment:

> "The best data we have are exactly what I would have predicted, had I had nothing to go on but the five books of Moses, the Psalms, the Bible as a whole."[20]

Amid all the talk about the science of the Universe, it is good to remind ourselves of whose creation it is!

3.5 Overview of the standard model of cosmology.

Our current understanding of how the Universe was born, and how it has developed over time is referred to as the standard model of cosmology. A simplified diagram of the features of the model is shown in Figure 3.6, with time increasing from the BB (on the left, here called the time-zero event) to the current epoch (on the right). Such a depiction has its limitations of course, the main one being that the three dimensions of space at any time are represented by a circular two-dimensional spatial slice. Notwithstanding this, the diagram is useful in showing the trend of the expansion, and the main features of our current understanding of the cosmos within which we live.

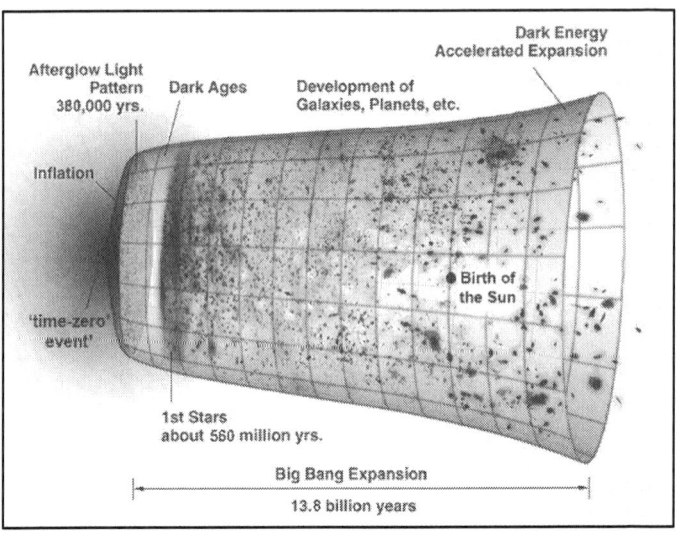

Figure 3.6 The timeline of our current understanding of the standard model of Big Bang cosmology. Credit: NASA.

The 'time-zero' event is currently beyond our abilities to analyse or understand as we do not yet have a theory of quantum gravity (see section 2.5). However, we do know with good confidence that this event occurred 13.8 billion years ago. There are some common misunderstandings about the expanding Universe, the main one being the nature of the bang. One of these is the idea that, at the time of the BB, the Universe was essentially an infinite expanse of space, and at some moment in time, and at a particular point in space, an explosion occurred. Thereafter, all the matter (galaxies) in the Universe moved away from each other, and from a common point in space-time (the location of the BB), so gradually filling the huge expanse of space-time. However, the current theory advances a different view of the BB. Rather than thinking of the Universe as an explosion in a pre-existing space-time, we need to think of it as the expansion of the fabric of space-time itself. Current theory posits that everything – space, time, matter and energy – came into being at the instant of the Big Bang, with space-time continuing to expand ever since.

Two curious consequences arise from this. Firstly, that questions like 'where is the centre of Universe?' or 'where in the Universe did the BB take place?' have no meaning. According to the theory, every point in our current Universe corresponds to the centre. Also, we cannot ask questions like 'what happened before the BB?', as, according to the standard model, time itself did not exist prior to the BB.

Returning to Figure 3.6, immediately following the time-zero event, there was a period of very rapid expansion which cosmologists refer to as cosmic inflation. This was an extraordinary and very brief era in the history of the Universe when space-time expanded at **superluminal** speed. Indeed, it was this process that put the bang into the Big Bang, and I shall return to this crucial era in cosmic history later in this Chapter.

As mentioned earlier, it was about 380,000 years after the bang (ATB) when the Universe had cooled sufficiently for the fog to clear, which allowed the afterglow radiation to propagate unimpeded throughout the cosmos. Information about the physical state of the Universe at this time is carried by the afterglow radiation and this is imprinted on the sky-map of the cosmic microwave background – referred to as the afterglow light pattern in Figure 3.6. After this was an era referred to as the Dark Ages, when the Universe continued to expand and cool. It was not until about 560 million years ATB that the cooling clouds of predominantly hydrogen and helium began to merge and collapse under the influence of gravity to form the first stars. Thereafter, the four fundamental forces (see section 2.4) acted upon the matter and energy content of the Universe to engineer the development of vast gravitationally bound systems of stars we now call galaxies.

To put our own Sun (and Solar System) into temporal context, a concordance of a variety of dating methods places its birth at around 9.2 billion years ATB. Put another way, this is about 4.6 billion years ago – one-third of cosmic history. Over this span of time the Sun has maintained a relatively stable output of energy, which has been so advantageous in the process of the development of life on planet Earth. Moreover, the Sun has sufficient resources to maintain this output for further five billion years or so.

A surprise in recent years has been the discovery that the rate of expansion of the Universe is accelerating, as indicated at the right-hand end of the timeline in Figure 3.6. Since gravity is an attractive force, the expectation is that as the cosmos ages the rate should either steady to a constant value, or decrease. The discovery of an accelerating expansion has led to speculation that empty space itself contains energy, and this admits the possibility of a repulsive force which drives the acceleration (see the next section). This revelation marks the return of Einstein's cosmological constant, which he abandoned in 1927 as his biggest mistake (see earlier explanation of Einstein's introduction of Λ). Currently, we have no idea what this vacuum energy is – it has been simply labelled dark energy.

Another significant constituent of the Universe that does not feature in Figure 3.6 is something called dark matter – again a convenient label, as no one currently knows what this is either. While dark energy is a relatively recent player in the cosmic story, the history of dark matter goes back more than a century. The basic evidence for its existence is that gravitational interactions within, and between galaxies cannot be accounted for simply by the matter that shines, such as stars. For example, when you look a typical galaxy, its brightness distribution suggests that most of its mass is concentrated at its centre. If this were so, the speed of stars as they orbit the galaxy would be expected to be greatest near the centre, and slower further out in the galactic suburbs. This pattern is echoed in our own Solar System, with Mercury orbiting the Sun much more rapidly than distant Neptune, for example. However, when the speeds of stars in galaxies were determined, the expected pattern was not found. Rather, stars were found to be travelling at similar speeds whether they were close to the galactic centre or further out. One possible solution to this enigma is to propose that galaxies are immersed in a roughly spherical distribution of dark matter, so that its mass is not concentrated in the bright central region. Further, evidence in the form of the dynamics of galaxies within galactic clusters strengthens the evidence for dark matter, and current studies suggest that it is actually far more abundant than 'normal' matter comprised of atoms. Physicists are baffled by what dark matter may be, but one favoured option at the moment is that it is comprised of a yet undiscovered particle of matter. These are called weakly interacting massive particles (or WIMPs) reflecting their expected physical characteristics.

3.6 What banged?

Despite the remarkable success of the BB theory, it is incomplete in its original form, as proposed by Friedmann and Lemaître. Even the name Big Bang theory is a misnomer as it is not a theory of a bang at all! This is expressed rather well by American physicist Brian Greene:

> " ... according to the ... theory, the bang is what is supposed to have happened at the beginning, [but] the big bang [theory] leaves out the bang. It tells us nothing about what banged, why it banged, how it banged, or, frankly, whether it ever really banged at all." [21]

The original theory has done well to describe how the early Universe expanded and cooled, and how gravity shaped matter into the structures, such as stars and galaxies, that we see today. However, it says nothing about the process that initiated the expansion of the Universe, which is indicated in Figure 3.6 as the era of 'inflation'.

The physics of cosmic inflation

The underlying mechanism of this explosively-rapid expansion of space-time is wrapped up in some quite esoteric physics, which is the focus of this section. Please feel free to pass over this material, as a detailed understanding of it is not necessary to progress through the text.

The theory of cosmic inflation was first developed in 1979 by an American physicist, Alan Guth, at Cornell University, USA, who realised that empty space (the vacuum) could provide a mechanism to account for the expansion of the Universe.

Vacuums are not what they used to be! When Newtonian physics reigned, a vacuum was space that was devoid of any content. But now physicists say that there is no such thing as empty space. We have seen that in the presence of matter, empty space acquires a curved geometry, and actively participates in the physics of how things move in a gravity field. Although it may seem strange to ascribe an energy content to a vacuum, particle physicists see the vacuum as a complex physical state, rather than a state of nothingness. As a consequence of Heisenberg's uncertainty principle (section 2.5), we now know that particle-antiparticle pairs are constantly and spontaneously appearing and disappearing in what would otherwise be considered a vacuum. Moreover, with the discovery of the Higgs Boson in 2012 (section 3.3), there is an associated Higgs field which fills the Universe. As each species of fundamental particle passes through this, it interacts with the field in proportion to its mass. Primarily, the Higgs field is the mechanism by which particles acquire their mass. So, both the soup of particle pairs and the Higgs field infuse the vacuum with energy, effectively doing away with the concept of empty space. American physicist Lawrence Krauss described this situation very aptly as 'much ado about nothing'[22]. In contemporary physics, less is indeed more.

Before we continue, we need to review a little terminology, and discuss what we mean by energy density. You may be more familiar with mass density: if we know the mass of something (kilograms, or kg) and have measured its volume (cubic metres, or m^3), then we know its mass density. For example, the mass of a cubic metre of water is 1,000 kg, so its mass density is 1000 kilograms per cubic metre (or kg/m^3). Similarly, we can consider energy density in the same way – if we have a specific amount of energy (**Joules**, or J) contained within a volume of one cubic metre, then we have an energy density of so many Joules per cubic metre (or J/m^3). For example, a region of near-Earth space will contain a stream of electromagnetic radiation from the Sun, and so will have an energy density associated with this radiation.

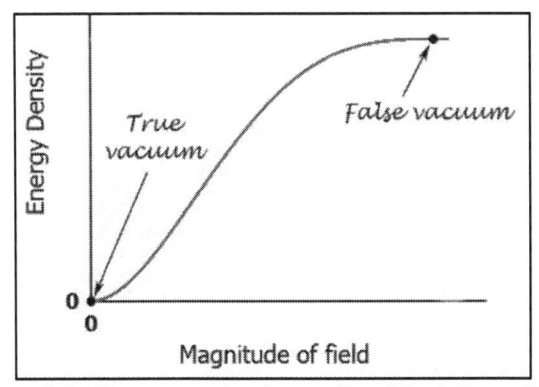

Figure 3.7 The energy density profile of the inflaton field.

Returning to our discussion about cosmic inflation, it was Guth's inspired idea that for an instant in the early Universe, space-time (or at least a small region of space-time) was pervaded by a form of energy which physicists later christened the inflaton field (this is not a misprint – the field driving inflation is called the 'inflaton field', in keeping with the historical pattern invoking names ending in 'on' – e.g. electron, proton, muon, etc.). The required energy density of this field takes a specific form, a typical example of which is shown in Figure 3.7. The essential property that makes cosmic inflation possible is the existence of such a field that has a high energy density that persists for a short period of time. Physicists refer to this state of affairs as a false vacuum. Given time, the field will roll down the curve to a point where the energy density has reduced to zero – a state referred to as the true vacuum. How long this takes will depend upon the shape of the plateau region of the curve.

So, if the early Universe acquired a nugget of false vacuum, in which space was permeated by a large, constant energy density, then how does this drive the swelling of space-time, and give the Big Bang a bang? The peculiar properties of the false vacuum arise from consideration of its pressure. To understand this, Guth proposed a thought experiment[23] in which he imagined a volume of false vacuum in a chamber. The volume of the chamber can be varied by moving a piston in or out, as shown in Figure 3.8. Initially the chamber contains a specific amount of energy, due to its constant energy density. If the volume of the chamber is now increased by pulling the piston outward, then the chamber has more energy in it than it had before because it has more volume. Where did the extra energy come from? This is provided by the work done by the force applied to expand the volume. And that is exactly how negative pressure is defined – a volume has negative pressure if it requires work to expand it (a volume with the more familiar positive pressure requires work to compress it). This manifests itself as a kind of suction, or, in other words, a negative pressure that pulls inward.

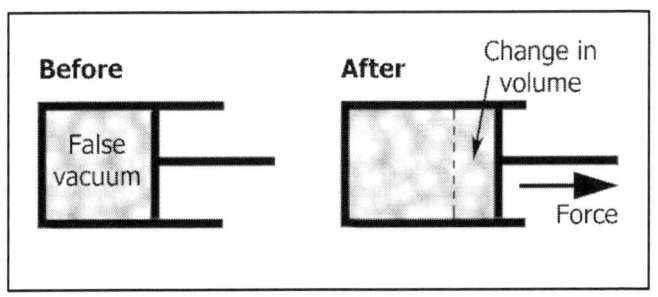

Figure 3.8 Thought experiment involving a volume of false vacuum.

However, this negative pressure (or suction) generated by the inflaton field does not seem, at first sight, a good mechanism to drive the outward expansion of space-time. The key to understanding this lies in the recognition of the sources of gravity in Einstein's theory of gravity. As we mentioned in section 3.3, pressure generates gravitational fields, and in particular a positive pressure creates what we might consider to be normal attractive gravity. However, the negative pressure of the false vacuum creates a repulsive gravitational field, which is the mechanism behind cosmic inflation. Once again, Einstein's cosmological constant Λ makes an entrance, this time in the physics of the early Universe.

The extraordinary events of the inflation era

In inflationary cosmology, it is assumed that a tiny volume of the early Universe – very much smaller than a proton – came to be in a false vacuum state. Once this happened, the repulsive gravitational effect caused this tiny nugget of space-time to swell exponentially, before the energy density decayed to acquire a true vacuum state, bringing the inflationary period to an end. This growth lasted for a period of about 10^{-35} seconds (an unimaginably short period of time). To produce a Universe with the characteristics that we observe today, the expansion factor must have been at least about 10^{30}, although the inflation theory does not place limits upon the amount of expansion permitted. The inflation mechanism generates a very short and very rapid expansion of space-time, providing an appropriately impressive bang for the BB theory. To give an impression of what this degree of expansion means, if you expand a human egg cell (circa 0.15 mm diameter) by a factor of 10^{25}, you end up with something about the size of the Milky Way galaxy!

Perhaps it is worth pausing for a moment again to take in what has just been said about the inflationary era of the birth of the Universe – a process way beyond my ability to imagine.

Once the false vacuum decayed, the energy that was stored in it was released to produce a hot, dense swarm of matter particles, providing the starting point of the traditional BB theory[24]. Bill Bryson's poetic description of the era of inflation perhaps does more justice to this extraordinary event than my attempt to describe the physics:

> "In a single blinding pulse, a moment of glory much too swift and expansive for any form of words, the singularity assumes heavenly dimensions, space beyond conception. The first lively second ... produces gravity and the other forces that govern physics. In less than a minute the universe is a million billion miles across and growing fast. ... We have a universe. It is a place of the most wondrous and gratifying possibility, and beautiful, too. And it was all done in about the time it takes to make a sandwich." [25]

3.7 What does the Universe look like now?

Geometry and density

On cosmic scales of billions of light years, the Universe appears to be homogeneous and isotropic. In other words, it appears the same at all locations and in all directions. These attributes are referred to as symmetries by physicists, and in this case, they are extremely powerful in limiting the number of possible geometries that the Universe can have to just three. When I mention geometry, I am referring to the curvature of space as we considered in the earlier discussion of Einstein's gravity theory (section 3.4), but this time on a cosmic scale. These geometries are illustrated in Figure 3.9. The first of these corresponds to a

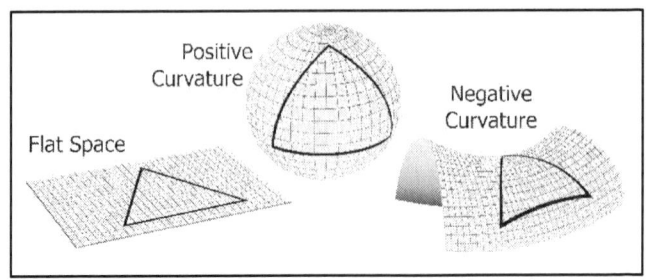

Figure 3.9. The cosmic curvature options for the Universe. Credit: NASA/WMAP Team.

globally flat Universe in which the ancient rules of Euclidian geometry apply – a geometry with which we are intuitively familiar. In other words, the included angles in a triangle add up to 180°, parallel lines do not meet, and so on. The second option, referred to as positive curvature, has a spherical surface as a two-dimensional analogy. Now we have a non-Euclidian universe in which the sum of included angles in a triangle exceeds 180°, π is less than the familiar value, and parallel lines converge. The final option is a negatively-curved cosmos, with a saddle-shaped 2D analogy, in which included angles are less than 180°, π is greater than the familiar value, and parallel lines diverge.

Which of these options corresponds to our Universe depends on the average universal density. The flat option is a half-way house between the other two, and corresponds to a universe in which the density takes a particular value, called the critical density. A straight-forward calculation gives this as about 10^{-26} kg/m^3, or of the order of 5 hydrogen atoms per cubic metre. If we define a density parameter W as

$W = density/critical\ density$,

then $W = 1$ defines a flat universe. This is referred to as an open universe that will continue to expand, but (in the absence of dark energy) the expansion will slow to a halt after very long times. If the density is less that the critical value ($W < 1$), we have negative curvature, which corresponds to an open universe in which the expansion will continue indefinitely. Finally, if there is enough matter corresponding to a density greater than critical ($W > 1$), then a positively-curved, closed universe will result which expands to a maximum extent, and then contracts, ending in a 'Big Crunch'. The 2D analogy corresponding to this case, the surface of a sphere, is effectively finite, but unbounded – you never fall off the edge of a spherical Earth, no matter how far you travel. In the same way the space-time of the closed universe is finite but unbounded. If you set off in a starship to journey the universe in a 'straight line', the positive curvature will bring you back to the point of departure.

In 1997 the first direct measurement of the global curvature of the Universe was made, based on detailed measurements of the cosmic microwave background (CMB). The idea was to construct the biggest cosmic triangle ever considered, and then determine whether it was Euclidean (flat), or otherwise. The CMB is a radio frequency signal, spread uniformly across the entire sky. However, there is structure in the sky map of the CMB, corresponding to tiny temperature variations in the soup of particles and radiation at around 380,000 years ATB when the CMB radiation was released.

As I write, it is a dull day with a fairly uniform overcast sky. However, when I look into the sky, I can discern features in the cloud structure. In the same way, the variations in the temperature of the CMB reveal structure in the afterglow light pattern referred to in Figure 3.6. With knowledge of the physics of that era, it is possible to estimate the absolute size of the CMB features, and at the same time estimate how far away they were, taking account of the billions of years of subsequent cosmic expansion. In this way, it is possible to construct a long, very thin triangle of cosmic dimensions to test the global curvature of the Universe. Over the years, the CMB has been studied with ever increasing precision, and the current estimate is that the sum of the included angles in the triangle is very close to 180°. So, current research suggests that the global curvature of the Universe is flat, to good accuracy.

Universal composition

From the discussion above, a consequence of the observed Universal flatness is that $W = 1$. In other words, that the average cosmic density is, to a good approximation, equal to the critical value. As far as the traditional BB theory is concerned, this is problematic. In this version of the theory the expansion takes place with attractive gravity, with the consequence that the density is driven away from the critical density value as the expansion proceeds (more on this in section 4.3).

However, the cosmic inflation process helps to explain why, at the current epoch, we have a flat universe with a critical density. The huge exponential growth during the inflation era, driven by the repulsive gravity of the false vacuum, causes any initial wrinkles in the curvature of space-time to flatten out, and drives the density towards the critical value. A good analogy is to think of a small curved object, say, a tennis ball, and then imagine blowing it up to the size of the Earth (an approximate inflation factor of a mere 10^8). The initial curvature is ironed out so that the surface becomes flatter and flatter. We can clearly see the surface flatness of a large sphere (the Earth) if we look out of a window.

So, if we have a universal, average density approximately equal to the critical density, what does that imply about the matter and energy content of our Universe? Do our observations of the Universe measure up to this constraint? Well, the answer is yes and no.

The average density of normal matter (electrons, protons, neutrons etc) can be estimated by looking at luminous objects (like stars) and darker regions (like gas and dust). If we do this, we find that the average density is about 5% of the critical density. Clearly, we need a bit more of something to make up the deficit. In section 3.5 we discussed the existence of dark matter, implied by its effects on the gravitational interaction within and between galaxies. Using this, and other more exotic methods, we can estimate the universal average density of dark matter at around

25% of the critical density. So, although the flatness of space is telling us that the average total density is the critical density, nevertheless looking out into the Universe it seems we can only account for about 30% of the expected matter content.

So, where is the absent 70%? The clue to this lies in the recent discovery that currently, the universal expansion is accelerating (see Figure 3.6). This acceleration is driven by something, and physicists have proposed that the vacuum of space itself processes a small, positive energy density − similar to, but very much smaller than the inflaton field that governed the inflation era of the early Universe. Such an energy density would produce a repulsive gravitational effect that would cause the observed recent acceleration. This constituent of the Universe is the dark energy that we also mentioned in section 3.5. In the same way that we do not, as yet, understand dark matter, so it is with dark energy. We believe it is there but do not know what it is, although it appears to behave in a way that is governed by something like Einstein's cosmological constant Λ.

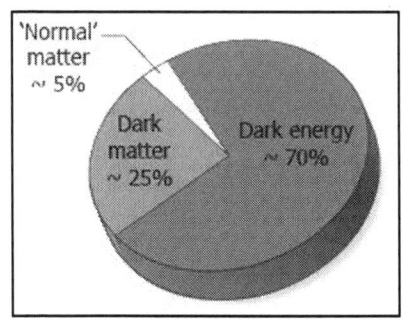

Figure 3.10. Current estimate of universal matter/energy composition.

Just when you feel we are making progress in comprehending the origins and evolution of the Universe, what we actually find is that 95% of the Universe is made of things that we do not yet understand − see Figure 3.10. I am reminded of a quote by Douglas Adams:

"There is a theory which states that if anyone discovers exactly what the Universe is for and why it is here, it will instantly disappear and be replaced by something even more bizarre and inexplicable. There is another theory which states that this has already happened." [26]

But seriously, on the positive side, this mystery is a great spur to the physics community to uncover the nature of dark matter and dark energy. It would seem that the route to this understanding is probably through the examination of the microworld of quantum physics.

Coda
After all this science, I hope you have gained the strong impression that I love the processes of trying to understand, and explain the wonders of physics in general, and cosmology in particular. Even if we have not grasped all the details, I hope that you have gained some insight into the beauty and intricacies of the Universe (both on the large and small scales) that science has revealed. I make no secret of my belief that scientific revelation reveals the splendour and awesomeness of the Universe in which we live, which I regard as God's creation. Through this process, I believe also that we can see something of the nature and character of our awesome creator God.

Obviously for me, standing under a clear, dark sky, and seeing the majesty of that creation is not only a cerebral celebration of the science of astronomy, but also a spiritual experience – an appreciation of who God is in creating the heavens. I recall one evening at Lee Abbey, a Christian conference and holiday centre situated on the North Devon coast near Lynton, UK. This coastline is on the edge of the Exmoor National Park Dark Sky Reserve, and that night the sky was glowing with stars, with our home galaxy, the Milky Way, stretched across the zenith. I was gathered around a firepit with a group of fellow believers, as the glowing embers from the fire rose on the warm air into the starry sky. At that point, it seemed so appropriate that one of the group read King David's words from the book of Psalms:

> "When I consider your heavens, the work of your fingers, the moon and the stars, which you have set in place, what is mankind that you are mindful of them, human beings that you care for them?" [27]

What a moment! David's words echoing down the millennia, inspiring awe at one of the most spectacular manifestations of God's power and wisdom in creation. When I pray, it's always good to remind myself with whom it is that I am speaking. On the other side of the coin, as Psalm 8 implies, this awesome creator God is also interested in, and cares for 'little ol' me'. This enigma of an all-powerful God, who nevertheless is also personal, is something that I, and many other Christians, experience personally. The story of how this happened I would like to share in the next chapter.

Chapter 3 endnotes:

[1] Carl Sagan, Cosmos, Club Book Associates, 1981, p. 247.
[2] Quoted in Frank Johnson, In the words of Neil deGrasse Tyson: The Inspiring View of Science, Amazon Book Store, 2014.
[3] Contemporary Bible scholars do not attribute the Creation accounts in Genesis to Moses. They were written in the 6th or 7th centuries BC, several centuries after the presumed dates for the life of Moses and the Exodus. It is also widely held that the account in Genesis Chapter 2 is older than that in Chapter 1. See, for example, Graham I. Davies, 'Introduction to the Pentateuch', in the Oxford Bible Commentary, John Barton & John Muddiman (Editors), Oxford University Press, 2007.
[4] For example, recent offerings include:
Ernest Lucas, Can we believe Genesis today?, Inter-Varsity Press, 2007.
Andrew Parker, The Genesis Enigma, Black Swan, 2009.
John Lennox, Seven Days that Divide the World, Zondervan, 2011.
[5] Interstellar, Paramount Pictures, 2014.
[6] Many ancient cultures had creation myths which implied a beginning of the Universe. It was only when these creation myths in their various forms were discarded that the Universe became to be regarded as eternal.
[7] F. W. Dyson, A. S. Eddington, and C. Davidson, A determination of the deflection of light by the Sun's gravitational field, from observations made at the total eclipse of May 29, 1919, Phil. Trans. R. Soc. Lond. (1920), Vol 220, pp. 291–333.
[8] Jeremy Bernstein, Einstein, Fontana, 1973, p. 120.
[9] For an explanation of the influence of 'time warping' upon GPS operation see Graham Swinerd, How Spacecraft Fly – spaceflight without formulae, Springer, 2008, pp. 21-22.
[10] YouTube has videos showing this kind of analogy. If you search for 'Einstein's gravity visualised', or similar phrase a variety of videos

result, for example, https://www.youtube.com/watch?v=uRijc-AN-F0 shows a good demonstration by American physicist Brian Greene.

[11] Attributed to John Wheeler, eminent American theoretical physicist.

[12] Alexander Freidmann's publications: Zeitschrift für Physik (1922), Vol. 10, p.377; Zeitschrift für Physik (1924), Vol. 21, p. 326.

[13] Georges Lemaître's publication of 1927 originally appeared in a little-known Belgium Journal. It subsequently appeared in 1931 in a Journal of the Royal Astronomical Society: Georges Lemaître, Mon. Not. R. Astron. Soc. (1931), Vol. 91, p.483.

[14] The Hubble-Lemaître Law was formerly known as Hubble's Law. The resolution that the name be changed to recognise Lemaître's important contribution was discussed at the General Assembly of the IAU (International Astronomical Union) in Vienna, Austria in August 2018. The recommendation that the title be changed was subsequently accepted, with 78% of the votes in favour, in an electronic vote of members.

[15] Edwin Hubble, A relation between distance and radial velocity among extra-galactic nebulae, Proc. Natl. Acad. Sci. USA (1929), Vol. 15, pp. 168-173.

[16] Isaac Newton was the first to split white light into an array of rainbow colours using a glass prism. Many years after Newton's discovery, it was found that the Sun's spectrum was not just an array of primary colours but it also contained many dark lines at particular wavelengths. These spectral lines were the signatures of particular elements in the solar atmosphere. As light passes through the gaseous atmosphere on its way to Earth, the various elements (hydrogen, helium, etc.) absorb the light at specific wavelengths, and a precise set of such absorption lines identifies the presence of a particular element residing in the solar atmosphere. So, what do we mean when the light is red-shifted as Hubble observed? As the distant galaxies are moving away from Earth, he found that the series of absorption lines corresponding to, say, hydrogen were shifted towards the red (longer wavelength) end of the visible spectrum, compared to laboratory-determined results. The magnitude of this shift allowed Hubble to estimate the galaxies' recessional speed using the Doppler effect.

[17] What Hubble observed is something we now call the cosmological red-shift. This is caused by the stretching of the fabric of space itself, so that objects with effectively fixed positions in space become separated. The wavelength of light emitted by these distant objects also stretches as space expands, producing the red-shift in their spectra.

[18] Ralph A. Alpher and Robert C. Herman, On the Relative Abundance of the Elements, Phys. Rev. (1948), Vol. 74, pp. 1737-1742.

[19] Nobel Laureate Steven Weinberg wrote an accessible guide to this era

of cosmic history: Steven Weinberg, The First Three Minutes (2nd Edition), Basic Books, 1993. Inevitably, the subject matter has moved on since 1993, so some parts of the discussion are a little dated.

[20] Attributed to Arno Penzias in an interview in the New York Times, 12 March 1978.

[21] Brian Greene, The Fabric of the Cosmos, Penguin Books, 2004, p. 272.

[22] Lawrence M. Krauss, A Universe from Nothing, Simon & Schuster, 2012, p. 55.

[23] Alan Guth, Inflation and the new era of high-precision cosmology, MIT Physics Annual (2002), pp 28-39.

[24] At this point you may be wondering where all the energy that makes up our Universe came from? The total energy increases by the cube of the expansion factor, so assuming an expansion factor of 10^{30}, this means an energy increase by a factor of 10^{90}. So, how does this accord with the law of energy conservation? The answer to this puzzle can be found in the behaviour of the energy of the gravitational field. In both Newtonian and Einsteinian gravity, the energy of the gravity field is always negative. During the expansion, while the energy of the inflaton field increases by a factor of 10^{90}, the energy of the gravitational field becomes more and more negative to compensate. The total energy, therefore, remains constant and very small, or indeed could even be precisely zero (in a Universe with a flat geometry). This leads to the extraordinary conclusion that inflation theory allows a means of creating and developing a Universe from just a tiny amount of embryonic matter – or indeed from nothing at all. As Alan Guth is quoted as saying "If inflation is right, then the Universe can properly be called the ultimate free lunch".

[25] Bill Bryson, A Short History of Nearly Everything, Black Swan, 2004, p. 28.

[26] Douglas Adams, The Restaurant at the End of the Universe, Pan Books, 1980, preface.

[27] The Holy Bible (NIV): Psalms, Chapter 8, verses 3 and 4.

From the Big Bang to Biology – where is God?

4 A Cosmos fine-tuned for Life.

"The laws of nature form a system that is extremely fine-tuned, and very little in physical law can be altered without destroying the possibility of the development of life as we know it."
Stephen Hawking[1]

*"Amazing grace! (how sweet the sound)
That sav'd a wretch like me!
I once was lost, but now am found,
Was blind, but now I see."*
John Newton

Graham writes ...

4.1 Introduction.

In this chapter there are two very contrasting themes: one, a striking, technical topic called cosmic fine-tuning, and the other, a very personal story of my coming to faith in November 2001. For me, these two themes are inextricably connected as science was very influential in my journey to the Christian faith. This is not as strange as it may seem, as often science leads us to the big questions, even though science *per se* may not be capable of answering them. In what follows, I will recount how this happened.

For the moment, I will give a brief summary of what cosmic fine-tuning is all about – I hope to flesh out some of the details as we go through this chapter. The essence of the argument is that, in recent years, physicists have discovered that the fundamental constants of nature – those special numbers upon which everything depends – have to be just right in order for life as we know it to be possible – not just here on planet Earth, but throughout the Universe. This universal impression of design, sometimes referred to as the Goldilocks enigma, is remarkable to the degree that it is a challenge for the physics community to explain why this is so. A great many instances of fine-tuning have been discovered, so that the Universe in which we live would appear to be a very unlikely place. In this chapter we consider the arguments and counter arguments, and hope to explore why this is so, what it means and why it is important. However, before we get into the details, I would like to say something about my personal journey.

In retelling my story, I am very fortunate that I took the time in the summer of 2002 to produce a written account of the extraordinary events of 2001. These events created such a huge change in my life that I felt I needed to put on paper – and do justice to – the story of how it all happened. However, at the time, I was unsure of my motivations in recording the events. Was I doing it to capture something important for myself? Was I doing it in response to the encouragement from others to do so? One thing I hoped for was that it would be of interest, and possibly help, to sceptical and Christian readers alike. This last point is one of the main reasons for my involvement in this book with John.

4.2 My story – from agnosticism to deism*.

Transformative events
As we go through life, we all experience transformative events – some good, some bad – that have an influence upon how our lives play out. For me, such an event occurred in the September of 1995 when my father died. Poor Dad's death in St. Thomas' Hospital, London, from a failed heart bypass operation, was a great shock. Prior to the event, I was convinced that the operation would be successful, and that it would give him a new lease of life. This made it all the more shocking – the event itself and the

---
* See glossary.

aftermath were painful for everyone who loved him. I found the situation traumatic, and very hard to deal with, from the perspective of a person without faith.

The reader might infer that this led to a change in my philosophy of life, with an active search for the meaning of life, perhaps a belief in a god. In fact, this was not the case at all. My life continued along its normal track, deeply entrenched in the agnostic view of a Universe where God's existence, or otherwise, was not at all relevant to the things that were happening to me (or indeed anyone else). However, I do believe that the events of September 1995 were transformative, awakening in me a subconscious desire to find answers to personal, fundamental questions about my life. Such events open a new chapter, and create a greater awareness of one's own mortality. Regrettably, at the time, this was submerged in the general busyness of life – all the usual distractions for someone caught up in the business of doing a job, and supporting a family. This was a convenient refuge to protect me from the hurt, and to distract me from the implications of what had happened. So, any transformative influence remained latent in me until the year 2001 when some extraordinary things began to happen.

Summer vacation

The next events occurred in the unlikely setting of a family holiday in Guernsey, an island off the coast of northern France. The holiday was a late booking, and it was pretty arbitrary where we would spend it, by the time we got around to booking. As it happened, we spent a very pleasant week in a Guernsey hotel in the August of 2001.

The weather was reasonable, and I spent quite a lot of time reading, while sitting by the hotel swimming pool in the sun. Holidays for me were a great time to read for pleasure – during the rest of the year I spent so much time reading at work, that I tended to do other things with leisure time. So this was an opportunity to find a large interesting book to plough through – this time a large biography of Einstein, the author of which I cannot recall. It was well-written, and I enjoyed the account of the young Einstein as he developed his early ground-breaking theories of relativity and gravitation. As the book developed, and as

Einstein grew older, the focus moved from physics to politics (pacifism, Zionism, etc.) and my attention wandered, and finally I have to admit I did not stay the course to the end.

However, as I read the book, a great deal of my life-long interest and knowledge of astrophysics and cosmology was brought to mind, and I began to think about things in a new way. I do not think that the book had a great deal to do with this, but it was catalytic in stimulating a startling insight about the nature of the Universe. I am not usually prone to having startling insights, so this was a rare event! The revelation by the poolside is captured by the simple observation that *the Universe is defined by our existence within it.*

So, what do I mean by this? If you confine the argument to planet Earth, then all the diversity of life here is well adapted to the environment because of a process called natural selection, famously proposed by Charles Darwin and Alfred Russell Wallace. Most people are familiar with Darwin's theory, and the way that the power of natural selection of species ensures that living organisms are well adapted to their environment. The idea is that a particular species will change gradually over time due to mutations (changes) in the genetic code that defines that species. If the mutations are beneficial – in other words, give the organism a reproductive advantage in its natural environment – then it will tend to survive (be naturally selected) while the original, now relatively disadvantaged organism will tend to die out. We can see this principle in operation all around us in the natural world. Although I am not a biologist, this process of evolution seemed to be a perfectly respectable solution to the observation that life on Earth is fine-tuned (biologists prefer the term adapted) to its environment.

However, my thoughts by the poolside in Guernsey took the argument to a new level that had not occurred to me before: the universe is fundamentally well suited to the existence of us, not just planet Earth. If the laws of nature were modified slightly, the complex chemical and physical organisms we call people would not be able to exist. Indeed, any complex life form could not exist anywhere in the Universe. In those precious moments by the pool, the process of the fine-tuning of the laws of nature that govern the Universe was revealed to me. I now sincerely believe this process

A Cosmos fine-tuned for Life

of revelation was a master-class by the Holy Spirit, in which He used the rare opportunity of this quiet time in Guernsey to fulfil His purpose. In retrospect, it is clear that I did not have the vocabulary then to express such a sentiment.

An example of this attribute of fine-tuning can be illustrated by considering the law governing the gravitational force (see Text Box 2.1). If Newton's famous inverse square law is modified just a tiny bit, then the orbits of things around other things would no longer be stable. I learnt this in my first-year studies as an undergraduate student, but of course I never thought about the philosophical implications of this mathematical exercise. If Newton's law of gravitation was not as it is, then the moon would not be able to orbit the Earth, the Earth would not be able to orbit the Sun, the Sun would not be able to orbit around our own galaxy, and so on. There would be no stable astronomical structures. The Earth would not enjoy the stable equilibrium which it currently does. If this were the case, life clearly would not exist anywhere in the Universe. Similarly, if the other forces of nature (to do with electromagnetism, and the interactions between the sub-atomic particles) were a bit stronger or a bit weaker, or the masses of the particles which comprise us were a little more or a little less, then complex chemical and biological structures would not be stable, and again the existence of life would be compromised. I am skimming over the detail here (but examples are discussed later) in order not to cloud understanding of the fundamental issue: that the laws of nature which govern the immense Universe are in some way fine-tuned in order that life can exist in this tiny corner which we call Earth.

Pondering the options

The next, and most obvious question for me was – why should this be so? To account for the laws of nature appearing to be so finely tuned to our existence, I needed some hypotheses. Sitting by the pool, the three I came up with were:

1. One day in the future, physicists will come up with a theory of everything (see section 2.5), in which all the parameters which define the laws of nature will be uniquely determined – and when this occurs these parameters will just happen to take on the required values to allow life to exist.

2. That there are in fact an infinite (or at least a very large) number of universes, all coexisting alongside each other, each universe having slightly differing physical laws. This collection of universes was called the multiverse by Astronomer Royal, Martin Rees. This hypothesis might seem exotic, but it is one that is entertained by contemporary physicists. We, of course, exist in this Universe because it happens to be the one that can sustain the existence of life, or put another way, we are just winners in a cosmic lottery.

3. That the Universe was designed in such a way that it would be well-suited to the existence of life, by some agency that we would call a Creator (the God hypothesis).

Many scientists are hard-headed about this and take the view, quite correctly, that the Universe has to be the way it is because, if it were otherwise, then we would not be here to contemplate such things (see discussion about the **anthropic** principle in the next section). However, for me, back in 2001, there were so many crucial aspects of the natural laws that were finely tuned that the probability that it occurred by chance was negligible. It raised the question: why is the Universe such an unlikely place? Just how unlikely is intimated by American physicist Lee Smolin[2]:

> "We have already discussed one piece of evidence ... : the apparently improbable values of the masses of the elementary particles and the strengths of the fundamental forces. One can estimate the probability that the constants in our standard theories of the elementary particles and cosmology would, were they chosen randomly, lead to a world with carbon chemistry. That probability is less than one part in 10^{220}."

Smolin implies that carbon chemistry is a necessary prerequisite for the development of life as we know it, but of course his argument takes no account of life forms as yet unimagined. Also, I have no idea how he made his estimate. Back by the poolside, I was unable to make such a quantitative estimate, but just knew intuitively that fine-tuning needed an explanation. What if you were watching someone with a pack of cards, who shuffled them thoroughly, and then dealt them out in perfect numerical order – hearts first, then diamonds, spades and finally clubs. The probability of this happening by chance is of course very small indeed. If I have got my sums correct then there is a one in 10^{68} chance of doing this. If you witnessed this you would probably question how such a thing could happen – and suspect that there was something more going on than pure chance. And for me, it was the same with the Universe – there must be more to it than pure chance.

Hypothesis No. 1 seemed as unlikely as the idea that the Earth was the centre of the universe, and indeed, if this hypothesis was correct, I felt it would reinforce the impression of design. At present, physicists' quest for the ultimate theory of everything (TOE) still seems a long way off. Currently our laws of science are expressed in terms of the fundamental constants that define our models of the Universe. These theories rarely provide a means to determine the values of the constants themselves[3]. In other words, these values are determined by experiment and then plugged into the theories. There is no indication that this *modus operandi* is changing, or that a TOE will resolve the issues posed by fine-tuning. Hypothesis No. 1 did not seem to be a strong contender.

The multiverse – hypothesis No. 2 – does, at least, provide a scientifically respectable explanation of why we inhabit a Universe fine-tuned for life. As I commented in Chapter 2, I am really not sure that nature does infinity. In the context of a multiverse, if there were an infinity of other universes coexisting alongside our own, then it would be a certainty that, somewhere in the multiplicity of other universes, at this moment in cosmic history, there would be another version of you reading this book which was co-authored by another version of me. I have to say that I believe such a scenario to be pure fantasy, and that consequently I believe the multiverse could contain a very large, but finite, number of other universes. However, getting back to my thoughts by the pool, my main objections to the multiverse were:

- Even an infinite number of universes may not give the attribute that is required – that is, a cosmos fit for life. As John Polkinghorne commented, the infinite sequence of even numbers, for example, is distinctly short of oddness.
- The multiverse seemed philosophically extravagant.

- Finally, and most crucially, the multiverse is scientific speculation. Such a hypothesis is untestable, and is therefore outside the realm of scientific method.

Exploring this last point, and taking account of more recent developments, it is difficult to see how there could be direct observational evidence for a multiverse. If there are other universes, they are what physicists call causally-separated from us, so that no information can pass from one universe to another. So it would appear that the notion of a multiverse is, by definition, outside the domain of physics. Without the passage of information, can there ever be direct evidence of other universes?

Effectively, there are two things going on here – on the one hand, the multiverse hypothesis has explanatory power to account for fine-tuning. But then, on the other, it is outside the domain of science. Some prominent scientists, such as Martin Rees and Steven Weinberg, are seduced by its explanatory power. For example, Physics Nobel Laureate Weinberg embraces the multiverse:

"According to the 'chaotic inflation' theories of Andrei Linde and others, the expanding cloud of billions of galaxies that we call the big bang may be just one fragment of a much larger universe in which big bangs go off all the time, each one with different values of the fundamental constants. In any such picture, in which the universe contains many parts with different values for what we call the constants of nature, there would be no difficulty in understanding why these constants take values favourable to intelligent life. There would be a vast number of big bangs in which the constants of nature take values unfavourable to life, and many fewer where life is possible." [4]

Other physicists, such as Smolin reject the multiverse hypothesis on the basis that it is untestable:

"The only problem with this kind of explanation is that it is difficult to see how it can be refuted. As long as your theory yields a large number of universes, you only need there to be at least one like ours. The theory makes no other prediction apart from the existence of at least one universe like ours. But we already know that, so there is no way to refute this theory. This might seem good, but actually it is not because a theory that cannot be refuted cannot really be part of science." [5]

Still others are more vehement in their opposition to the multiverse hypothesis, for example, the cosmologist George Ellis writes:

"The extreme case is the multiverse proposal, where no direct observational test of the hypothesis is possible. Despite this, many articles and books dogmatically proclaim that the multiverse is an established scientific fact." [6]

Back in 2001, I appreciated that hypothesis No. 2 (the presence of a multiverse) did at least provide an acceptable explanation of why we inhabit a finely tuned Universe. The third hypothesis, that a Creator engineered the physical Universe to be a suitable cradle for life, was anathema to me then, so I was rapidly running out of options. It had come down to a choice between two effectively untestable hypotheses. However, there was another factor that I found influential in my thinking. It was clear that an explanation for cosmic fine-tuning was posing a significant challenge to the physics community. Back then, by the poolside, the multiverse was a convenient, if unlikely, proposition devised by physicists to shut the door firmly on the God hypothesis.

Given this dilemma, I briefly appealed to Occam's razor, a device I first came across during my graduate studies in the 1970s. It is often used in a scientific context to establish the most likely theory to account for a set of observations, and is along the lines of all other things being equal, the simplest explanation is probably the correct one. But the problem here was not really one of science, but rather a choice between a metaphysical option and a theological one. And how can you judge the relative complexity of a multiverse compared to a creative deity? Clearly this is not possible, and making a choice between two untestable options has to be a subjective process.

My fundamental aversion at that time, to the multiverse option was the consideration that brought resolution. Was it really possible for there to be an infinite number of other universes residing alongside our own, with all that that entailed? In such an ensemble of universes, all things are possible, including fanciful realities that stretch credibility to the limit. Further, if our total physical reality comprises a multiverse, what would be the point of doing physics? The existence of all possible theories of everything becomes a certainty.

As time went by, the likelihood of the God hypothesis seemed to grow as I struggled to bring resolution. It certainly seemed more credible – certainly to the billions of people who professed a faith in such a deity. Drawing a line under the process, hypothesis No. 3 became my reluctant choice. To be honest, I am not sure that I would make the same choice now, in light of our greater understanding of the theoretical basis of the multiverse. In other words, I would probably have been captivated by its explanatory power, and rejected any kind of Creator God. However, it also needs to be said that, just because something can be modelled theoretically, it does not mean that it inevitably becomes part of physical reality. In retrospect, I believe that a providential hand was steering my thoughts in a particular direction so, although the science seemed very important at this juncture, it ultimately became irrelevant in the longer term. The important outcome of this story was that, in 2001, I had become more comfortable with the idea of a Creator God as the engineer of the observed fine-tuning of the cosmos.

I have found it quite difficult to summarise my thought processes, and what I have said probably suggests that it was rather matter of fact and straightforward to arrive at this conclusion. In fact, it took what seemed then to be a long time beyond my August stay in Guernsey. Generally, it was a struggle and, given my background, it was a conclusion with which I was not comfortable. The other thing to say, of course, is that the personal academic discussion above certainly does not constitute a proof that God exists.

At this stage in September 2001 all I knew was that, for the first time in my life, I was receptive to the notion of the existence of a Creator God. I had made a journey from agnosticism to deism.

I really didn't have any idea about what kind of God this was. Clearly, there was a further journey to be made from this Creator God to a theistic God, such as that of Judaism, Christianity or Islam. I will continue my story later in the text, but before that I would like to put some more flesh on the bones concerning some of the more technical aspects of cosmic fine-tuning.

4.3 Cosmic fine-tuning.

A sharper edge

What do prominent scientists say about the impression of design in creation? The majority make no comment at all, but some find the impression so striking that they feel compelled to acknowledge that there is something that requires explanation. One such is Freeman Dyson, a British-born American physicist, who commented:

> "The more I examine the universe and the details of its architecture, the more evidence I find that the universe in some sense must have known we were coming." [7]

Dyson, who worked at the Institute of Advanced Studies at Princeton University, USA prior to retirement, was a Christian church-goer, and he saw no conflict between this and his science.

British theoretical physicist and astrobiologist, Paul Davies, has contributed to academic and popular debate on issues such as the origin of life and extra-terrestrial intelligence, and on the topic of fine-tuning he offers these often-quoted unequivocal remarks:

> "There is for me powerful evidence that there is something going on behind it all ... It seems as though somebody has fine-tuned nature's numbers to make the Universe ... The impression of design is overwhelming." [8]

> "The laws [of physics] ... seem to be the product of exceedingly ingenious design ... The universe must have a purpose." [9]

Interviews with Davies suggest that he is not a believer in the traditional sense, but rather professes something close to **pantheism**, identifying God with the order and majesty that he sees in nature.

The notion that the laws of nature (section 2.4) must be constrained by the existence of life in the Universe has been with us for some time, in the form of something called the Weak Anthropic Principle, which can be summarised as:

The natural laws that govern the Universe are constrained by the necessity to allow human existence.

Some kind of fine-tuning of the laws of nature has always been recognised as necessary simply because we are here to think about it. So, what is the big deal in discussing this further? Well, the issue for me in 2001, and even more so now in 2020, is the degree to which the laws and fundamental constants need to be finely tuned for life to flourish. As we intimated before, the probability of a Universe such as ours coming about by random processes is so small as to be negligible. Furthermore, as time goes by and observational technology steadily improves, the anthropic principle has a sharper edge. As we learn more about the Universe we inhabit through more precise forms of data gathering, the more cosmic fine-tuning becomes a challenge.

The explosion in observational technology
To put this into context, it is helpful to think about the status of technology when I was born in 1950. At that time, there was nothing in orbit around the Earth, apart from the moon. Space exploration was yet to begin. It was just 30 years beforehand that Arthur Eddington first made the suggestion that the Sun's energy might be produced by nuclear fusion reactions. The most capable astronomical observatories were the 100 inch (2.55 m) aperture Mount Wilson telescope (as used by Edwin Hubble), and the 200 inch (5.10 m) Mount Palomar telescope, first operational in 1949. There was no internet.

The years leading up to 1975 when I completed my Ph.D., were however exciting times. The Space Age had begun in 1957, and human exploration of the moon had happened and was over. The building blocks in understanding the Universe were in place, and the cosmic microwave background had been discovered and studied, and its significance realised.

My graduate studies were in the area of gravitational waves, supervised by George McVittie, who himself had been supervised by Arthur Eddington — my claim to fame? In 1975 there was an appreciation that if gravitational waves existed, they would be extremely weak and their detection was not considered to be feasible for the foreseeable future. Consequently, my research was theoretical. However, it took the engineers just 40 years to catch up with the theoreticians, with the first detection of gravitational waves in September 2015. This illustrates the huge strides made in observational technology in the last four decades or so, resulting in ever increasing degrees of observational precision.

Perhaps the most obvious advance has been the development of space-borne astronomical observatories, of which the Hubble Space Telescope (HST) is the most iconic. This was launched in April 1990 and has been gathering data ever since. Something like 15,000 scientific papers have resulted. The HST is about the same size and mass as a single decker coach and has a mirror aperture of 2.4 m. This makes it slightly smaller than that of the Mount Wilson telescope used by Hubble, but the big advantage that the HST has over its terrestrial counterpart is that it operates above the obscuring blanket of the Earth's atmosphere.

At the time of writing, HST has been operating for 30 years and is approaching the end of its useful life time. Its replacement, the James Webb Space Telescope (JWST – named after the NASA Administrator from 1961 to 1968), has been in development for many years. The new observatory will have an aperture of 6.5 m (about 2.7 times larger than that of the HST), and is currently due to be launched in 2021. It is anticipated that the results from JWST will challenge and revolutionise our knowledge of the Universe, as did its earlier counterpart. It should also be acknowledged that there has been an armada of other space-borne astronomical missions that have acquired data across the entire electromagnetic spectrum.

At the same time, ground-based observatories have also improved. Currently, the most advanced terrestrial optical observatory is the aptly-named Very Large Telescope, or VLT, which is located atop a 2600 m high mountain in the Atacama Desert of Northern Chile. The high altitude ensures that the observatory is above the densest part of the Earth's obscuring atmosphere. The VLT is managed and operated by a 16-nation research organisation called the European Southern Observatory (ESO). On site there are four large 8.2 m aperture telescopes, and four smaller, movable 1.8 m aperture telescopes (see Figure 4.1). These 8 telescopes can work together to produce images that rival, or exceed, the resolution acquired by space-borne instruments.

A ground-breaking innovation at the VLT is the use of adaptive optics to combat the obscuring effects of the atmosphere. This relies on four bright lasers attached to one of the large telescopes that shoot 30-centimetre-wide orange beams into the sky that excite sodium atoms in the atmosphere, creating artificial guide stars. The light from these is then analysed to determine how it is being disturbed by turbulence in the atmosphere. To counteract the disturbance, commands are fed-back to a deformable mirror that constantly changes shape to reduce blurring.

Figure 4.1. The VLT in operation, showing the four large Unit Telescopes and four Auxiliary Telescopes. Credit: ESO/S. Brunier.

The ESO is also constructing another large optical observatory called the ELT (Extremely Large Telescope – someone in ESO has a sense of humour!), which is close to the VLT on a neighbouring mountain top. Building began in June 2017, and completion and operation is expected in 2025. The aperture of this telescope will be an extraordinary 39 m, made up of 798 smaller mirror segments, and the system will benefit from the VLT experience of adaptive optics. It is hoped that these incredible developments in optical astronomy will allow study of the first stars and galaxies formed after the dark ages about 500 million years after the Big Bang (see Figure 3.6), and contribute to the understanding of the mysterious dark matter and dark energy constituents that seem to dominate the dynamics of the Universe.

These engineering developments, both in space and on the ground, demonstrate the progress made in the precision of the astronomical tools used to observe and examine the very large. Similar progress has been made in engineering of the means to explore the very small – the world of particle physics – as discussed in section 3.3. The Large Hadron Collider (LHC) is the world's largest and most powerful particle accelerator, and the most complex experimental facility ever built. This has provided sufficient energy to allow ground-breaking discoveries, such as that of the Higgs Boson in 2012. Proposals for more powerful particle accelerators have been tabled, principally by Europe, the USA and China, with the near-term aim of creating a Higgs Boson factory – machines that can produce Higgs particles by the millions in order to characterise their properties in detail. What discoveries these facilities can make in the longer term is a matter of speculation. But no doubt nature, as always, will surprise us with quantum realities beyond our ability to imagine.

Examples of fine-tuning

There are many instances of cosmic fine-tuning, and I will briefly outline a few examples. For more detail, I recommend Martin Rees's concise and accessible book *Just Six Numbers*[10]. Although, Rees writes from a secular perspective, the book echoed my own thoughts on fine-tuning, which was very encouraging when I first came across it in 2006.

- *The initial conditions of the Big Bang (BB)*

As you may recall from the discussion in section 3.7, the initial conditions of the traditional BB theory (as originally proposed by Friedmann and Lemaître) would require fine-tuning in order to produce the attributes of the Universe that we observe today. In particular, this relates to the initial value of the universal density – the combined density of mass and energy. At a time just after the Big Bang, we can imagine all the mass and energy going out in an expanding bubble of space and time. Of course, the matter and energy content has its own gravitational influence, which slows the expansion down. So, if the initial density is too high, the Universe expands but then it contracts again too quickly to allow the formation of stars and galaxies. On the other hand, if the initial density is a bit less, then the expansion would be so rapid that stars and galaxies would not condense. The surprising thing is that if the initial value of the density at 1 second after the Bang is changed by more than one part in 10^{15} (a million billion), then the Universe would not have the flat geometry we observe today, and, more importantly, we would not be here to think about it.

Fortunately, as discussed earlier, this fine-tuning requirement of the traditional BB theory can be relaxed by the introduction of inflationary cosmology (see section 3.6). However this does not wholly remove the problem. Another fine-tuning requirement is introduced, albeit less extreme, to do with the initial conditions that control the inflationary phase of the early Universe, such as the attributes of the inflaton field's energy density curve (see Figure 3.7). Paul Steinhardt, a co-worker with Alan Guth on the development of inflationary cosmology, commented:

> "From the very beginning ... I was concerned that the inflationary picture only works if you finely tune the constants that control the inflationary period. ... The whole point of inflation was to get rid of fine-tuning ... The fact that we had to introduce one fine-tuning to remove another was worrisome. This problem has never been resolved." [11]

- *The strength of the strong nuclear force*

The energy radiated by the Sun, that sustains all life on Earth, originates from nuclear reactions deep within its core. These are referred to as nuclear fusion reactions. In this process hydrogen atoms, and **isotopes** of hydrogen, are fused together to form helium atoms. Figure 4.2 shows a schematic of the hydrogen atom and the helium atom, indicating the number of protons, neutrons and electrons in each, and their respective electric charges. Note that to build a helium atom, you need, at some stage of the process, to bring together two positively charged protons. Since like-charges repel each other, this is difficult to achieve. However, the extreme conditions of high temperature and density in the core of the Sun are ideal in overcoming the mutual repulsion of the protons. This allows them to be in close proximity for long enough so that another fundamental force, the very short range strong nuclear force (see section 2.4), can act to hold them together to allow the formation of helium.

So where does the output of energy come from in this process? In the fusion reaction 0.7% of the mass of the helium atom is converted into pure radiate energy. This is the equivalence of mass and energy, as described by Einstein's equation $E = mc^2$ (see Textbox 3.2). As discussed earlier, the Sun has produced a stable output of energy over a period of 4.6 billion years, and, in that time, it has converted the equivalent of about 100 Earth masses

A Cosmos fine-tuned for Life

into radiate energy in the process. The Sun's stability is a balance between, on the one hand, the thermal pressure pushing outwards produced by the nuclear reactions in its core, and on the other, the inward pull of gravity. Effectively, our star is a gravitationally-bound fusion reactor.

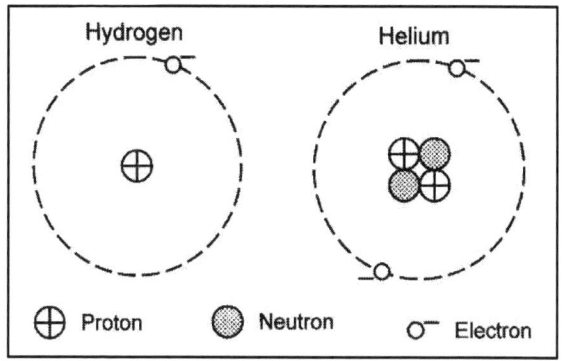

Figure 4.2. An illustration (not to scale) of hydrogen and helium atoms.

The magnitude of the 0.7% efficiency of the fusion reaction is directly related to the strength of the strong nuclear force. One could ask – what would happen if the efficiency was varied by ±0.1% (one part in a thousand)?

- If efficiency was reduced to 0.6%, the strength of the strong nuclear force would be diminished, and the hydrogen to helium reaction would be unstable. The result of this would be a Universe of hydrogen, with the path to all heavier elements closed off. The outcome would be pretty boring chemistry, and no life.
- Conversely, if the efficiency was increased to 0.8% the fusion reaction would be more robust, so that no hydrogen would remain after the Big Bang. The main consequence for us would be that there would be no water, and again no prospect of life as we know it.

Remarkably, no complex physical and biological entities, such as people, could exist if the efficiency of the fusion reaction was less than 0.6% or more than 0.8%. It would seem that the fusion reaction efficiency of 0.7% is just right.

- *Stellar nucleosynthesis*

You may recall (section 3.4) that the elements hydrogen, helium and a smattering of lithium were formed during the first few minutes following the Big Bang, in a process called 'primordial nucleosynthesis'. This prompts the question concerning the origin of the heavier elements, such as carbon, nitrogen and oxygen, which are vital for the more complex chemical and physical processes required to make life.

In the preceding subsection, we discussed briefly how nuclear reactions in the Sun produce helium by 'burning' hydrogen, with the associated release of energy that makes the Sun shine. This explanation for the Sun's prodigious energy output was first proposed in the 1920s, and the out-working of its theoretical basis was undertaken in the years that followed. However, a detailed understanding of the origin of the heavier elements beyond helium, were not understood until the 1950s when a general theory of stellar nucleosynthesis was developed, principally by Fred Hoyle. Hoyle is mainly remembered for his failed Steady State theory, as discussed in section 3.4, but arguably his greatest contribution to astrophysics was his amazing mathematical insights into the origin of the heavier elements.

So, what does stellar nucleosynthesis mean? Essentially, it is the process by which the heavier elements are cooked-up in the nuclear furnaces of stars. Just as for the Sun, the stability of any star is a balance between the outward thermal pressure caused by fusion reactions in its core, and the relentless inward pull of gravity. The reactions producing helium from hydrogen generates this outward pressure, but what happens when there is little hydrogen fuel left in the core? The reaction slows, and the outward pressure reduces. At this point gravity takes the upper hand, and squashes the star causing the density and temperature in the core to rise. This creates the necessary conditions for a new form of nuclear reaction to take place, this time fusing helium into carbon.

If the star is large enough, with a mass in excess of around eight times the Sun's mass, the cycle will repeat. In other words, when the helium in the core is almost depleted, the nuclear reactions slow once again, and gravity takes over. This inward force will cause the core density and temperature to rise still further, initiating a new reaction to produce a new, heavier element. This cyclic process continues, creating an onion-like structure in the star, with the composition of each concentric layer effectively comprising a different element. The process comes to an end with a particular reaction that converts silicon into iron, creating a central core comprised of iron. At this point, fusion reactions can no longer take place as energy input is required for the process to continue. The energy enabling the outward thermal pressure is lost, and the fate of the star is now in the hands of gravity.

For such a massive star, the gravitational force is unopposed, and the core of the star cannot sustain itself. A huge amount of energy is released when the core collapses to the tiny size of a few kilometres, becoming either a black hole or a neutron star. The outer layers of the star are ejected violently, creating a huge explosion called a supernova. In this cataclysmic event, conditions are sufficiently extreme to produce heavier elements beyond iron. The remnant of this event is an expanding gas cloud enriched with the heavy elements required to make life possible. Around 4.6 billion years ago, and light years away, a star we now call the Sun formed from such a gas cloud. Planets also formed, some of them rocky, and on one of them life began and established itself, enabled by the necessary mix of heavy elements. To use the well-worn cliché – we are indeed star dust![12]

Hoyle's great legacy is the development of the theoretical details which allowed an understanding of this incredible process of stellar evolution from birth to death, that made life on Earth possible. However, this development was not without its problems. For example, in 1952, there was a potential show-stopper with the theory, which suggested that the synthesis of carbon and oxygen in stars was very unlikely. Clearly, the existence of human beings attested to the fact that these elements are relatively abundant in the Universe, so Hoyle had to re-examine the theory to explain this. As a consequence, he proposed a modification to the theory which implied an enhancement effect in the fusion reaction related to the creation of carbon from helium – effectively, a nifty application of the weak anthropic principle. Subsequently this was confirmed. Referring to the resolution of the problem, John Polkinghorne later commented:

"It's only possible because of a very large enhancement effect, called a resonance in the trade, which makes [the reaction] go much quicker than might be expected. And that resonance is there because the laws of nuclear physics take a very specific form ... That's a very striking example of how finely tuned the Universe has to be for us to be inhabitants of it."[13]

Hoyle's response to this turn of events was one of surprise, even dismay, since he was an atheist throughout his life. Despite this he later wrote:

"Would you not say to yourself, 'Some super-calculating intellect must have designed the properties of the carbon atom, otherwise the chance of my finding such an atom through the blind forces of nature would be utterly minuscule. A common-sense interpretation of the facts suggests that a super-intellect has monkeyed with physics, as well as with chemistry and biology, and that there are no blind forces worth speaking about in nature. The numbers one calculates from the facts seem to me so overwhelming as to put this conclusion almost beyond question.' "[14]

Such a declaration might suggest that Hoyle had found, at least, a creator God in his mathematics, but as far as I know, he remained an ardent atheist to the end.

I could go on, but I will not. There are many other examples, which make our Universe a very unlikely place. To wrap-up this section on fine-tuning, I would like to give Gribbin and Rees[15] the last word:

"If we modify the value of one of the fundamental constants, something invariably goes wrong, leading to a universe that is inhospitable to life as we know it ...The conditions in our universe really do seem to be uniquely suitable for life forms like ourselves"

4.4 My story – from deism to theism[†].

After my poolside reading in August 2001, and subsequent deliberations, the next steps in my journey to faith were taken in an Alpha Course led by Rev. Julian Williams, who was then vicar of St. John's church, Rownhams, near Southampton, UK, in the autumn of 2001.

[†] See Glossary.

A Cosmos fine-tuned for Life

I have always referred to my wife Marion as a 'cradle Christian'. She has been a Christian for as long as she can remember, and when we had our two lovely children, Vicky and Jamie, she wanted to bring them up in the church. I had no objection to this (I was obviously a tolerant agnostic!) so when we moved to Southampton for my job at the University in 1987, they started to attend a small, beautiful Victorian church just a short walk away from our new home in Rownhams. The kids did their growing up in Rownhams, before leaving home to attend University in the early years of the new millennium. During those years, the three of them attended St. John's church regularly, whereas it was my habit to meet them at the church after the service to enjoy a chat, a cup of coffee and whatever eats were available. This routine suited me fine. No pressure to attend was applied, and I got to know and make friends with a lot of people in the church. However, very gentle pressure was applied every year by Marion who regularly suggested that I might like to attend an Alpha Course. This was run each Autumn term by the church, and every year I politely declined. It was clearly something that was not for me!

However, in the Autumn of 2001 things were different. When I heard the course was running again I was very comfortable with the idea of going, since I had known, and developed warm friendships with many of the people at St. John's church over a long period of time. Also, with my embryonic belief that there may be a Creator God fresh in mind, I was very keen to hear what Christianity could add to my understanding. As the reader might suspect from what has gone before, at this stage my belief was rational, rather than spiritual. My approach was all head and no heart, and my mind was full of questions about how a Creator God could be set within the context of Christianity.

I am pleased to mention the Alpha Course in my testimony, as I feel that this has come in for some bad press over the years. I guess any particular course is only as good as those who run it, and some may be poorly organised highly-pressured events. However, I'm pleased to say that the one I attended, was a very open, relaxed and informative affair, with no pressure applied to guests. If you haven't been on an Alpha Course, I can certainly recommend it. The format was very comfortable – the evening started with a drink and a chat as people arrived, followed by a full meal. Then, a talk was given on the evening's topic, followed by discussion groups, where questions were encouraged. I found the atmosphere always convivial and constructive, and I have to thank the people on my discussion table for their patience in tolerating my inquisitive approach to everything.

Discussion Group

I was blessed with a lovely group on my discussion table, mostly committed Christians, who made the whole experience comfortable and stimulating. The group was led jointly, and very ably, by Marion (not my wife!) and Andy. Marion I knew before – in the Spring of 2001 I did a paint job on her garage and porch! Andy had just moved to Southampton, so I did not know him prior to the course, but subsequently he has become a good friend. However, it was good that there was another fellow seeker, among the discussion group with whom I shared a certain empathy and healthy scepticism. It was comforting to have another person there who was not immersed in the Christian faith, and who could identify with my deficit in spirituality and faith.

I attended each week, with each evening's topic following the Alpha course handbook. Some of these were factual – for example, Who is Jesus? covered the historical evidence for Jesus's existence and why he had such an impact on the subsequent 2000 years of human history. Others, although interesting, I thought related to people who were already steadfast Christians – for example, How can I be sure of my faith? or How does God guide us?. During the early days of the course, I felt that perhaps it should be called the Omega Course, and someone else should do a real Alpha Course for people like me!

As the weeks passed by, I really looked forward to those Wednesday evening sessions. The talks Julian gave were always stimulating, and the discussion groups afterwards always seemed to end too early, just as things were warming up. During the early weeks, I had so many questions about the Christian faith, as if on a quest to understand everything before I believed. In retrospect, I feel that I should have apologised to other group members for monopolising the discussion time. I know that this was a source of exasperation for some of them. However, this is the joy of the course, when people with very different views can meet, discuss, and have respect for each other's points of view.

The Alpha Away-Day
On a Saturday in mid-November 2001, I attended the Alpha Course away-day on the topic of the Holy Spirit. At the time, I was feeling particularly low, having had a rare bout of flu which had left me with a nasty chest infection. The doctor had diagnosed it as a viral infection, and had therefore not prescribed antibiotics – so it was a case of go away and cough a lot! In an attempt to aerate my lungs, and to try to rid myself of the awful cough, I decided to cycle to the away-day.

I arrived rather wearily on my bicycle that morning. The first session, Who is the Holy Spirit?, took the usual format of a talk followed by a discussion group, and was followed by lunch. During the morning, something Julian said would have a significant impact. I can't remember in which session he said it, but it was a quote attributed to St. Augustine, Bishop of Hippo – which was simply along the lines of 'I believe in order that I might understand'[16]. This immediately struck me as exactly the reverse of the approach to Christianity that I had taken up to that point. I had been attempting to understand everything first, and then believe! I can now appreciate the naivety of this approach. St Augustine's simple quote urged me to do something that was alien to me – to take leap beyond the security of reason. For some reason, on that day, I was ready to accept this and take a step of faith to see where it would lead.

The day was full of surprises for me, and the next turning point occurred in the afternoon session of the away-day. If you haven't been on an Alpha Course yet, then watch out for this session! It doesn't take the usual format, but is a practical session in which the question is asked: How can I be filled with the Holy Spirit?

Encounter
The session was introduced and led by Julian. Without going into all the details, the main focus was to invite the Holy Spirit to 'fill' those present. Since initially I was expecting the usual meeting format, what came next was not only a surprise, but it was also to change my life! In the still atmosphere of the gathering, it

was clear that things were beginning to happen. As Julian continued to invite the Spirit, while encouraging us to be receptive, the first indication of His presence manifested itself in a friend. He began to behave rather strangely, which at first I found quite alarming until I realised he was also very happy. Then, as I stood quietly, eyes closed, it soon became clear that the Spirit was inviting *me* to participate actively in the session! It is difficult for me to find the words to describe the event that took place that afternoon. With the benefit of hindsight, I would now be more comfortable with such an encounter. However, at that time, nothing like it had ever happened to me before – something was going on that I didn't understand, and as such I was fearful of it. It wasn't just fear of the unknown, but also fear of surrendering control as I could perceive was happening to others around me. My fear and inhibitions won out on the day and I did not accept what was being offered. Although I can understand this instinctive reaction, I still regret not surrendering myself in that moment. However, regret was not my overriding emotion that afternoon; I was uplifted to learn a powerful lesson – that there is more to life than just the rational bits described by the physicists!

All this sounds like a bit of a 'road to Damascus' experience, but on the day my outward reaction to it was almost zero – in the moment I did not want to acknowledge that anything had happened. But it did leave its mark, and, along with St Augustine's philosophy, it opened my eyes to a spiritual dimension to life.

Recently, I asked my discussion group leader, Andy Ball, to write something about how he saw the events that day, as he had been through the whole thing with me. I know I was asking a lot of him, as it was a long time ago. However, he did remember in some detail the events of that day:

> "As I recall I was sitting near Graham, when we stood to invite God to send His Spirit to move among us. I put a hand on his back to pray for God to fill him with His Spirit and during this prayer I felt a lot of heat coming from my hands. From my experience, this is usually a good indicator that God is present and doing something. God was quite tangibly present. However, when I looked at Graham there didn't appear to be any visible sign of God working in him – no change in facial expression, no deep peace, or altered breathing, no emotion, nothing. Having prayed this prayer previously, Graham's unresponsiveness to God's manifest presence totally baffled me at

the time and I wondered how I had got it so wrong. How could God be so obviously present, and yet, looking at his face, there was nothing to suggest God was touching him at all. Unperturbed, I continued praying, now harder, in the hope that there would be some discernible breakthrough, but it didn't appear to happen ..."

Poor Andy was as confused as I was! The 'Provider' was there, but the recipient was not responding to the gift offered.

As I left the venue at the end of the day, I was particularly touched by a friend, Glennis, who gave me a big hug, and said how happy she was to see me there on that day. And as I came back down to Earth, riding off into the cold, dark afternoon on my bike, I was confused and perhaps a little cross – the events of the day were not part of the script for my life! My wife Marion recalls the moment I returned home that afternoon. My head was buzzing with questions, mostly about the Holy Spirit, in an attempt to make sense of what had happened. Who was this person with the power to disturb my complacency? She took the brunt of most of the questions – the ones that she could answer. Over the coming days, I calmed down and was more accepting of the remarkable events at the Alpha away-day. After all, if the awesome God that created the Universe had placed a metaphorical hand upon my shoulder, how then could I ignore what had happened. That precious **numinous** moment had changed my life. There was no going back.

As we approached Christmas of 2001, the Alpha Course ended. Many people on the course, including myself, had benefited greatly from attendance, and would miss our Wednesday evening Christian fellowship. This hole was filled, however, by Julian Williams running the 'ABC course' from January 2002. I started attending it as a 'considering confirmation' course, and ended it as a preparation for baptism and confirmation, which took place at St John's church, Rownhams on 17 November 2002 – exactly the first anniversary of the Alpha away-day.

This is not the end of the story, but just the beginning. In the years since 2001, so much has changed. If you had told me then, the sorts of things that I would be doing now – such as writing a book such as this – I would not have believed you. I think it is fair to say that my story is a good example of God meeting people wherever they happen to be in their lives. Mine seemed to have no room for God, and was surrounded by an apparently impregnable, and long-standing, wall of agnosticism. The process by which He reached me, which I have tried to convey in these pages, is pretty extraordinary.

4.5 Concluding remarks.

There is inevitably much talk of science in my story, so a reasonable question to ask is – what if the science changes? What if somehow we were able to confirm the reality of an infinite number of parallel universes, or other discoveries are made to change subtly the logic of all that I have said? Regarding my own faith in the Christian God, Jesus Christ, I would say that it is not dependent upon what is going on in the world of science. I believe that God used the science to hook me, but subsequently He has revealed himself to me in so many other ways that He and the spiritual realm are now part of my reality. I have been on a scientific and spiritual journey, and arrived at a point where I cannot deny Him. Both Marion and I have received remarkable physical healing through prayer (something that can be confirmed by our GP), and we have witnessed transformation and healing in so many other people in our roles as pastoral carers.

One thing I have learned from all this, and in particular in the context of courses such as Alpha, is that people are convinced not by endless academic discussion of the issues, but rather by the simple means of personal experience of God's transforming power in their own lives, and in the lives of others.

Having set the stage with a cosmos fine-tuned for life, I now hand over to my co-author John to tell us about the amazing and beautiful diversity of life on planet Earth.

Chapter 4 endnotes:

[1] Stephen Hawking and Leonard Mlodinow, The Grand Design: new answers to the ultimate questions of life, Bantam Books, 2010, p. 205.
[2] Lee Smolin, Three Roads to Quantum Gravity, Basics Books, 2001, p. 201.
[3] One exception to this is String theory. The fundamental premise of the theory is that the subatomic world is not populated by point particles, but by tiny, string-like, vibrating filaments. These have different modes of vibration, corresponding to the different species of particles. Built into

the theory is a methodology to allow the characteristics (mass, charge, spin, etc.) of all subatomic particles to be calculated. However, the method is dependent upon knowing the geometry of spatial dimensions, which are themselves so tiny as to be unobservable in the foreseeable future. So, the current technique of determining the particle attributes by experiment and inputting them into our current models is still the best we can do. For a good lay-person's account of String theory see, for example: Brian Greene, The Hidden Reality, Penguin Books, 2011, Chapter 4.

[4] Steven Weinberg, A Designer Universe, 1999. An article based on a talk on cosmic design given in April 1999 at the Conference of the American Association for the Advancement of Science in Washington DC, USA. Physics & Astronomy Online: www.physlink.com/education/essay_weinberg.cfm.

[5] Lee Smolin, Three Roads to Quantum Gravity, Basics Books, 2001, p. 199.

[6] George Ellis, Opposing the Multiverse, Astronomy & Geophysics (2008), Vol. 49, Issue 2, pp. 2.33-2.35.

[7] Freeman J. Dyson, Disturbing the Universe, Harper & Row, 1979, p. 250.

[8] Paul Davies, The Cosmic Blueprint, Simon and Schuster, 1988, p. 203.

[9] Paul Davies, Superforce, Simon & Schuster, 1983, p. 243.

[10] Martin Rees, Just Six Numbers: the deep forces that shape the universe, Phoenix, 2000.

[11] Paul Steinhardt's quote from interview with John Horgan, Scientific American online, 1 December 2014

[12] The Holy Bible (NIV): Genesis, Chapter 2, verse 7.

[13] John Polkinghorne, God: New Evidence, Focus, 2010. A series of short videos exploring aspects of fine-tuning: www.focus.org.uk.

[14] Fred Hoyle, The Universe: Past and Present Reflections, Engineering and Science (magazine), November 1981, pp. 8-12.

[15] John Gribbin and Martin Rees, Cosmic Coincidences, Black Swan, 1991, p. 269.

[16] Centuries later, St. Anselm of Canterbury, echoed his statement in similar fashion: "I do not seek to understand in order that I may believe, but I believe in order to understand."

From the Big Bang to Biology – where is God?

5 Life in the Goldilocks Zone.

"An insect is far harder to understand than either an atom or a star."
Martin Rees[1], FRS, Astronomer Royal.

"To understand how all of this works we will need something more than merely lists of components ... the great difference between the telephone directory and a Shakespeare play is that, while both have a grand cast of characters, only the play has a plot."
Sydney Brenner[2], FRS, Nobel Laureate, part of the group who deciphered the working of the genetic code.

John writes ...

5.1 Just right.

In the previous chapter we saw how the starting conditions at the Big Bang were very precisely defined and that precision allowed for the formation of a Universe with stars and planets and much else beside. We have also looked at the synthesis of carbon, the element that has ideal properties for forming large and complex molecules such as we see in living organisms. At first, its very existence seemed improbable. As we saw in section 4.3, Fred Hoyle's atheism was shaken when he realised just how finely tuned the laws of physics need to be to produce the abundance of carbon that we see today. But there is more than that: the Earth itself is a very special planet. I will give here only a partial list of distinctive features, those that are most relevant to thinking about life on Earth. For anyone who wishes to delve deeper, I thoroughly recommend *The Goldilocks Enigma* by Paul Davies (Penguin Books, 2007).

The first thing to say is that the Earth is in the optimal range of distance from its star, our Sun. The temperature range that we experience means that water can exist in liquid form (an essential for the biochemistry of life) over most of the planet. It is neither too hot, nor too cold but just right. Recalling the children's story *Goldilocks and the Three Bears,* we say that Earth is in the 'Goldilocks Zone' (or in more formal terms, the circumstellar habitable zone). Then there is the structure of the planet itself. During its formation, so much radioactive material was incorporated that its iron-rich core will remain molten and mobile for billions of years. Currents in this molten core create a magnetic field that protects the Earth from external sources of radiation such as solar flares. The molten core is not covered by a fixed lid but a mobile covering consisting of **tectonic plates.** Their mobility (and associated phenomena such as volcanoes and earthquakes) recycles materials, especially carbon, giving us a dynamic and self-renewing planet with a range of different types of terrain on its surface. This provides a wide variety of habitats in which living organisms can exist and evolve.

Our large moon is also special and is important because its gravity helps stabilise the angle of tilt of the Earth's axis. The axis of rotation of the Earth is not perpendicular to the plane of its orbit around the Sun but is tilted by about 23°. It is this tilt of the axis that gives us seasons (and wider variation in habitat), but large changes in the angle of tilt would lead to dramatic climatic fluctuations. The moon's gravitational field also gives us tides (again creating more habitats) and provides some protection against asteroid/meteorite impact.

This very special planet, set in a finely tuned Universe, is thus set up for life. Paul Davies, a physicist who writes widely about fine-tuning and associated topics has said "To a physicist life looks nothing short of a miracle. It's just amazing what living things can do."[3] How then did that miracle happen and what does it look like now?

5.2 Life is based on information.

The beginning of life on Earth (abiogenesis) remains what Darwin might have called an abominable mystery (he actually said that about the origin of flowering plants). We can do experiments to demonstrate the feasibility or otherwise of particular mechanisms but none of them have given really incisive insights into the process. Paul Davies calls it 'The Fifth Miracle' [4] adding that "the origin of life is one of the great outstanding mysteries of science". Others have alluded to biology's hidden Big Bang. It is a question that is genuinely within the constituency of science but which science has yet to answer. However, we are all in agreement that, whatever the means by which life started, it is certainly based around molecular information in the form of a very special molecule, DNA (deoxyribonucleic acid). The role of DNA as the carrier of genetic information was conclusively demonstrated in 1944. Until then, that role had been tentatively ascribed to other types of molecule within **chromosomes**. We now know that all living organisms on the planet use DNA as their genetic material (although some viruses, which are difficult to classify as either living or non-living, use the very closely related molecule, RNA – ribonucleic acid).

DNA is an extraordinarily clever molecule – indeed, it has been rightly described as the most extraordinary molecule on Earth. The molecular information – the genetic code – within DNA consists of the order in which its four building blocks (known as bases[5]) occur along the length of the molecule. A specific linear array of bases is a **gene** and thus the DNA component of a chromosome is a linear array of genes. If an individual's total set of genes – its **genome** – is regarded as a library, then we might say that an individual chromosome is like a bookshelf. This library of genes contains all the information necessary for the development and minute-by-minute activity of an organism but the information is in code. I describe below how the code is translated but here I want to emphasise again the cleverness of the DNA molecule in relation to passing genetic information on to the next generation. This is something that has to occur every time a cell divides: each daughter cell must have a full copy of the genetic information. The ability to do this is based on the overall structure of the DNA molecule. The molecule is actually not just one linear array of bases but two, intimately associated together in the famous double helix. This is where it gets really beautiful. A base in one of the strands pairs with a base in the other strand, but the base pairing rules are very specific. The base adenine (A) can only pair with the base thymine (T)[6] and the base guanine (G) can only pair with the base cytosine (C) (I've often thought that ATGC would be a great name for a rock band!). This means that one strand automatically dictates the structure of the other. When DNA is being copied (replicated) in preparation for cell division, the two strands separate and each acts as a template for a new partner strand (Figure 5.1). This leads to the formation of two daughter molecules each with the same array of bases as the original parent molecule. Consequently, the genetic information is conserved and passed on. As James Watson and Francis Crick wrote, with uncharacteristic modesty, "It has not escaped our notice that the specific pairing we have postulated immediately suggests a possible copying mechanism for the genetic material"[7]. If this had been invented by humans, we would describe it as work of sheer genius.

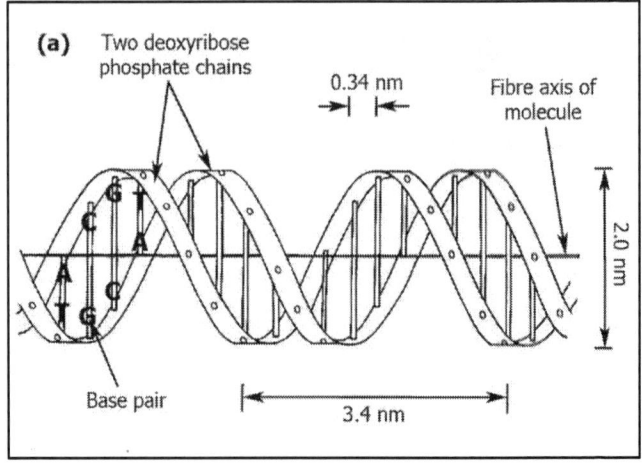

Figure 5.1a. The DNA double helix consists of two DNA strands that are wound round each other. The backbone of each strand consists of the

Life in the Goldilocks Zone

sugar deoxyribose (the D in DNA) linked to phosphate. Each deoxyribose phosphate is joined to a base (A, T, G or C) and the two strands are held together by weak chemical linkages between the bases in one strand and the bases in the other (represented by the cross-bars in the diagram; if this depiction were shown in vertical orientation, the cross-bars are like the rungs of a ladder). A sequence of bases is depicted on the left-hand side of the diagram. The horizontal black line indicates the central axis of the molecule, were it actually to be stretched out straight. Note: 1 nm = 1 nanometre = 1 thousand-millionth of a metre. Credit: Figure based on Figure 1.2b in John A Bryant, *Molecular Aspects of Gene Expression in Plants,* Academic Press, London and New York, 1976.

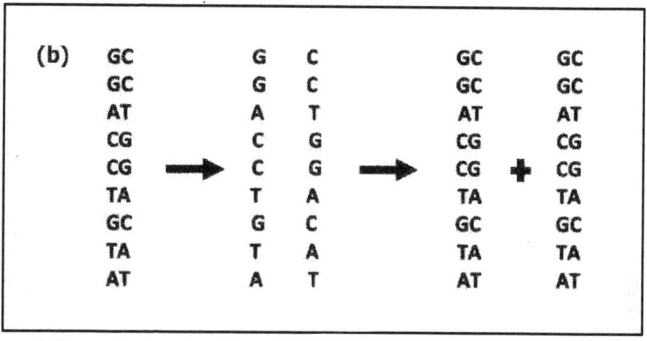

(b)								
	GC		G	C		GC		GC
	GC		G	C		GC		GC
	AT		A	T		AT		AT
	CG		C	G		CG		CG
	CG	➡	C	G	➡	CG	✚	CG
	TA		T	A		TA		TA
	GC		G	C		GC		GC
	TA		T	A		TA		TA
	AT		A	T		AT		AT

Figure 5.1b. A simple diagram illustrating the key features of DNA replication or copying of DNA. On the left, a very short section of a double helix is represented by two linear arrays of letters which represent the bases. In order for the DNA to be copied, the two strands of the helix separate (centre). Each one is now able to act as a template (via specific base-pairing) for synthesis of a new strand. This results in two DNA double helices, each containing one old strand and one new strand (right).

5.3 Life is also based on energy.

Before thinking a little more about how the information system in DNA works, I need to mention that all living things need to be able to extract sources of energy from their environment (which, for photosynthetic organisms is the Sun, and for most other organisms is their food). They also need to convert environmentally derived energy into forms that can be used in life processes. In individual cells, these life processes include making all the molecules that contribute to cell structure and function –

DNA, **proteins**, lipids (fats) and many more. In his seminal book, *The Vital Question* Nick Lane points out that whatever primary energy source is used and whatever the overall chemical/biochemical pathway employed to convert it to a useful form, all living organisms have the same biophysical mechanism at the heart of the process. That mechanism is the generation of an excess positive charge (i.e. an excess of protons) on one side of a membrane so as to give what is effectively an electrical potential across the membrane. It is the controlled passage of the protons back through the membrane, through a tiny turbine, that is the final step in synthesising the cell's energy currency. This currency is a molecule called **ATP** (adenosine triphosphate) which drives nearly all the energy-requiring biochemical reactions in cells. This basic mechanism of generating a difference in positive charge across a membrane is called **chemi-osmotic coupling** and when it was first proposed by the British biochemist, Peter Mitchell in the 1960s, it was not widely accepted. However, we now know that, as mentioned above, this basic mechanism is universal and in recognition of the importance of the discovery, Mitchell was awarded a Nobel Prize in 1978[8].

When we look at the mechanism in detail, for example in our own cells, it is truly beautiful. Who would have thought that a turbine with moving parts could be made of protein, making it the smallest turbine on the planet! This protein is called **ATP synthase** and is actually composed of 18 different protein chains; some of these are represented more than once so that there are in total, 29 protein chains in a single ATP synthase turbine in human cells[9]. ATP synthase is located in the mitochondria, the compartments within cells that generate biochemical energy. Each turbine, driven by protons returning from one side of a membrane through a pore in the ATP synthase, rotates at 120 revolutions per second, making three ATP molecules for each complete rotation[10]. For readers especially interested in this, there is a very neat animation available via endnote [9] (use 'molecular animations' in the search box). The number of ATP synthase turbines per cell depends on the type of cell; muscle cells for example have several thousand. Overall, ATP synthase makes approximately our body's weight of ATP each day. Stop to think what this actually means: a person weighing 65 kg makes about that weight of ATP per day, an astonishing amount. The ATP is in a constant cycle of being made, being used and being re-made. As Lane says, the overall beauty and complexity of the process has led some people to believe in God – but not him. He sees the 'wonder of natural selection' in generating this 'wondrous machine.' But actually, belief in God and in natural selection are not alternatives; natural selection is a set of mechanisms, God is the agency behind those mechanisms (see also section 5.6).

5.4 How does the genetic code work?

Mention of natural selection brings us back to DNA and the genetic code. The first point to make is one that gives biologists shivers of excitement. The code is the same in all living organisms, from the simplest bacteria to the most complex vertebrates. Even those viruses that have RNA as their genetic material have the direct equivalent of the DNA code in their RNA. For biologists, this is consistent with the idea that every living thing on Earth is descended from one common ancestor, known as the Last Common Ancestor (LCA). That is not to deny the possibility that there were other life forms in existence on the early Earth prior to or at the same time as the LCA but if there were, they did not survive. We also note in passing that the universality of the code makes it possible to carry out genetic modification/genetic engineering. Thus, a human gene that encodes the hormone insulin can be transferred into bacterial cells, and the bacteria can subsequently use the gene as if it was one of their own. They can decode it because their DNA reads the code in the same way as human DNA does.

Secondly, the information in the genetic code enables the cell to make proteins[11]. These are the ideal choice for being the cell's working molecules. With twenty different **amino acids** (the building blocks of protein) available and an infinite array of possibilities for the number and order of the amino acids, a huge variety of different proteins is possible. And they do indeed come in a wide variety, each with its own specific role. Thousands of them (and I do mean thousands) are **enzymes** which are proteins that carry out biochemical reactions. Others are structural, such as collagen in cartilage and bone, or keratin in hair; some are carriers of other molecules, exemplified by haemoglobin in the blood; there are also sensors, hormones, regulatory proteins (including those that control the activity of genes), membrane components, pumps, contractile proteins (as in muscle) and even, as we saw above, a small complex of proteins that form tiny turbines. Biologists amongst our readers will know that this is a simplified list but even a simplified list tells us something about the biochemical complexity of life, all of which is encoded in DNA.

Thirdly, the essentials of the mechanisms that translate the code are similar in all organisms but some of the details differ slightly, for example between bacteria and all other life-forms. Here we will just focus on the essentials, in order to give a flavour of the beauty of the decoding mechanism. The first step is to copy one strand (based on the same specific pairing as discussed above) of a particular gene into a molecule that will carry the code from the DNA into the rest of the cell. This molecule is called a messenger and is made of RNA. In all cells except bacteria and **archaea**, the genes are located in a compartment within the cell called the nucleus. The **messenger RNA** is transported out of the nucleus into the **cytoplasm** in order to instruct the manufacture of proteins via the genetic code. To do this, the messenger RNA associates with small particles called **ribosomes**. These are made of proteins plus a type of RNA called ribosomal RNA. They are effectively the work-benches on which proteins are made and each of our cells has up to ten million of them.

As mentioned above, proteins are built from amino acids and the genetic code specifies which amino acids are incorporated, one at a time, into a growing protein molecule. The genetic code is written in bases, with three bases (a triplet) specifying each amino acid. With four types of base in DNA, the possible number of different triplets (known as **codons**) is 4^3, i.e. 64. There are only 20 different amino acids that are incorporated into protein so the genetic code has some built-in redundancy. Thus, most amino acids are encoded by several different codons and there are also codons that specify start and stop.

Nucleic acids are therefore ideal molecules for carrying the genetic code; and proteins are ideal molecules for performing a wide variety of roles within cells. However, there is no *a priori* reason for a sequence of bases in a nucleic acid to be related to a sequence of amino acids in a protein. For example, a protein cannot be assembled by individual amino acids finding and lining up with their specifying codon. There is no biochemical mechanism that would enable the two classes of molecule to associate in this way. At this point in time we cannot envisage how the relationship between nucleic acids and proteins developed and by what mechanism the first proteins were assembled. I want to emphasise this again: nucleic acids (DNA and RNA) are ideal molecules for carrying a code; proteins in their vast range of types are ideal molecules for the range of roles they perform in cells. However, we cannot even imagine how the order of bases in one type of molecule came to specify the order of amino acids in another type of molecule. The evolution of the genetic code has thus been described by molecular biologists as a profound problem. The best we can do is to describe what happens now (and which has been happening, as far as we can tell, since the first cells were formed) – and even then we cannot envisage how these mechanisms began to evolve. Thus Paul Davies is not alone in thinking that the whole system looks designed.[12]

Since free amino acids will not line themselves against the appropriate codon, how does it happen that the presence of a particular codon leads to the incorporation of the correct amino acid into protein? The answer is remarkable as becomes evident when we look at a specific example. One of the two codons that specifies the amino acid *glycine* is GGC (see earlier for full names of the bases); an adapter molecule recognises the codon and brings the glycine to the ribosome. The adapter molecule is called **transfer RNA** (tRNA) and there is a specific tRNA for recognition of each codon (each tRNA is encoded in a gene). In our example, the relevant codon is recognised because the corresponding tRNA has an **anti-codon** consisting of the bases CCG; this will pair with the codon by the rules of base-pairing mentioned earlier. Prior to associating with the messenger RNA in this way, the tRNA has been joined (temporarily) to a glycine molecule by a specific enzyme which recognises both the tRNA and the glycine. The enzymes that do this, one for each type of amino acid, are thus very sophisticated in their ability to recognise the right molecules and there is a good deal of speculation as to how they evolved. Thus Carl Woese and his colleagues, leading experts in this field, write 'the code is far too highly structured to have been ordered merely through the evolutionary wanderings of these enzymes'[13].

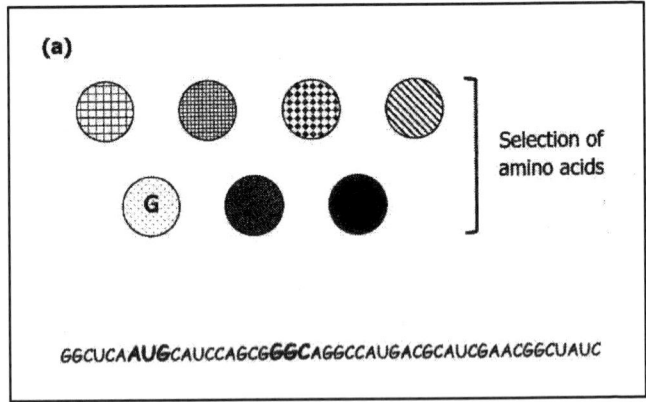

Figure 5.2a. Figures 5.2a and 5.2b show the key steps in building a protein. In 5.2a we see part of the genetic code of a messenger RNA molecule. This is a working copy of a gene that carries the genetic code to the site of protein synthesis. Note that the base T in DNA is replaced by U in RNA. This functions in the same way as T. The code is organised in triplets of bases: a particular triplet specifies a particular amino acid. The diagram also contains a small selection of amino acids; there are actually 20 different sorts that are used for making proteins. In real life, the 20 different sorts vary extensively in size and overall shape whereas in the diagram they differ in patterns of grey (with glycine indicated by G). The amino acids do not on their own line up in the right order to build a protein. There is no biochemical mechanism known that enables a free amino acid to line up against a specific triplet of bases.

(b)

```
                CCG
GGCUCAAUGCAUCCAGCGGGCAGGCCAUGACGCAUCGAACGGCUAUC
```

An enzyme recognises both the adaptor molecule and the correct amino acid and joins them together.

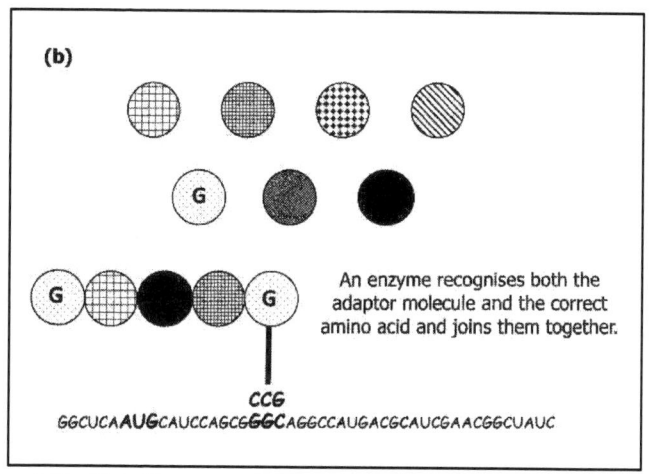

Figure 5.2b. This illustrates the mechanism that solves this problem. A codon is selected that specifies the simple amino acid glycine. Glycine cannot recognise its triplet codon, GGC but the codon can be recognised, using the 'rules' of specific base-pairing, by another RNA molecule that carries the three bases that will pair with GGC, namely CCG. This RNA molecule, known as transfer RNA is thus an adaptor. At this point the process becomes even more remarkable: an enzyme (which, you will remember is a protein that carries out a biochemical reaction) recognises both that this tRNA specifies glycine and also the glycine itself and joins them together. The transfer RNA can then take the glycine to the site of protein synthesis where it is joined into the growing protein chain. Thus the synthesis of proteins requires the prior existence of proteins, proteins which in terms of their actions, are very sophisticated. As many commentators have noted, this is a classic chicken and egg situation. Sharp-eyed readers will have also noticed another glycine at the start of the growing protein. This is specified by a different codon, AUG, which only occurs at the start of the coding sequence in messenger RNA. It effectively tells the cell to start reading the code here.

Despite our inability to understand the evolutionary origins of these enzymes one thing is clear: they *have* evolved. Thus, this vital mechanism enables the tRNA to bring the appropriate amino acid, glycine in our example, to the ribosome to be joined on to the growing protein molecule (Figure 5.2). As I write this, I cannot help but think that we biologists are so used to this that we have become a little blasé. It is an amazing mechanism. We note that there are many steps in the process where, starting at the gene and ending with the finished product, the synthesis of proteins requires the existence of pre-existing proteins – enzymes, transport proteins and structural proteins. How were the first proteins synthesised? We also note the sheer beauty of the way in which base-pairing is used to bring the correct amino acids for incorporation into a growing protein chain.

This description of how genes work is a summary of a set of mechanisms that are in reality far more complex. Text box 5.1 is for readers who want to learn more about this topic.

Foreshadowing our discussion of evolution later in the chapter, we should stop to ask: how did all this arise?

5.5 DNA and the origin of life.

Life as we know it is based on the use and transmission of information contained in DNA. Some aspects of that were described above. We sometimes call DNA a self-replicating molecule but that is not strictly true. What is true is that its structure enables the order of the bases – the code – to be preserved during DNA replication[14] thus ensuring that the embedded information is passed from generation to generation. But DNA is not *self*-replicating. The copying of DNA is carried out by several enzymes and is regulated by several other proteins. Where do these come from? Well, they are made by the same decoding and protein synthesis mechanisms that I have just described. The enzymes and other proteins are encoded in the DNA and are made by the standard cellular mechanisms, the components of which are also encoded in the DNA. That then is the puzzle. The working of DNA requires the prior working of DNA. And it goes further than that. Although molecular biologists can carry out in test tubes specific reactions (or several linked reactions) that are involved in DNA replication or in the working of genes, the full range of functions of DNA requires the pre-existence of a cell (see Text Box 5.2 and endnote[15]). All the components of that cell are encoded directly or indirectly[16] in the DNA. DNA cannot work without a cell but the existence of a cell requires the working of DNA.

So, even if we can envisage the existence on the early Earth of a molecule that was actually at that time self-replicating, it is still a very long way from understanding how that chemical hardware

---

Text Box 5.1: And there's more ...

- Associated with every gene is a regulatory tract of DNA called a promoter. Some promoters allow the relevant gene to be active in all or nearly all cells. These are the genes that code for the proteins which all cells require; we call these genes 'house-keeping' genes.

- However, many promoters are responsive to cues which may be, for example, developmental, positional, nutritional, temporal (as in diurnal rhythms) or environmental. Some genes may be switched on by such cues, others may be switched off.

- In eukaryotic organisms (i.e. all organisms except for bacteria and archaea) the coding sequences of genes are interrupted by non-coding tracts of DNA called **introns**. In some genes, in more complex organisms such as vertebrates, the total length of the introns may be much larger than the total length of the coding portions (which are called **exons**) of a gene.

- This means that when a gene is copied, the molecule that is synthesised is not actually messenger RNA (mRNA) but pre-mRNA.

- Pre-mRNA must be edited (biologists call this step *splicing*) in order to form the version of mRNA that leaves the nucleus to direct protein synthesis.

- Many pre-mRNAs may be spliced in different ways to give different mRNAs. Alternative splicing is one of the ways in which the relatively few genes that mammals, including humans, possess (about 20,000) can code for so many different proteins.

---

came to be used essentially as informational software that could direct the synthesis of a cell and all its components. On several occasions Paul Davies has said it is like a kite evolving into a radio-controlled aeroplane. That mystery makes us aware of yet one more: did proteins exist before cells or were they a product that could only be synthesised in cells? It has been calculated that the chance of even a small protein assembling itself correctly from a solution of amino acids is so small as to be non-existent. As Paul Davies puts it: "… when you put the numbers in you find, to your absolute horror, that you could wait almost forever just to get a

---

Text Box 5.2:

Clever work but not the creation of life.

In 2010, the American biochemist and entrepreneur Craig Venter announced that he and his team had created life. This was a bold claim but essentially untrue. What they had achieved was the chemical (i.e. not using enzymes) synthesis in the laboratory of a complete bacterial genome. Although bacterial genomes consist of only one relatively short DNA molecule, this was a great step forward for **synthetic biology**. They then transferred the DNA molecule into a cell of a closely-related bacterial species *from which its own DNA molecule had been removed*. The 'artificial' DNA molecule functioned perfectly in this cell, to which Venter gave the name *Synthia*. He said, with characteristic panache, that this was the first living organism whose parent was a computer (in that a computer had controlled the construction of the artificial DNA molecule). However, whatever else they had achieved, Venter's team had not created life. The new DNA molecule required a pre-existing cell in which to work.

---

single protein. The odds of shuffling amino acids at random into just one short protein are one in 10^{130} …" [17] And even if the chances were much better than this, we still need to ask from where did the amino acids come? Were they generated from simpler molecules in reactions caused by lightning strikes or ultra-violet light? We do not know.

At this point, I need to emphasise that neither I nor my co-author hold to a God of the Gaps viewpoint, i.e. the things that we do not know are ascribed to God, while science has explained the rest. For us, God is the God of the whole of creation and science is providing us with information on how it works. And that brings us back to the origin of life. Everything that I have mentioned so far points to the possibility that the whole system is designed and that in turn implies a designer (however, I am not talking about the Intelligent Design viewpoint held by some of the opponents of evolution – which we will discuss in Chapter 7). It is interesting that some scientists struggle with this because it goes against everything they want to believe or disbelieve. The astronomer Fred Hoyle called the Universe a 'put-up job' as if some 'superior intellect' had been involved in generating the laws of nature. Paul Davies writes that "Scientists are slowly waking up to an inconvenient truth – the Universe looks suspiciously like a fix"[18] and actually goes further in saying "… the impression of design is overwhelming."[19] In connection with the origin of life he writes "The peculiarity of biological complexity makes the genome seem almost like an impossible object – yet it must have formed somehow. I have come to the conclusion that no familiar law of nature could produce such a structure from incoherent chemicals" [12]. From the Big Bang to biology there are strong pointers to the existence of God.

5.6 Energy and the origin of life.

In the previous section, we focussed on the information system based in DNA. However, there is another view. As mentioned in section 5.3, biochemist Nick Lane has pointed out that in every living organism, the same core process lies at the heart of their energy transduction mechanisms. That process is the creation of electrical potentials based on the generation of differences in proton concentration on either side of a membrane. Lane makes a convincing case that under very particular environmental conditions, such electrical potentials can be generated by purely chemical means and thus might provide energy to make some larger molecules non-biologically (rather than the energy coming from lightning strikes or UV light, as mentioned earlier). He goes on to suggest that lipids (fats) formed in this way might themselves act as membranes and thus be in effect 'proto-cells'. So in his view, the ability to generate an electrical potential based on differences in proton concentration represents the basic activity of living things, rather than the possession of a self-replicating information-carrying molecule (DNA). However, there has to be a large jump from a hollow lipid sphere behaving like a proto-cell to even the simplest of bacteria. We need proteins, proteins whose function is dependent on the order of the building blocks (amino acids) from which the proteins are built. Energy to build the proteins is not enough; information to guide their building is essential (remember the calculated odds against the assembly of a sequence of amino acids presented earlier). The ATP synthase turbine mentioned earlier is a classic example. Nick Lane believes that it is the oldest protein in the world but even the simpler forms of it are very complex and cannot be envisaged to have been formed by random assembly of amino acid building blocks. We are back to the problem of how the information in DNA became the code that enables the cell to build protein.

Overall then, both information and energy are needed to replicate cells. The possession of DNA as the genetic material embodying a universal code plus the use of chemi-osmotic coupling in all living things suggest that these were both part of the earliest cells on Earth. And there we have to leave it.

5.7 Life on Earth – a brief overview.

The origin of life remains unknown but we do know that there have been living organisms on Earth for a very long time. As mentioned in section 3.5, Earth was formed about 4.6 billion years ago, within the circumstellar habitable zone of its star, our Sun. The first identifiable fossil cells date back 3.8 billion years but it has been claimed that geochemical analysis reveals the presence in 4 billion year old rocks of molecules that today are only made by living cells. In relation to the age of the Earth, life started only a short time after the birth of the planet, during the long geological era called the pre-Cambrian (see Tables 5.1 and 5.2). These earliest living things were simple single-celled organisms much like modern Gram-positive[20] bacteria. These cells gave rise to two further lineages, Gram-negative bacteria and archaea (sometimes known as archaebacteria) both of which arose early in the history of life on Earth. The scene is now set for the generation of the abundance and diversity of life on our planet. As a prelude to more detailed discussion in section 5.9, the major events are summarised in Table 5.2.

Table 5.1 The Geological Periods

Period	Millions of Years before Present
Pre-Cambrian	4,600 to 570
Cambrian	570 to 505
Ordovician	505 to 438
Silurian	438 to 408
Devonian	408 to 360
Carboniferous	360 to 286
Permian	286 to 245
Triassic	245 to 208
Jurassic	208 to 144
Cretaceous	144 to 66.4
Tertiary	66.4 to 1.8
Quaternary	1.8 to present

5.8 Natural selection and evolution.

It is a major premise of biology that the development and diversification of life on Earth, briefly summarised above, has happened by the processes of natural selection and evolution. This topic has assumed a perhaps disproportionate prominence in the science-faith debate and thus needs a full discussion. However, before doing that I need to comment on the phrase 'The Theory of Evolution'. A scientific theory is not a hunch or hypothesis yet to be supported by adequate evidence. It is a well-supported, very firmly established understanding of an aspect of the natural world that can be tested by scientific method and which allows one to make predictions which may also be tested (see section 2.3).

Table 5.2 Major events in life on Earth

Event	Millions of Years before Present
Origin of Life	4,000 to 3,800
First photosynthetic organisms	2,800
First complex (eukaryotic) cells	2,000 to 1,800
First occurrences of sexual reproduction	1,100
First vertebrates	530
Invertebrate animals invade land	500
Green plants invade land	472
Vertebrate animals invade land	397
First trees	385
First dinosaurs	225
First mammals	200
First birds	150
First flowering plants	130
Extinction of dinosaurs	66
First great apes	14
First 'modern' humans (*Homo sapiens*)	~0.25 (250,000 years)

Charles Darwin's book, *On the Origin of Species by Means of Natural Selection*, published in 1859, became an immediate best seller. It was almost as if educated Victorian society was waiting for something like this. And in a sense it was. In the previous century, geologists had shown that the Earth was older, very much older than the 6,000 years in Bishop Ussher's interpretation of the early chapters of Genesis[21]. Further, the existence in rocks of fossil animals and plants that were no longer extant, was already very well known. Indeed, 'dragon bones', now known to be parts of fossil dinosaurs, were reported in China as long ago as 300 BC. By the time *The Origin of Species* was published, palaeontologists and fossil hunters such as Samuel Goodrich and Mary Anning had established the existence of many more species of fossil animals. Further, in the previous century, half-formed ideas about the descent of complex animals from simpler forms were evident in the writings of amateur scientists, including Charles Darwin's grandfather, Erasmus (who was a doctor in Lichfield). The contribution of Charles Darwin (Figure 5.3) and Alfred Russell Wallace was to use their detailed observations of the natural world to formulate a coherent theory. This has subsequently become known as the Theory of Evolution and Darwin's book is still regarded as the foundation of modern evolutionary biology – an amazing legacy.

Figure 5.3. Charles Darwin, 1854.
Credit: Henry Maull and John Francis (public domain).

Darwin's ideas were formed during the voyage of HMS Beagle[22] and particularly, but not exclusively, during a visit made by the ship to the Galapagos Islands, 1,000 km off the west coast of Ecuador. Differences between what were obviously closely related species of mocking birds and of 'finches'[23] and between varieties of giant tortoises were associated with different lifestyles on the different islands (see Figures 5.4 to 5.6). These observations led him to propose that amongst the varieties present within any one species, some are more suited to their environment than others and that these would enjoy greater reproductive success (although the advantage may actually be quite small). This was the basis for the idea of Natural Selection. Varieties which enjoyed more reproductive success would come to dominate a population, and thus succeeding generations would eventually become different from the ancestral population. Darwin called this 'Descent with Modification'. Further, this process would lead to the establishment of clearly different varieties – and eventually different species – all of which were descended from an original founding population or common ancestor. This process of speciation would be accelerated if different populations were at least partly isolated from each other (but see later in this section).

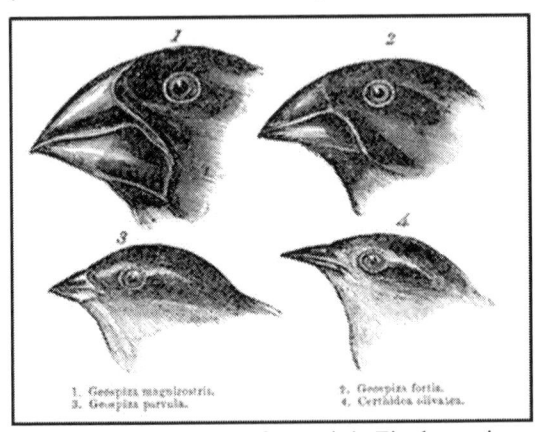

Figure 5.4. Four of Darwin's Finch species:
1. Large Ground Finch, 2. Medium Ground Finch, 3. Small Tree Finch, 4. Warbler Finch. Credit: drawing by John Gould in The voyage of the Beagle (public domain).

Darwin backed up his ideas not only from observations of the fauna of the Galapagos Islands but also from general observations of anatomy, physiology and ecology and to a much lesser extent from his knowledge of fossils (he had studied geology for a year at Cambridge). However, he was concerned about the puzzle of heredity. How could the blending of characteristics between two parents preserve the identity of specific traits so that they could be passed on unchanged to the next generation? There is a certain irony that between 1856 and 1865, a monk, Gregor Mendel, was working at Brno in Czechoslovakia on the inheritance of particular traits in pea plants. He concluded that these traits were based in physical factors (later called genes) that were passed on to the next generation via pollen and ova. He published his work in 1866 and had Darwin known about it, it would have solved his 'puzzle of heredity.' However, Mendel's work was not initially widely known because it was published in a rather obscure journal. It was not until its rediscovery and confirmation by three different scientists in 1900 that the concept of genes started to gain traction – and by that time, Charles Darwin had been dead for 18 years.

Figure 5.5. The Hood Mocking Bird, named after Hood island in the Galapagos archipelago, where it lives. The name of the island is now Española. Credit: John Bryant.

We can now say that genetic variation within populations is a key element in natural selection and evolution. There is much misunderstanding of the scope of this variation and to address that misunderstanding I have summarised different types of genetic variation in Text Boxes 5.3 and 5.4. However, I will only deal with the most common type of variation, namely differences in the base sequence of a particular gene between individuals in a population. As mentioned earlier, the structure of DNA itself directs the faithful copying of the sequence of bases from one generation to the next. However, from time to time, the wrong base is inserted as the new molecule is built up. In the vast majority of cases, the cell's proof-reading machinery recognises this and the mistake is corrected but occasionally some escape the proof-reading and thus a **mutation** occurs (although the word mutation has taken on sinister undertones, it actually only means change). Because of the way that the genetic code works, many of these changes will have no detectable effect on the organism itself: the system of replication embodies a good deal of resilience. Thus, if we compare the base sequence of specific genes between two individuals we may well find minor differences which are undetectable at the level of gene function.

Figure 5.6. A Galapagos giant tortoise. Tortoises from different islands differ morpho-logically from each other, but they can interbreed, so have not yet evolved into separate species.
Credit: John Bryant.

Text Box 5.3: Genetic Variation.

Genetic variation takes many forms, including:
- At its simplest, it is the substitution of one base for another – straightforward mutations, many of which are neutral in effect.
- It can also involve deletion (loss) or insertion (gain) of individual bases or sequences of bases.
- Gene duplication.
- Duplication of whole genomes (polyploidy).
- Horizontal gene transfer, i.e. the insertion into the genome of a gene (or genes) from another organism or from a virus (genetic modification occurs in nature!).
- Movement of sequences from one part of the genome to another ('jumping genes' or transposons).

> **Text Box 5.4: An example of a genetic mutation.**
> **Lactose tolerance in humans.**
>
> We often hear from those opposed to the Theory of Evolution that mutation always leads to loss of genetic function. However, there are mutations which cause a gain of function and further there are genetic changes which actually add DNA/genes to the genome (as in previous text box).
> To illustrate some of the complexities associated with genetic change we can consider lactose tolerance/intolerance in humans
> In mammals, the ability to digest lactose (the sugar that occurs in milk) disappears after an individual is weaned. Drinking milk after weaning has deleterious effects. Humans are mammals and so the same should be true of us and yet in many countries nearly all adults can drink milk. What has happened? A mutation has occurred in a gene that regulates other genes. This mutation removes its ability to switch off the gene that encodes lactase (the enzyme that digests lactose) although its other regulatory activities are not affected. The presence of lactase enables us to drink milk without harm. So we have a partial loss of function in the regulatory gene but a gain of function associated with the lactase gene. The mutation, initially rare, has spread through those cultures in which milk and milk products are widely used as food sources. The mutation is clearly advantageous in such cultures; people who still have the original version (the wild-type) of the regulatory gene are lactose intolerant and may be somewhat disadvantaged by this.

However, some genetic changes actually give a detectable (and sometimes visible) effect; in genetic language, we say that a change in **genotype** causes a change in **phenotype**. For example, in Mendel's experiments with peas, smooth, round seeds are the usual form but seeds with wrinkled coats also exist. So we can say that in any population of a species there is likely to be genetic variation; many genes can potentially exist as two or more versions or **alleles**. For many differences in the genotype, the effects on the phenotype may be small, while for others, the differences may be as obvious as the round versus wrinkled seed coats in Mendel's experiments[24].

Focussing for the moment on small differences, we can see that some may result in small advantages or disadvantages in specific habitats. Thus, in any species, for example of bird, there is a range of sizes of the organism. In many species the range is small but in others, including humans, the size range is larger. Although some features, including size, may also be influenced by environmental factors (for example, food supply), a significant proportion of the quantitative variation may be ascribed to genetic variation. In most situations small differences in size will not confer advantage or disadvantage but, nevertheless, it is certainly possible to envisage situations in which larger or smaller individuals may be at an advantage.

Returning now to evolution, we can say that populations are subject to natural selection: in a given environment there are features or traits which make reproductive success more or less probable (remembering that the differences in success rate may be small). The predominant basis for the variation in those traits is genetic variation within the population. Some genetic variants are more reproductively successful than others. Over time, this may lead to formation of separate species, especially if there is some form of isolation between different sub-groups within a population (as in an archipelago such as the Galapagos Islands)[25]. Indeed, at this level, we can clearly see evolution working. On islands it is often found that particular organisms have diverged from a parent population on the mainland to form sub-species and eventually species. In the UK, for example, there are species which differ from their very close relatives in mainland Europe. Amongst birds, the Scottish crossbill and the red grouse (derived from the willow grouse) are examples. There are also subspecies on off-shore British islands that differ from those on mainland Britain. Again taking birds as a source of examples, there are different identifiable sub-species of wren on the Shetland Isles, on

Fair Isle and on St Kilda.

It is clear then that in the natural world we have evidence of speciation in action. However, we can see the effects of selection even more vividly when we consider plant and animal breeding. Domestication of animals and plants mostly started about 12,000 years ago[26], although there is evidence dating back at least 15,000 years for domestication of dogs (for hunting) in Central Asia. With domestication came selection of the variants that best suited the needs of the farmers or pastoralists. Even before attempts at hybridising different varieties, the domesticated plants or animals came to be very different from their wild progenitors (because of intense selection for particular traits). Many of our crop plants cannot now interbreed with those progenitors. In other words, they have become new species and this is reflected in new Latin names. Further, even within some of those domesticated species, typified by dogs, selection of favoured traits has resulted in strains or breeds that differ so markedly from each other that it is doubtful whether some individuals of some breeds are physically capable of mating with individuals of other breeds, even if still genetically compatible. A breeding barrier has been set up because of trait selection and this is a step towards speciation.

The processes that I have just described are often grouped together as micro-evolution, whether they occur naturally or as a result of human intervention. In nature, micro-evolution is evident all around us, including the acquisition of antibiotic resistance in bacteria, the loss of sight in cave-dwelling fish and the formation of sub-species and species on islands. But the big question is whether micro-evolution can lead to macro-evolution. It is the view of biologists that over the billions of years during which life has been present on Earth, there is enough time for the accumulation of sufficient changes for the formation of new groups of living organisms. It is clear from the fossil record that the history of life on Earth is characterised by the appearance from time to time of new major groups of organisms that differ markedly from pre-existing life-forms. We can also see that, overall, the range of types of organism has increased. Thus, amongst vertebrate animals, we now have fish, amphibia, reptiles, birds and mammals. In general, the most recently appearing forms, mammals and birds, are more biologically sophisticated than earlier appearing forms such as fish. It appears then that there has been a progression towards complexity. Further, by detailed comparison of the extant (currently living) groups with each other and with fossils and with knowledge of the geological period in which groups first appeared, we can build up a picture of the origins of each group. Amongst the items of evidence for those origins are transitional or intermediate forms both in the fossil record and amongst extant animals and plants.

Although the fossil record was only one small strand of evidence used by Darwin in formulating *The Origin of Species* we may concede that the absence of known transitional forms at that time was a weakness in the theory. However, the situation is very different now. We can identify certainly hundreds and possibly thousands of transitional forms amongst fossils, along with many living fossils. These organisms have retained a number of ancestral characteristics over many million years and include, amongst many others, the *Gingko* tree, hoatzins (a type of bird), lungfish and mudskippers. However, I note that some commentators suggest that, because evolution is a dynamic, ongoing process, there is a sense in which every extant organism may be regarded as a transitional form.

Mention of currently living organisms brings us back to the topic of genetics. Comparisons of individual genes (and more recently of whole genomes) between different organisms gives us a very clear picture of the degree of relatedness of those organisms. Further, when data from whole genomes are compared we can pinpoint the key genetic changes that were involved in the divergence of one group from another. For example, Figure 5.7 shows an outline family tree for Darwin's Finches, indicating that the ancestral species was a warbler finch-like bird. Further it is now clear that different variants of two genes, known as *ALX1* and *HMGA2*, are the major contributors to the differences in shapes and sizes of beaks.

This approach, called molecular phylogeny, can be applied on a much wider scale than just to one group of birds. When this is done, we see a remarkable picture of the relationships of different groups and of their ancestry, as indicated by 'family trees' and calculated genetic distances. The data are strongly supportive of the view that macro-evolution has led to the present diversity of life on Earth. Indeed, some commentators have stated, perhaps over-enthusiastically, that we do not even need to call on the fossil record for support when genetic and genomic data themselves provide such strong evidence for evolution. The fossil record is written very clearly in genomes: our evolutionary history is in our genes. It is the view of the vast majority of biologists (somewhere between 99.3 and 99.9%) that the evidence for the Theory of Evolution is so extensive and so well-founded that we cannot envisage genuine alternatives. With that in mind, we return to the big picture of the evolution of life on Earth, focussing on some of the key events.

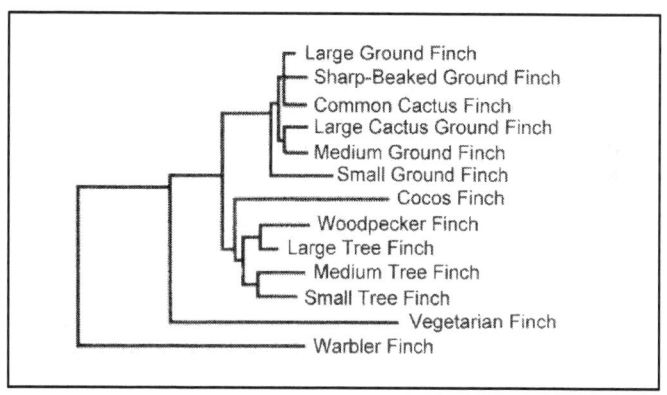

Figure 5.7. A simplified 'family tree' of the major Darwin's Finch species. Drawn from data presented by A. Sato, et al (1999)[27].

5.9 Evolution of life on Earth: some key events.

The first point is that we cannot separate the evolution of living things from the evolution of Earth itself: they are intertwined. The origin of life itself gave rise to organisms that needed nutrition and sources of energy. Thus early metabolism would have started, in a very small way, to utilise and to modify the existing chemistry of the planet. As already indicated, we have no idea about how those first organisms originated but we do know something about the next key event, the arrival of photosynthetic organisms, in water/oceans 2.8 billion years ago. These were very similar to blue-green bacteria. Their blue-green colour is caused by the presence of the green pigment, chlorophyll and the blue pigment, phycocyanin[28], both of which are involved in photosynthesis. The importance of photosynthesis cannot be overstated. It enabled organisms to use an energy source external to the Earth, the Sun, to make carbohydrates from carbon dioxide (CO_2) which was very abundant in the atmosphere of the early Earth. As is now well-known, CO_2 is a greenhouse gas and its use by these early photosynthetic organisms led to a significant cooling of the planet. As photosynthesis also results in the release of oxygen into the atmosphere the multiplication of photosynthetic organisms led to the 'great oxidation event' with the atmospheric concentration of oxygen reaching 15% by volume. This led to two further effects. First, oxygen in the stratosphere was (and still is) converted to ozone in a process driven by ultra-violet radiation from the Sun. Thus, Earth now has an ozone layer which prevents a large amount of the DNA-damaging ultra-violet radiation from reaching the surface of the planet. Life is now being protected. Secondly, it led to the evolution of *aerobic* organisms, organisms that were able to utilise oxygen in cellular energy conversions, in processes that were much more efficient than anaerobic metabolism. For many reasons it is true to say that had photosynthesis (and later its occurrence on land) not evolved, we would not be here.

The next major event on which I want to focus is the evolution of complex cells, between 1.8 and 2.0 billion years ago. We call them **eukaryotic** cells (from Greek words meaning good/true and nucleus) because they have within them a separate compartment called the nucleus in which the genetic material is located. The earliest stages of their evolution are still not clearly known. One view is that cells in the archaeal (archaebacterial) lineage (see earlier) began to develop complex internal membrane systems and a nucleus, to become what we might call proto-eukaryotes. How the nucleus was actually formed is still mysterious but current thinking is that it was derived from the cell's endo-membrane system (the folds of membranes that exist within eukaryotic cells)[29]. However, the next step is very clearly understood, based on extensive evidence from present-day cells and from wide-ranging genetic and genomic analysis. Proto-eukaryotes engulfed aerobic (oxygen-using) bacteria which initially lived inside the proto-eukaryotes as **endo-symbionts**[30] (the word *symbiosis* means living together – but in this case living together involved one single-celled organism living inside another – endo-symbiosis). The hosts gradually took into their nucleus most of the genes of the endo-symbionts which became mitochondria, the cell compartments that carry out aerobic energy metabolism (some journalists call them the cell's batteries).

This gives us the basic structure of all eukaryotic cells, the cells of which fungi (including simple, single-celled fungi such as yeasts), animals and plants are built. But for plant evolution there was one more step: a second engulfment-endo-symbiosis-take-over event occurred. This time the endo-symbionts were photosynthetic cyanobacterial cells (see above) which became chloroplasts. Today the resemblance between the genes that have been retained in chloroplasts and the genes of cyanobacteria is remarkable, giving us an insight deep into the evolutionary past.

It is widely thought amongst biologists that it was the arrival of eukaryotic cells which made many more things possible[31] and in particular, the building of multi-cellular fungal, plant and animal bodies. Multicellularity implies cell division and it is in eukaryotes that we see **mitosis**, a highly organised process in which each daughter cell gets one set of the newly duplicated chromosomes (following duplication of the genome). We also see extensive division of labour between different types of cell and between different parts of the body. Vertebrate animals, especially birds and mammals show the most sophistication in respect of this feature. The structure and diversification of eukaryotic cells also made sex possible (sexual reproduction originated about 1.1 billion years ago). I do not mean sexual intercourse, but the merging of two cells from different individuals within a species in order to create a new individual. It is immediately apparent that this will create more genetic diversity: the two individuals contributing the sex cells are likely to vary from each other and thus sexual reproduction brings two variants together in new combinations. However, sex also brings with it a major problem. The merging of two cells gives rise to new individuals with twice the amount of genetic material; eukaryotes keep their DNA in structures called chromosomes; the merging of two cells doubles the chromosome number. This cannot go on. It needs a very special and remarkable type of cell division called **meiosis** to correct the problem (see Text Box 5.5). I do not want to go into meiosis in any detail here except to say that it ensures that the chromosome number is halved in each gamete and that each new cell has the correct number of chromosomes. Further, it does not distinguish between the two parental sources of the chromosomes so that although each new cell has a full set, that full set is a mixture of chromosomes from the two parental cells, again generating genetic variety[32]. As to how it evolved we do not know.

We now jump forward several hundred million years. Fungi

Text Box 5.5: Meiosis.

Haploid and diploid.

In most multicellular eukaryotes, the organism that we see carries a double chromosome set in its cells. For humans this means that our cells contain two sets each of twenty three chromosomes. We use the term **diploid** to describe this state and it applies to all the cells that make up our bodies. However, when gametes (sperm or eggs) are made, meiosis occurs so that the gametes have only one set of chromosomes; the term **haploid** is used to describe this. When a sperm and an egg merge in fertilisation, the diploid state is restored. This arrangement pertains amongst all animals and amongst most plants.

---

started to colonise the land about 700 million years ago; invertebrate animals took another 200 million years to take that step. But then an event occurred that is regarded as one of the most important in the deep history of the planet: green plants, very similar to modern liverworts, started to invade the land about 472 million years ago, helped in this by fungi with which they formed a cooperative relationship[33]. This greening of the land had profound consequences. There was, in the words of the American botanist Linda Graham, "a quiet but relentless transformation of terrestrial landscapes"[34], creating a whole range of new habitats and ecosystems, giving rise to new opportunities for speciation and evolution among all groups. Furthermore, photosynthesis was now occurring on land as well as in the oceans, causing, amongst other things, an increase in atmospheric oxygen concentration and hence a strengthening of the ozone layer.

In some snapshots of later periods, we see the forests of non-flowering plants in the Carboniferous period which gave rise to coal. We see forests of tree ferns, cycads and gymnosperms (conifers) in the Cretaceous, about 130 million years ago. Also in the Cretaceous, the first flowering plants appeared. These early flowering plants were almost certainly pollinated by beetles (beetles are by far the most abundant type of animal on Earth), but over millions of years relationships with several other types of pollinators including wind pollination have evolved[35]. There are some remarkable examples of co-evolution, establishing very strong inter-dependencies between some plants and their pollinators. Further, the production of seeds has provided sources of nutrition for many animals, including humans who utilise several species of flowering plants as crops. In the poetic language of the story of creation in Genesis 'I give you every seed-bearing plant ... and every tree that has fruit with seed in it. They will be yours for food'[36].

Returning to the Cretaceous period (from 130 million years ago), we see that the most abundant and dominant vertebrate animals were reptiles, especially dinosaurs, pterosaurs, plesiosaurs, mosasaurs and ichthyosaurs. The latter three groups were marine reptiles. The ichthyosaurs became extinct in the mid-Cretaceous era. Birds (which had evolved from dinosaurs) and mammals were also present but did not occupy the dominant positions they do now. However, at the end of the Cretaceous, about 66 million years ago, a major extinction event occurred and all the major reptile groups that I have just mentioned died out.

Other reptiles, including snakes, lizards and crocodiles survived the extinction as did birds and mammals. Indeed, the latter two groups began to expand and diversify from the start of the Tertiary period, leading to the range of birds and mammals that we see today. For mammalian evolution, the extinction of the dinosaurs was especially significant. Mammals were now able to become the dominant terrestrial vertebrates and to occupy many different habitats[37]. This led to extensive diversification, including the arrival on the scene of great apes, fourteen million years ago. The scene is being set for evolution towards **hominins**, eventually culminating in the arrival of the first modern humans, only 250,000 years ago – the topic of the next chapter.

5.10 Concluding remarks.

As we look at the big picture of life on Earth it is apparent that amongst many groups of organism there has been a trend to greater complexity as evolution proceeds. It is as if a beautiful picture has emerged from less complex previous versions, like an artist creating a landscape on canvas. Now, if natural selection and evolution were just about reproductive advantage then this move towards greater complexity might be seen as disadvantageous. Vertebrate reproduction is not straightforward. If we want to see reproductive efficiency, we only have to look at bacteria which, after copying their genome, simply split into two. It can be very rapid; in some bacteria the doubling time is as short as 20 minutes. This feature, plus their great metabolic flexibility, has enabled bacteria to occupy almost every possible habitat on the planet, living unseen (but not necessarily undetectable as anyone who has eaten food contaminated with *Salmonella* will know!) alongside, on and even inside more complex organisms. But the presence of those complex organisms brings us back to the question of why they have evolved, and to ask whether we can see purposeful progress in evolution. Immunologist Denis Alexander suggests our modern understanding of evolution demolishes the view that biology is based on purposeless chance but rather that we can detect purpose and that purpose is divine[38].

With that in mind, let us return to the extinction of the

dinosaurs. The key role of this event in the evolution of mammals, eventually leading to humans, has already been mentioned. So how did it happen? The current view, widely supported by evidence, is that a large asteroid collided with the Earth, striking land on the Yucatan Peninsula in Mexico. The impact created a huge crater and spewed tonnes of dust and other debris into the atmosphere. Deposits resulting from this have been found in several places globally – deposits that contain material that could have only come from an asteroid. The density and composition of the cloud of dust and debris was such that the amount of solar radiation reaching the Earth's surface was severely reduced. A lengthy period of global cooling ensued and the dinosaurs, and their close relatives were not able to survive this. Now, here is something to think about. Had the asteroid impacted a few tens of seconds earlier or later, the impact would have occurred in the ocean. This would undoubtedly have caused a huge tsunami along global coastlines, but there would have been little global cooling. The dinosaurs would presumably have survived except where they succumbed to the tsunami. It appears then that the event which allowed mammals to flourish and hence eventually for humans to evolve, was dependent on chance in relation to its specific timing. Or was that timing part of a bigger plan? I leave our readers to ponder that before moving on to the next chapter.

Chapter 5 endnotes:

[1] Ruth Valerio in conversation with Sir Martin Rees, YouTube, January 2020, https://www.youtube.com/watch?v=gAHf-isYdV0.
[2] Sydney Brenner, Loose Ends, Current Biology (1994), Vol. 4, No. 2, p. 188.
[3] Big Think Interview "With Paul Davies". Interview with Austin Allen, bigthink.com, April 15, 2010.
[4] Paul Davies, The Fifth Miracle: The Search for the Origin and Meaning of Life, Touchstone (Simon & Schuster), 2000.
[5] The bases are in fact part of larger structures called deoxyribonucleotides.
[6] In RNA, thymine (T) is replaced by uracil (U).

[7] J.D. Watson and F.H.C. Crick, Molecular Structure of Nucleic Acids: A Structure for Deoxyribose Nucleic Acid, Nature (1953), Vol. 171, pp. 737-738.

[8] I had the privilege of meeting Peter Mitchell in the late 1980s and talking with him about chemi-osmotic coupling and ATP synthesis (which, by chance, was the topic of my next lecture in our first-year biochemistry course). It was a wonderful experience for me.

[9] Cambridge biochemist John Walker was awarded the Nobel Prize in 1997 for his work on elucidating the structure and mechanism of ATP synthase. Animation at http://www.mrc-mbu.cam.ac.uk/projects/2245/atp-synthase.

[10] For those who want to delve more deeply, there is lot of information here: http://www.mrc-mbu.cam.ac.uk/projects/2245/atp-synthase.

[11] We must get away from the word 'blueprint', much loved by the media. DNA does not provide a blueprint. It is more like a library of recipe books, with the vast majority of the recipes giving instructions on making proteins

[12] Paul Davies, The Fifth Miracle: The Search for the Origin and Meaning of Life, Touchstone (Simon & Schuster), 2000.

[13] CR Woese, GJ Olsen, M Ibba and D Söll, Aminoacyl-tRNA Synthetases, the Genetic Code, and the Evolutionary Process, Microbiology and Molecular Biology Reviews (2000), Vol. 64, pp. 202-236.

[14] During my academic career, much of my research focus was on the enzymes and other proteins involved in DNA replication and on the genes that encode them.

[15] D. G. Gibson, et al., Creation of a bacterial cell controlled by a chemically synthesized genome, Science (2010), Vol. 329, pp. 52-56; see also J. Craig Venter Institute (2010) https://www.jcvi.org/media-center/first-self-replicating-synthetic-bacterial-cell-constructed-j%C2%A0craig-venter-institute.

[16] Many major cell components such as lipids and carbohydrates are not encoded in DNA. However, the enzymes that make these compounds are encoded in genes.

[17] Paul Davies (2018), In Search of Eden, http://www.abc.net.au/science/morebigquestions/stories/s540242.htm.

[18] Paul Davies (2007a), The Guardian, 26 June 2007, https://www.theguardian.com/commentisfree/2007/jun/26/spaceexploration.comment.

[19] Paul Davies (2007b), The Cosmic Blueprint: New Discoveries in Nature's Creative Ability to Order the Universe, Templeton Press, 2007.

[20] Gram-positive and Gram-negative are terms that simply refer to whether or not cells can be stained with Gram's stain. (Dr Hans Christian Gram, 1853-1938, was the inventor of the staining method).

[21] John Bryant and Michael Reiss, 'Creationism'. In The Sage Encyclopaedia of Higher Education (editors M. E. David and M. J. Amey), Sage Publications (Thousand Oaks, California), pp. 311-314.

[22] As detailed in 'Voyage of The Beagle', Darwin's 'Journal and Remarks' about the voyage, published in 1839.

[23] These have become known as 'Darwin's Finches' but in strict ornithological terms, they are Grassquits.

[24] Some of the mutations and genetic variations that cause more obvious changes may be seriously harmful to the organism, as discussed in the next chapter.

[25] Note that the isolation or separation of sub-populations does not have to be geographical. In some instances of speciation amongst plants, some variants within a population differ from each other in the time of flowering. This very effectively prevents inter-breeding and thus 'fixes' the separateness of a particular genetic variant.

[26] Alice Roberts, Tamed – ten species that changed our world, Windmill Books, 2018.

[27] Akie Sato et al., Phylogeny of Darwin's finches as revealed by mtDNA sequences, Proc. Natl. Acad. of Sciences USA (1999), Vol. 96, No. 9, pp. 5101-5106.

[28] Although phycocyanin is involved in photosynthesis in blue-green bacteria, it is not involved in green plants, including algae.

[29] See discussion in John Bryant 'Mysteries, Molecules and Mechanisms'. In Plant Nuclear Structure, Genome Architecture and Gene Regulation, D.E. Evans, K. Graumann and J.A. Bryant (Editors), Wiley-Blackwell, 2013, pp. 1-17, 2013.

[30] Note that some biologists, including Nick Lane, author of 'The Vital Question', think that the endosymbiosis event occurred before the development of internal membrane systems.

[31] Nick Lane, The Vital Question – why is life the way it is?, Profile Books, 2016

[32] Intermixing of genetic material from the two parents also involves recombination, adding still further to genetic variety. Discussion of recombination lies outside the scope of this book except to say that it introduces more complexity to the process and adds to our uncertainty about how meiosis evolved.

[33] See https://www.astrobio.net/origin-and-evolution-of-life/fungi-helped-plants-move-to-land/
(and note that symbiotic relationships between fungi and plants are still very widespread).

[34] Linda Graham, Journal of Plant Research (1996), Vol. 109, pp. 241-251.
[35] M.J. Hodson and J.A. Bryant, Functional Biology of Plants, Wiley-Blackwell, 2012.
[36] The Holy Bible (NIV): Genesis, Chapter 1, verse 29.
[37] R.B. Scully, Extraordinary fossils show how mammals rose from the dinosaurs' ashes, New Scientist (24 October 2019), https://www.newscientist.com/article/2221128-extraordinary-fossils-show-how-mammals-rose-from-the-dinosaurs-ashes/.
[38] Denis Alexander, Is There Purpose in Biology?, Lion Books, 2018.

6 What makes us Human?

"I viewed my fellow man not as a fallen angel, but as a risen ape."
Desmond Morris[1]

"Like the universal background radiation that points to the Big Bang origin of our universe, the notion of humankind made in the image of God is constantly there in the background ... reminding us of the intrinsic value of human personhood."
Denis Alexander[2].

John writes ...

6.1 A brief introduction.

The human species, *Homo sapiens*, appeared in East Africa about 250,000 years ago. The accepted date has, over the past two decades, been slowly pushed back from an earlier estimate of 100,000 years as more evidence is uncovered (and indeed, some authorities would push the date back still further). A term that we encounter in the literature is 'anatomically modern humans', identified as our species from a number of anatomical features that we all share. These features include, for example, an arrangement of the pelvis that facilitates the particular way we walk (gait). We are thus anatomically distinct from even our most recent ancestors. But what else is there that makes us human? The rest of this chapter attempts to address this question.

6.2 Biological background.

We finished the previous chapter with a brief discussion of the extinction of the dinosaurs and their close relatives. Whatever we think of the events that led to the extinction, it seems clear that it made room for other vertebrates to thrive – birds (which are actually flying dinosaurs) and mammals, both diversified extensively in the Tertiary period. As noted in the previous chapter, this diversification, combined with increasing sophistication, led to the arrival of the great apes about 14 million years ago and thus eventually to hominins and to humankind. I want to emphasise at this point that in terms of biology, humans are just as much part of the evolutionary history of life as any other animals. In common with other Christian biologists[3], I take issue with the view that humans were a special separate biological creation, distinct from the general flow of evolution – a view presented by mathematician and Christian apologist John Lennox[4], amongst others. This is a strange position to hold, namely that everything else evolved but humans did not. Our biology, our genetics and the fossil evidence give every indication that we arrived here via evolution.

Let us look at that biology in a little more detail. Humans are mammals, warm-blooded vertebrates that give birth to live young who are initially fed on milk produced by their mothers. It is therefore no surprise that we share a good deal of our general genetic makeup with other mammals. Thus, we have in common with the mouse all those genes that specify mammalian function. That is not to say that those genes held in common have identical sequences. The genes may have the same function but mice have the mouse version and we have the human version. Further, there are differences at the detailed level in gene regulation. Michael Snyder of Stanford University, an expert on genomics, summarises this as: "In general, the gene regulation machinery and networks are conserved in mouse and human, but the details differ quite a bit"[5]. In addition there are those species-specific genes that make a mouse a mouse and a human a human; these amount to about 3% of each genome. Overall, however, our genomes place us firmly in class Mammalia, the flourishing of which followed the disappearance of the dinosaurs.

Further, we are also part of the advanced mammalian order called **Primates**. Within that order we are a member of the family Hominidae, which also includes the orang-utan (found in Asia) and the African great apes. We can see in our genes, the divergence of the hominins from the chimpanzee-**bonobo** lineage (one of several groups diverging from the original great apes) which took place between 5 million and 7 million years ago. The detailed genetic evidence for this common ancestry with chimpanzees and bonobos has been extensively described by other authors and I do not need to repeat those details here. However, two points need to be made. Firstly, it is yet another example of evolutionary history being written in the genes. Secondly, we emphasise that we have not descended from chimpanzees, nor indeed from any other extant group of great apes. Just as an individual human is not descended from their first cousin, but rather shares common ancestors with that cousin, so we are in effect evolutionary cousins with the chimpanzees and bonobos. The theory of evolution has never claimed that we descended from chimpanzees.

6.3 Hominins and humans.

From that divergence point (of hominins from chimpanzee-bonobos) we can assemble, primarily from fossil evidence but with some genetic clues, a branching tree of hominin evolution with the eventual appearance of a major branch that included our immediately pre-human ancestors, *Homo erectus* (2 million years ago) and then *Homo heidelbergensis* (700,000 years ago). The latter is regarded by many as the common ancestor of both *Homo neanderthalensis* and our species, *Homo sapiens*. The status of more recently discovered hominin fossils, the Denisovans (named after the Denisova cave in Siberia where the first discovery of specific remains was made) is not yet clear. However, evidence is pointing to the view that this is a third species descended from *Homo heidelbergensis*. We need to note that in some interpretations of the data, *Homo heidelbergensis* is regarded as having branched off the main lineage that led to *Homo sapiens* rather than being a direct ancestor of humans. These two ideas about relationships are shown in Figure 6.1.

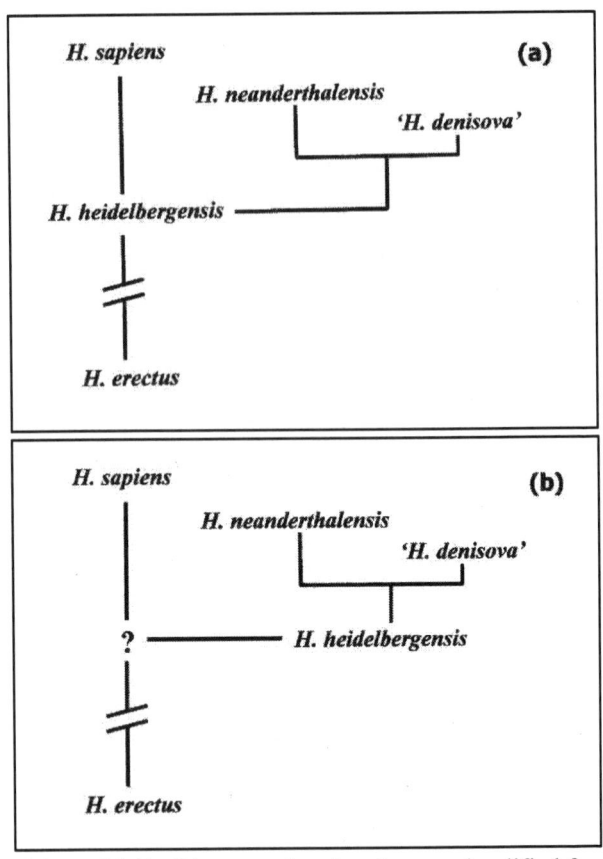

Figure 6.1a and 6.1b. Diagrams showing, in very simplified form, two of the current views about the relationship between humans, *Homo sapiens* and other recent closely related *Homo* species. Each diagram omits possible intermediates between *H. erectus* and *H. heidelbergensis* /*H.sapiens*.

Despite some uncertainties, it is clear that for part of our history we existed at the same time as Neanderthals and Denisovans. Indeed, both humans and Neanderthals are known to have also, at some time, lived in the Denisova cave. We are actually able to obtain DNA from some Neanderthal fossils and

Denisovan fossils. This means that the comparative anatomy of fossil hominins can, for these species, be supplemented with genetic information. There is, for example, genetic evidence for a limited amount of interbreeding between humans and Neanderthals[6], between Neanderthals and Denisovans and possibly between humans and Denisovans.

Homo erectus and *Homo heidelbergensis* both had large skulls capable of accommodating large brains, but not as large as the brains of modern humans (circa one litre as compared to circa 1.4 litres). We do not know whether they possessed a particular gene, *ARHGAP11B*, known colloquially as the 'big brain gene' but it seems unlikely, based on brain size. In *Homo sapiens*, this gene enables the extensive expansion of the neocortex, (the region of the brain that is associated with cognitive activity), leading to the formation of a highly folded organ packed with neurones[7]. We know that Neanderthals and Denivosans also possessed this gene, indicating that their brain capacity may have been equivalent to that of humans. However, we also need to note that the manner in which neurones are used is also important, especially the ways in which they wire and unwire with each other to make flexible networks. The ability to do this is a function of the genes expressed in the neurones, but which networks are formed lies outside genetic control.[8]

We have no direct way of telling whether Neanderthals and Denisovans were able to use their brains in the same way that we do. Nevertheless, their possession of the big brain gene leads us to ask questions about the intellectual and emotional lives of these other two hominin species. It is certainly apparent that Neanderthals had a rich family life and were effective hunters who were able to make good use of natural resources (e.g, in using plant fibres to make string or rope). There are also signs that they had burial rituals with evidence that flowers were placed on graves. Indeed, it is possible that they had some religious or ritual practices before humans did. Archaeological evidence indicates that first Denisovans, then Neanderthals originated in the savannahs of East Africa and migrated from there before the origins of anatomically modern humans. It was later in their history that Denisovans and Neanderthals encountered modern humans as humans spread out of Africa.

6.4 Human distinctiveness.

Our early history is thus intertwined with that of Neanderthals and at this point we need to ask again what it is that makes humans special. For some people it is speech. Humans have communication abilities that far exceed those of any other animal. Speech makes possible a vast range of abstract thought that is not possible if communication relies on gestures plus a limited range of sounds. It also makes it possible to communicate those thoughts in detail, alongside all the other things about which humans communicate. It is these abilities to speak and to think, coupled with manual dexterity afforded by, amongst other things our opposable thumbs, that have enabled humans to live in every terrestrial environment. By contrast our nearest living relatives, chimpanzees and bonobos, are endangered species restricted to the rainforests of Africa.

But when did speech actually originate? The conventional view is that it arose in anatomically modern humans (*Homo sapiens*), about 250,000 years before present[9]. In order to try to pin this down, we need to look for several factors. First, our primate relatives are unable to speak because of large air sacs (vocal pouches) in the throat. These are used to make the booming sounds that scare rivals away but render it impossible to make precise and detailed sounds. Members of the *Homo* genus from *H. heidelbergensis* onwards lack that air sac. Then there are some anatomical modifications, including changes in the inner ear that are associated with making or hearing sophisticated sounds. Thirdly, there are also a 'large number of nerve pathways from the brain, through the spine, to the diaphragm and the muscles between the ribs'[10]. These enact the fine control of breathing that is required for making sounds very precisely. Finally, there is the *FOXP2* gene, the human version of which enables us to control very precisely the movements of our face and mouth. If we take the presence of these features as signs of speech, then we would conclude, as several scholars have done, that Neanderthals may have had speech of some sort. If this is correct, then speech must have arisen before the separation of the Neanderthal and human lineages. The fact is that we can never know. However, what is clear is that the human species is fully adapted for spoken language and that this has contributed enormously to our social and technical development.

6.5 The brain and beyond.
Let us return for the moment to the brain. In terms of volume, the human brain is not the biggest in the animal kingdom but in terms of connectivity it is by far the most complex. Indeed, scientists have described the human brain as the most complex object that we know of in the Universe. The brain contains approximately 10^{11} neurones and each is, in theory at least, capable of making connections with all the others. That gives 10^{123} possible connections, which is more than the number of atoms in the known Universe.

The workings of this complex brain gives rise to three features that are much harder to pin down, namely consciousness, mind and awareness of self. All these rely on brain processes but are not brain. Human consciousness is much more than just being awake. It is an awareness of surroundings and the ability to respond to the information that arises from that awareness. It is a quality that is not confined to humans. All **sentient** beings have this quality to some extent. However, we distinguish consciousness from, for example, the ability of plants to respond to environmental signals which does not require the workings of a nervous system. Consciousness leads on to mind, the workings of which include the marshalling and storage of information and the processes that are involved in thought. As we have noted before, abstract thought requires complex language and it is a matter of debate as to whether we can describe animals that lack speech as having a mind. Certainly many mammals and birds are capable of learning and of problem-solving but whether we can equate these activities to those of a conscious mind is a matter for discussion. Even if some elements of mind are there, they fall far short of that possessed by humans. For example, as conscious human beings, we are also aware of our thought world. This leads us to consider awareness of self, the knowledge (and the associated feelings) that 'I am me', a separate conscious being. Linked with that is the paradox that I cannot know what it feels like to be you. Many animals do not possess this awareness of self, hence some birds will attack their own reflection as if it was a rival. However, mind is present, at least to the extent of being able to recognise self in a mirror, in a surprising range of vertebrates, including chimpanzees, bonobos, orang-utans, dolphins (and possibly other **cetaceans**), elephants, some dogs, Eurasian magpies (an advanced bird species) and manta rays (a fish with a large brain). Human babies do not appear to have an awareness of self; it is not until a child is between 18 months and two years old that this starts to develop, seen initially in the mirror test.

How are we to regard these features of consciousness, mind and awareness of self? For some, they are indistinguishable from the brain in that they represent brain phenomena. However, we cannot locate any of them to a physical entity within the brain, even though we can show that particular regions of the brain are active when a subject is thinking about particular things or carrying out a calculation or doing a puzzle. If we hold the view that mind and brain are of the same substance then mind must be located throughout the brain. On the other hand, there are those who support the idea of mind-body duality. Although the brain is essential for mind, mind emerges from the brain but is not the same thing. Pushing this further to self-awareness, this then becomes a non-material feature. If we take this view, using the words I or me introduces a non-material element into the conversation. Exactly this idea was expressed by the philosopher Roger Scruton in a discussion of his book *On Human Nature*[11] at the 2017 'Ways with Words' literature festival. This leads on to the view that a human person has a dimension of existence that cannot be pinned down in physical terms but which is nevertheless an embedded part of their whole. I will return to this in section 6.7 but in the meantime I want to consider briefly other features that are associated with being human.

Although, sadly, it is sometimes not apparent, humans exhibit high levels of altruism, compassion and empathy. These characteristics are known in other higher animals, for example, empathy at some level seems to be a general mammalian trait, while macaques exhibit clear altruism and elephants show compassion. However, these traits are much more extensively developed in humans[12]. Further, it has been suggested that the evolution of compassion and altruism is essential in developing complex human society and that alongside these a form of conscience also evolved. If these features are associated with culturally modern humans rather than anatomically modern humans, it would date their acquisition at about 45,000 years before present. It is interesting that some philosophers across the centuries have suggested that we have an inborn sense of right and wrong (Kant for example, spoke of 'the moral code within'), although it was usually attributed to God rather than genes (but I note that these are not mutually exclusive: if God is creator then he is the creator of our genes).

6.6 All in the Genes?

The fact that the initial development of compassion, altruism and empathy is regarded as part of our evolutionary history has been used by some commentators as evidence for genetic determinism or genetic essentialism. This is the view that everything we are, including behaviour, moral attitudes, personality and intelligence is written in our genes. It has been noisily propagated by some scientists, including Richard Dawkins who sums up this view nicely as 'DNA neither cares nor knows. DNA just is. And we dance to its music'[13]. And certainly, the acceptance that characteristics such as altruism and compassion have arisen as part of our evolutionary history lends some weight to this idea, which I often call the Genes-R-Us hypothesis. If a characteristic can be subject to natural selection and hence be involved in the evolution of the species, the implication is that it must be heritable. But this is only part of the story. The idea that we are totally determined by our genes, which implies amongst other things, that there is no free will, has lost a lot of support over the past 20 years or so. Indeed, I suspect that Richard Dawkins no longer holds this view nearly as strongly as his writing implies.

How much then do our genes contribute to these non-physical features of our personhood? The first thing to note is that behavioural and personality characteristics are quite hard to quantify because there are no obvious physical measures and also because the expression of some aspects of, for example personality, may vary from day to day. Nevertheless a range of tests has been developed which provide means of measuring these characteristics, albeit with not as much precision as we get in measuring height, weight and so on. This then enables us to use identical twins, non-identical twins, other siblings and adopted versus non-adopted children to compare the extent to which particular characteristics are shared[14]. Taking identical twins as an example, they have identical genomes so any differences between them cannot be ascribed to differences in genes. The heritability of the differences between the twins is therefore zero. Differences are due to non-heritable factors which may be environmental (in the widest sense of the word) but which may arise from free-will choices made within the same overall environment. For example, I know pairs of identical twins that have made very different choices in life, despite their very similar physical appearance and upbringing in the same home.

Without going any further into the methodology, we can say that identical-twin studies give us a baseline enabling us to make comparisons between non-identical siblings and so on. Overall it is found that approximately 50% of the differences in behaviour or personality or intelligence between any two people may be ascribed to differences in their genes: variation in these features has a heritability of 50%. Further, the number of genes involved is very large – about 200 are involved in intelligence for example – and only for a few of these do we have information about the molecular mechanisms involved. However, pieces of the jigsaw puzzle of neurogenetics are slowly being found. For example, we now know of about 20 genes which, working together, contribute about 5% to that inherited component of intelligence.

Neither must we ignore gene-environment interactions. It is well established that many of our genes are affected by environmental factors (again using that term in a very wide sense) but some interactions are very surprising. An example of this is the so-called warrior gene, a mutation in the monoamine oxidase A (MAOA) gene that leads to much reduced levels of the monoamine oxidase enzyme. This in turn affects the concentration of several neurotransmitters, including dopamine and serotonin, thus having an effect on brain function. A correlation between possession of the mutation and violent anti-social behaviour in men has been known for many years. But can we say that the mutant gene causes violent behaviour? The answer is not necessarily, because there are men with the mutant gene who are not violent. The situation turns out to be more complex than a simple Yes or No. Men with the mutation who were maltreated in childhood are likely to become violently and anti-socially angry when provoked even by mild stimuli in adulthood. The childhood emotional and social environment can thus affect the way that a gene works in adults[15].

Perhaps even more spectacular were the effects of severe deprivation in very early childhood in Romanian orphans in the 1980s: some aspects of brain development just did not happen. Being deprived of emotional and physical contact affected the expression of genes that control brain structure[16]. Further we now know that much milder instances of deprivation or neglect can also affect brain development, although not to the same extent as seen in the Romanian orphans.

Overall then, we can regard genes as providing the molecular information that allows us to develop and function as physical beings, members of the human species. This basic biological function is subject to environmental influences, such as nutrition and, surprisingly as mentioned above, emotional and social factors. Genes also provide, presumably through the structure and specific individual functioning of the brain, a framework in which our personalities, intelligence and behaviour patterns can develop.

6.7 But is there more?

I have recently been struck by some words from two different people who state firmly that they have no belief in God. The first was a well-known scientist who, on being asked whether she was a spiritual being, replied that she certainly was. The second was the author Raynor Winn, describing a visit to a tiny church in North Devon: "I sat in the graveyard and let the utterly peaceful place wash over me. It was profoundly spiritual, nothing to do with God or religion, but a deeply human spirituality ... Maybe there *was* some power there"[17]. In passing, I note the irony of sensing a deep sense of spirituality in a churchyard but dismissing the possibility that it has anything to do with religion. But what do these people who have no belief in God mean by spiritual? It seems that they are using the term in different ways. Our scientist seems to be referring to that inner life to which we referred earlier – our awareness of self, our consciousness and our mind and all that goes with those phenomena, such as creativity, intelligence, compassion and altruism, features that, either by their very existence or by the extent of their development in humans, mark us out from the rest of the animal kingdom. However, the author Winn adds a further dimension in that she sensed something greater than herself, outside of herself and she ascribed that to the presence of human spirituality around her in that particular place. In both statements, questions lurk in the background, even if unacknowledged by those making the statements.

The title of this book is also a question: *From the Big Bang to Biology: where is God?* We have discussed the Big Bang and the evolution of the Universe; we have discussed the origin of life on Earth and the processes of evolution that have given rise to an amazing array of life-forms. We have arrived at human biology and the answer to the question is that God has been there all along. His presence has been strongly hinted at as we have described 13.8 billion years of history and Graham has been very specific and open about the bigger questions that he was forced to deal with as he considered the way the Universe works (Chapter 4). Further, we have noted that particular aspects both of fine-tuning and of the origin of life have pushed unwilling minds to consider the possibility that life is designed, again forcing us to consider a bigger question: if life is designed, who is the designer?

As culturally modern humans searched for meaning, so an

awareness of God (and associated religious practices) slowly evolved. I have described this briefly in a previous book[18] and it is dealt with in more detail by Christian anthropologist Cara Wall-Schleffler[19] in a Faraday Institute lecture. We both make the point that the fact that religion has evolved does not invalidate it in any way. We have come to the understanding that God is the designer and creator of everything there is, and that humans are spiritual beings who are made in God's image. Both those latter terms need to be unpacked. By *spiritual beings* we do not mean that we carry an additional add-on feature. Spirituality, although non-material in nature, is embedded into our being just like mind, consciousness and awareness of self; indeed it may be the conflation of these that adds up to our spirituality and our ability to relate to God ("God is spirit, and his worshipers must worship in the Spirit and in truth."[20]).

The Image of God, as written in the original texts, implies that we are God's representatives or even his icons on this planet. The words do not imply that we look like God physically but that we carry something of God in our embodied selves. In particular, we are relational beings with free will. We exhibit altruism, compassion and empathy. We are able to make moral choices and to distinguish right from wrong. The image may be marred as is the image of the sovereign in an old and tattered bank note but it is still there. Now, sharp-eyed readers will have noticed that some elements of the image such as altruism, compassion, empathy and perhaps even conscience are to some extent part of our genetic makeup (but only to some extent – these features can easily be over-ruled by free-will choices that ignore our understanding of right and wrong). I have no problem with this; if some features of the image of God are embedded in our biological make-up that seems to me to be wonderful[21].

6.8 Concluding remarks.

One more thing needs to be said. The author Raynor Winn (quoted earlier) became aware of a presence outside herself and greater than herself. She put it down to the powerful presence of human spirituality. Her reason for reaching that conclusion was her lack of belief in God and therefore this sense could have nothing to do with God. But through the ages, individual humans and sometimes groups of humans have from time to time had this sense of a presence around them. We call this a sense of the numinous and in our view, it is a stronger than usual indication of the universal presence of God. And so here is the last point of this chapter. The creator God, who is completely beyond our understanding can be known and related to by individual humans, both through and in his creation and especially through Jesus Christ. That is one of the most astonishing things about being human.

Chapter 6 endnotes:

[1] Desmond Morris, The Naked Ape: A Zoologist's Study of the Human Animal, Jonathan Cape (London), 1967.
[2] Denis Alexander, Genes, Determinism and God, Cambridge University Press, 2017, p. 280.
[3] For example, Graeme Finlay (*Homo divinus:* the ape that bears God's image, Science and Christian Belief (2003), Vol. 15, pp.17-40) and Denis Alexander (Is There Purpose in Biology?, Lion Hudson, Oxford, 2018)
[4] John Lennox, Seven Days that Divide the World, Zondervan, 2011.
[5] https://www.nih.gov/news-events/nih-research-matters/comparing-mouse-human-genomes.
[6] In an earlier publication (John Bryant, Beyond Human?, Lion-Hudson, 2013) I indicated that this evidence was not reliable but it has now been confirmed by further investigation.
[7] Florio, M., Albert, M. Taverna, E. et al, Human-specific gene ARHGAP11B promotes basal progenitor amplification and neocortex expansion, Science (2015), Vol. 347, pp. 1465-1470.
[8] I recommend two excellent video clips by Christian neuroscientist Bill Newsome:
https://www.testoffaith.com/resources/resource.aspx?id=312 and
https://www.testoffaith.com/resources/resource.aspx?id=313.
[9] The dates given by different authorities for the first anatomically modern humans (*Homo sapiens*) vary between 200,000 and 300,000 years before present. However, very recent findings suggest that it was certainly longer ago than 200,000 years bp, hence I give a date of 250,000 years bp.

[10] David Robson, The origins of language discovered in music, mime and mimicry, New Scientist (2019), No. 3228, pp. 34-37.

[11] Roger Scruton, On Human Nature, Princeton University Press, 2017.

[12] Emma M. Seppälä, Emiliana Simon-Thomas, Stephanie L. Brown, Monica C. Worline, C. Daryl Cameron and James R. Doty, (editors), The Oxford Handbook of Compassion Science, Oxford University Press, 2017.

[13] Richard Dawkins, River out of Eden, Phoenix Books, 1995 (re-issued 2001, Science Masters' edition, 2004). I want to add that in general, Dawkins' writing about evolution itself is beautiful, even inspirational, but he allows himself too often to make philosophical and often anti-religious statements that the data do not support and that the context does not merit.

[14] Denis Alexander, Genes, Determinism and God, Cambridge University Press, 2017. A very good, detailed account of this topic.

[15] Mairi Levitt has written a nice account of the 'warrior gene' here: https://thebiologist.rsb.org.uk/biologist-features/158-biologist/features/903-crime-genes.

[16] Eliot Marshall (2015), Childhood neglect erodes the brain: https://www.sciencemag.org/news/2015/01/childhood-neglect-erodes-brain.

[17] Raynor Winn, The Salt Path, Penguin/Random House, 2018, p. 49.

[18] John Bryant, Beyond Human?, Lion-Hudson (Oxford), 2013.

[19] http://downloads.sms.cam.ac.uk/1571546/1571551.m4v.

[20] The Holy Bible (NIV), John's Gospel, Chapter 4, verse 24.

[21] Since arriving at this view, I was pleased to note that Denis Alexander takes the same position (and discusses it very fully) in Chapter 12 of Genes, Determinism and God, Cambridge University Press, 2017.

7 The Big Bang, Biology and the Bible.

"We have no need to try to prove that evolution is untrue or alternatively to try to show that Genesis can be reconciled with it. ...this [would mean] focussing on concerns other than the concerns God had in inspiring this story. Genesis 1 is a portrait, a dramatization, a parabolic story. This does not imply that it is not true; it means its truth is expressed in the manner of a parable. Painting this picture for people helps underline various aspects of the nature of creation."

John Goldingay[1]

John writes ...

7.1 Introduction.

In the preceding chapters we have presented current scientific understanding of the origin and working of the Universe and have noted the extreme precision required in the laws of nature for life to have emerged in it. We have shown how the biological data point so strongly to an evolutionary **paradigm** that it is very difficult think of it being negated and we have discussed the status of humankind within that paradigm. We also noted that in terms of our current biological understanding, we have no workable model for the origin of life; frankly, it looks impossible (a quick reminder: the theory of evolution by natural selection has never directly addressed the problem of the origin of life – abiogenesis – although a small number of evolutionary theorists have tried to do so; our understanding of evolution goes back to the first living cells and no further).

We have suggested that both the astrophysical data and the biological data are consistent with there being a creator. In the words of Einstein: "Everyone who is seriously interested in the pursuit of science becomes convinced that a spirit is manifest in the laws of the Universe – a spirit vastly superior to man, and one in the face of which our modest powers must seem humble." [2]

However, there is a problem. The scientific accounts that we have described appear to be at odds with the Biblical account of creation as presented in the early chapters of Genesis. Is there a conflict between science and faith? The rest of this brief chapter examines this idea.

7.2 Creationism and Intelligent Design.

The concept of God as creator is built into our Christian faith, as it is into Islam and Judaism. In that sense, all adherents of the Abrahamic faiths are creationists. However, as currently used, the term has a much more specific meaning. Creationism is a view of the world based on a literal interpretation of the early chapters of Genesis[3]. According to this view, the Earth is not very old, perhaps a few thousand years[4] and the many forms of life on the planet arose by special creation of the different kinds. That includes humankind, the last species to be created, according to the account in Genesis 1. Thus, evolution of the Universe, of Earth and of life on Earth is almost totally rejected. I say almost, because some creationists accept the idea of micro-evolution; that is changes within kinds leading to differences within those kinds that may sometimes lead to separate species. However, the time-scale during which such events may happen is regarded as very, very much shorter than we actually observe in nature.

Amongst creationists, evolution is very often described as atheistic: one either accepts evolution or one believes in God and the Bible. Thus any synthesis that accepts evolution but believes that God is the agency behind it is dismissed as mistaken.

According to this view, God is the agency behind creation but he did not do it by an evolutionary process. Interestingly, some of the more vocal science-based opponents of religion make a similar type of claim but obviously from the other side. You can believe in evolution or God but not both and since science has proved evolution then belief in God cannot be sustained. There is no understanding in that statement of the difference between process and agency.

It might be supposed that the current creationist movement grew out of opposition to Darwin, dating back to the publication of *On the Origin of Species by Means of Natural Selection*. However, that is not so. There was no widespread opposition to evolutionary ideas at that time and indeed, many Christians, including many clergy, welcomed the theory[5]. The first hints of the current creationist movement were seen in the USA around 1910 and included a growing opposition to teaching about evolution in schools. The infamous 1925 Scopes monkey trial[6] was a sign of that opposition. However, it was in the second half of the 20th century that creationism emerged as a vocal movement within Christianity and it was not until the 1980s that the term itself began to be widely used in the USA and the UK. In some areas, the movement has taken on a strongly anti-science position which, in the USA especially, is often also linked with denial of climate change (which will be discussed more fully in Chapter 8).

A new doctrine within the creationist movement called Intelligent Design (ID), arose in the 1980s and came to prominence from the mid-1990s onwards. This was heralded as a scientific challenge to the theory of evolution, claiming to show that evolution by natural selection could not have resulted in particular features possessed by living organisms. In an interesting parallel with traditional creationism, an attempt to introduce the teaching of ID as a science in high school led to a court case (which the proponents of ID lost)[7].

The Intelligent Design argument takes two forms. The first is 'irreducible complexity.'[8] This refers to structures that are made up of several parts and that can only work with all the parts in place. It is argued that they cannot have arisen by natural selection from a suite of gene products because it is so unlikely as to be impossible that all the required genetic changes should arise together. One of the several examples cited, is the bacterial flagellum, the whip-like structure that many bacteria use for locomotion. The existence of such structures means, according to ID, that they must have been especially designed.

The second line of argument is 'specified complexity'. Many discussions of ID lump this together with irreducible complexity (as I indeed have tended to do[3]). However, it is actually somewhat different. Specified complexity is linked with information theory and refers to biological structures, especially complex molecules such as proteins, that consist of many parts in which the order of the parts is essential for function (for proteins, the parts are the individual amino acids from which the protein is built). A long array of letters may be complex but the complexity is only specified if those letters are arranged to say something. Thus, in a widely quoted example, 'a Shakespearean sonnet is both complex and specified.'[9]

Both lines of argument are taken to show that evolution by natural selection cannot be the mechanism by which the huge range of living organisms came into being. There must be a designer, it is argued and although the designer is never named, the origins of the intelligent design movement show us that its proponents are talking about God as presented in the Bible. This reinforces the God versus evolution scenario that has been so significant a part of the creationist position.

7.3 What about the science?

In Chapters 2 to 6 we presented what we consider to be a majestic and awe-inspiring story. Working outwards, the evolution of life on Earth is inextricably interlinked with the dynamic state of the planet itself. The evolution of Earth is linked to the evolution of our Solar System which in turn is linked to the evolution of our galaxy and of the Universe itself, going back to the Big Bang, 13.8 billion years ago. The overall story results from observations, measurements and experiments of scientists working across many different disciplines and yet the picture that has emerged is beautifully integrated. In all aspects, that picture is by far the best fit to the data we have. That is not to say that we can close the book and say that it is done. There are still mysteries to unravel and it is one of the joys of being a scientist that these mysteries remain to be investigated. However, focussing now specifically on biology, nearly 100% of those working within the discipline, including Christians, believe that the theory of evolution is so well-founded that it is very difficult to envisage that it might be negated[10], although our understanding at the detailed level may change. The claim sometimes made by creationists that there are many leading authorities who oppose evolution is simply not true[11].

How then are we to regard the science in relation to the creationist view or, putting it the other way round, how do creationists view the body of scientific data that have led to our current understanding? I want to be very gentle and diplomatic here. It is not my intention to undermine anyone's faith but I do want to respond to some of the views that we encounter, especially in relation to biological evolution. The first thing is that science is not an atheistic enterprise. It may surprise some of our readers that I need to say this. I have heard scientific discoveries and theories across the board, including the Big Bang and of course evolution, described as atheistic. One necessary response is to say that when scientists talk in naturalistic terms, they are describing natural phenomena as they have been revealed by the scientific method. There is nothing sinister or anti-God about this, although of course scientists who are atheists do not admit the possibility of anything other than the material level of existence (as is discussed in Chapter 2). To use a simple analogy, if I describe how a car works I do not keep referring to the inventors of the internal combustion engine or fuel injection mechanisms. I simply describe the mechanisms as they are now; this approach neither denies nor affirms the existence of the inventors. In the same way, scientific accounts of how the Universe works neither deny nor affirm the existence of God. And in that context, the words of Darwin in relation to *The Origin of Species* are very apposite: "I see no good reasons why the views given in this volume should shock the religious views of anyone". He also stated that anyone who had read the book could immediately see that he had written it with "no relation whatever to theology."[12]

Despite this, creationists hold the view that because evolution contradicts the Biblical account, it must be wrong. But there is a vast body of data drawn from a wide range of biological disciplines from palaeontology to molecular genetics, which all point extremely strongly to evolution taking place on a planet that is 4.6 billion years old. Further, there is no evidence at all that supports the view that Earth is only a few thousand years old. During the course of many discussions over many years, I have heard three different creationist viewpoints. The first is the most extreme and is held by only a very few people but nevertheless it is out there, namely that the data have been made up and further that the media are complicit in the deception. If that were so, then we would have to invoke a conspiracy going back at least three centuries (when geologists started to realise that the Earth must be old). This does seem rather far-fetched. The second view is that the data are wrong or in other words that mistakes have been made in measurements, observations and experiments across the whole range of biological disciplines. But we note that results from those same biological disciplines are regarded as reliable in areas other than evolution, for example in relation to medicine or agriculture. Thirdly, there is the view that all these data have been misinterpreted. Again we have to say that this misinterpretation must go right across all those areas of science that have contributed to our current understanding. Just looking at the recent (in geological terms) history of the Earth, two examples serve to illustrate the difficulties in that position. First, ice cores taken from the Antarctic show annual layers. Counting back we can see that the past 10,000 years of annual deposits only occupy a very small space at the top of the ice core. Counting back further from there, we can go as far as hundreds of thousand years before present[13]. It is hard to envisage that the data from near the top of the core are interpreted correctly but that at some point below that, misinterpretation sets in. Is this feasible? Secondly, using straightforward and unambiguous methods, based on well-established laws of physics, we can show that light takes eight minutes to reach us from the Sun. We can also show that, because of the sheer size of the Milky Way, light takes about 80 thousand years to reach us from stars on the other side of the galaxy – so we can say unequivocally that those stars (and the Universe) existed at least 80 thousand years ago. If there is a misinterpretation of data, at what point between the Sun and the far reaches of the Milky Way did it occur?

There is a further problem with this viewpoint. Why are data gathered by established scientific methods misinterpreted? One way of dealing with this is that our standard interpretation of the data relies on a constancy of natural laws. If the laws of nature were not constant, the argument goes, it is quite possible that a young Earth appears to be old because we are assuming constancy. Once, in a discussion on BBC radio, a creationist with whom I was debating stated that God made the Earth (and presumably the whole Universe) with an appearance of great age. This implies that creation involved an act of deliberate deception. I leave our readers to their own thoughts on this.

I have tried to be as gentle as possible in dealing with these views, which all in different ways say that there is no evidence that evolution happened while at the same time providing no scientific evidence at all for the creationist view. This leads us to intelligent design which, its proponents suggest, provides a scientific objection to evolution. Dealing first with irreducible complexity, creationists postulate that certain multi-component structures or systems must have been designed because we cannot envisage all the individual components arising together by chance. Whether or not simpler structures are regarded as being designed is not mentioned. However, when we examine these multicomponent structures or systems it is apparent that they are built up from individual components that were already there, having arisen individually over the evolutionary history of the relevant organism (see Bryant and Reiss[3] and Bryant[8]). These examples certainly do not disprove evolution.

The other aspect of intelligent design, specified complexity, suggests that the chances of assembling structures like proteins and DNA with the building blocks in the correct order are so small as to make their existence more or less impossible, unless they were actively designed. As discussed in Chapter 5, the early synthesis and evolution of proteins right back at the beginning of life is certainly a mystery. Equally mysterious is how the order of bases in DNA came to code for the order of amino acids in proteins when there is no *a priori* reason for this in the structure of proteins or DNA. And yet each type of molecule is beautifully fitted for their particular roles. Thus, as indicated in Chapter 5, commentators have struggled to avoid concluding that life is designed. The idea of specified complexity fits in well with this general trend. There are two further things to be said. First, this does not disprove evolution and secondly, if life is designed then it is surely the whole of life, including evolution, which is the work of the designer.

7.4 Back to the Bible.
The creationist position is that the theory of evolution contradicts the Biblical account about the creation of living organisms (including humankind) and also contradicts Biblical views on the age of the Earth. Are either of these true? First we need to take an overall look at the relevant chapters in Genesis. I am concentrating mainly on Chapters 1 and 2 but other chapters will be considered. Although clearly written in pre-scientific times, Chapters 1 and 2 do not date back several thousand years; rather, it is thought, both were written during the time that the people of Israel were in captivity in Babylon during the 6th century BC. The second account (starting in verse 4 of Genesis chapter 2) is almost certainly the older of the two and they are stylistically different, to the extent of using different names for God and different words for make or create[14].

Chapter 1 (and the first three verses of Chapter 2) gives us much more detail. The Earth arises from a creative event: 'In the beginning, God created the heavens and the earth'[15]. As discussed earlier in this book, we can obviously equate the initial creation event with the Big Bang although it certainly would not have been in the mind of the writer(s) of Genesis. The story of the creation of the physical Universe then gives us a picture of the sky as a curved vaulted ceiling in which the stars were placed and across which the two great lights of the Sun and moon, make their regular journeys (we now know of course that the moon is a reflector, not a light). The curve of the vault brought it down to the edges of the Earth which thus appears to be a flat disc. There is water both above the vault and beneath the Earth. Intriguingly, light itself is created before the Sun (day one and day four respectively) and in terms of current understanding that is actually correct - there was light before the birth of our Solar System – but the writer of the chapter did not have that understanding. However, evenings and mornings and the transition from the darkness of night into the light of the day are mentioned from verse three/day one onwards which is also before the Sun was created.

This is a very much a picture of heaven and Earth as it appeared to ancient observers. Over the succeeding centuries this has been completely replaced by our current understanding of the overall structure of Earth, its relationship with its moon and the rest of the Solar System and of space in general. By 300 BC, the Greeks knew that the Earth was spherical and had made observations about the movement of planets in the heavens. A Greek mathematician, Aristarchus of Samos, proposed in about 200 BC that Earth goes around the Sun, an idea that lay dormant until the work of Copernicus in the 16th century and then of Kepler and Galileo early in the 17th century. Thus, the understanding of the structure of the Universe as it appeared to unaided observers in the 6th century BC had by 1650 been swept away and our modern views about the Universe started to take shape. Interestingly, despite the conflict between Pope Urban VIII and Galileo, the Christian church has been happy to accept the scientific understanding of the Universe. Calvin, for example, writing in the 16th century, stated that teaching us astronomy was not the purpose of the first chapter of Genesis. The exception to this general picture is that young-Earth creationists do not accept our current view of the age of the Universe (as discussed in the previous section).

Moving on to the biological part of creation, a series of events is described in Genesis Chapter 1, verses 11 to 31, starting on day three. Plants are made first, but before the Sun and stars are created; in relation to a literal reading, we would have to say that initially, photosynthesis must have used light in general (see above) rather than a specific source. Then came sea creatures and birds (day five), followed by land animals on day six; wild and domesticated species are made at the same time. Finally, also on day six, humans are made, creatures with responsibility, who carry the image of God. The term man (*a·dam* /*ha·'a·dam*) is used both as a singular and plural (we are not told how many humans there were) and to include both male and female. We thus understand it to mean humankind. Overall, this is a beautiful account of creation, written in grand language but it does not conform in any way to our current views on the origins of the remarkable range of biodiversity that we see on Earth now. The account in Genesis 1 is thus almost completely at odds with our current scientific understanding except that, in a very general way, we know that modern humans are the most recent major species to emerge on this planet and they certainly have the capacity to exercise dominion.

Genesis Chapter 2 mentions the heavens and the earth only in passing and actually focusses very strongly on the creation of humankind. There is no mention of the passage of days. Unlike the account in Chapter 1, the Earth is dry and God used the dust to make a man (*ha·'a·dam*). The Hebrew word for this individual man is the same as that used in Chapter 1 for humankind (*ha·'a·dam*) and is also very similar for the word meaning 'from the earth' (*ha·'a·da·mah*).

It was not until springs and then rain had watered the earth that plants could grow and these appeared in the form of a garden planted by God. After the garden has been formed, animals and birds are created and shown to the man (Adam) so that he can give them names. A female human is then made to be a helper for the man[16]. This account clearly does not map onto the account in the previous chapter, neither does it relate in any way to our current understanding of the biological world. Further, as we read on into Genesis Chapter 4 we see indications of a population, including a wife for Adam's son, Cain, who could not have possibly arisen one generation after the creation of just one human couple. Looking briefly at the creationist overall narrative, it takes in the days of creation in Chapter 1 but moves into Chapter 2 for the creation of humankind, using the Hebrew word *ha·'a·dam* to indicate the creation of just one man, Adam, rather than of humankind as implied in Chapter 1 (and indeed by that Hebrew word itself). The creationist narrative is thus a mixture of the two creation stories.

What then are we to make of all this? It would be too easy to dismiss the text as having no relevance because of its pre-scientific origins but that would be a mistake. Let us consider the genre of writing[17]. The early chapters of Genesis are written in different styles from the more historical reporting of the lives of the Hebrew patriarchs, described later in the Bible. Genesis Chapter 1 for example, has a repeating structure in which God establishes order in chaotic situations. It is not poetry, nor is it conventional prose. Over the centuries, going back as far as Origen in the third century and coming via Augustine and Calvin, right up to the 21st century, Christian scholars have interpreted these early chapters of Genesis as figurative narratives which convey basic truths about God, the creation and humankind (for more details, including references, please see Bryant and Reiss[3] and Lucas[17]). In that context, I rather like John Goldingay's description of the creation story as a parable[1].

This view is reinforced by comparing the Genesis texts with the creation myths of other cultures around Israel at the time, including those in Babylonian and Sumerian literature (the people of Israel, in captivity in Babylon, would be familiar with the former). There are both similarities to and differences from these other creation accounts[18]. For example, the structure of Earth and its relationship to the heavens is very similar in Sumerian and Babylonian texts to that described in Genesis 1. However, the differences are both very important and very striking. In the Sumerian myths, creation arises by a series of birthing events in which different parts of the creation bear other parts. Physical elements such as the ocean are regarded as personifications of gods in a large array of deities. Further, in some cultures, individual components of nature are deified. Think, for example, of the culture of ancient Egypt in which so many created things, including the Sun, moon and many birds and animals were regarded as gods.

In the Genesis accounts, God the creator is separate from the creation; created things, whether animate or inanimate, are not divine. Although we see the hand of God in nature – and are amazed by it – we recognise that the natural world, wonderful though it is, is the result of God's creativity but is itself not divine. Furthermore, God cares about the creation and also cares for humans who are capable of a relationship with Him. But humankind has spoiled that relationship and the image of God, referred to only in Genesis 1, is marred. These are foundational truths about the 'Who' of creation and not the 'How'. They are expressed in allegorical language, just as Chapters 39 to 41 of the book of Job speak of creation in powerfully poetic language (Job is also dated to the 6th century BC).

7.5 Concluding comments.

This has been a hard chapter to write but I felt compelled to do so. I have come across several people who struggled in their journey to faith because they believed that Christians deny the facts of evolution. Our scientific curiosity and the increasing ability to exercise that curiosity are gifts from God. As we wrote way back in Chapter 2, science is very good at doing what it is supposed to do. It is one approach to truth and we have nothing to fear from that type of truth; after all, it is truth about God's creation. However, simply to deny well established scientific paradigms because they apparently contradict what one reads in the Bible is not helpful – and indeed, because of the language sometimes used by those who deny evolution, may also be quite hurtful to scientists who are Christians. This then is a plea for respect for our scientific and Christian integrity.

Allow me then to return to section 7.4 where I said that the allegorical language of the early chapters of Genesis revealed foundational truths of a spiritual nature. These include God's plan to be in relationship with humankind. But the New Testament shows that there is more. When Jesus taught his disciples to pray to Our Father[19] ... he was saying, not only that the creator wants us to be in relationship with him but that he also allows us to call him 'Dad'. Awesome.

Chapter 7 endnotes:

[1] John Goldingay, Genesis for Everyone, Part I, SPCK London, 2010, p. 28.

[2] We are not claiming here that Einstein had a conventional Jewish or Christian faith – his spirituality was more complex, more akin to pantheism (see section 2.3).

[3] For more detail please see J. A. Bryant and M. J. Reiss, Creationism. In Sage Encyclopaedia of Higher Education, M E David and M J Amey (Editors), Sage Publications, Vol. 1, 2020, pp. 310-314.

[4] Confusingly, there are some old-Earth creationists who reject evolution yet accept that the Earth is older than a few thousand years. This contrasts with the majority of creationists who are thus young-Earth creationists.

[5] John Polkinghorne, Science and Theology: an Introduction, SPCK London/Fortress Press, 1998.

[6] A trial in which John Scopes, a supply teacher in a Tennessee high school, was accused of contravening the state's Butler Act, which had forbidden the teaching of human evolution in state-funded schools. Scopes was found guilty but never paid his fine because the verdict was overturned on the basis of a legal technicality.

[7] The Board of Education of the Dover Area school district in Pennsylvania voted to introduce the teaching of ID as science. Dissenting members of the board resigned; science teachers and many parents objected. Eleven parents filed a group action against the Dover Area school district (hence, colloquially, the 'Dover trial') and the court found in the parents' favour. The Board was forced to pay substantial costs to the plaintiffs.

[8] John Bryant, Intelligent Design Theory: New hypothesis or old idea in a new guise?, The Biochemist (2007), Vol 29, pp. 28-30; John Bryant, Intelligent Design, Resource (2009), Vol 14, pp. 14-16.

[9] William Demski, Intelligent Design: The Bridge Between Science and Theology, Inter-Varsity Press, 1999, p. 47.

[10] Kenneth Miller, Only a Theory: Evolution and the Battle for America's Soul, Viking Press, 2008.

[11] See, for example, N Matzke, Alleged scientific opposition to evolution, The Biochemist (2009), Vol. 31, p. 23.

[12] As with Einstein, we are not claiming that Darwin was a Christian. He eventually found it impossible to believe in a 'beneficent' God but we have his own word for it that he was not and never was an atheist.

[13] A 2.7 million-year-old ice core obtained in 2017 consisted almost entirely of ancient ice. See also http://www.antarcticglaciers.org/glaciers-and-climate/ice-cores/ice-core-basics/.

[14] See also https://biologos.org/articles/what-is-the-relationship-between-the-creation-accounts-in-genesis-1-and-2.

[15] The Holy Bible (NIV): Genesis, Chapter 1, verse 1.

[16] The English name for the 'first woman', Eve, is loosely derived from the Hebrew name *Chava*. This in turn is derived from a word meaning 'life' or 'living' because Eve was the 'mother of all living humans.'

[17] See Ernest Lucas, Can we believe Genesis today?: The Bible and the questions of science, Inter-Varsity Press, 2005.

[18] G J Wenham, The Perplexing Pentateuch, Vox Evangelica (1987), Vol 17, pp 7-22; G J Wenham, Genesis. In James Dunn, and John Rogerson, (Editors), Eerdmans Commentary on the Bible, Eerdmans Publishing Company, 2003, pp. 32-71.

[19] The Holy Bible (NIV): Luke's Gospel, Chapter 11, verse 2. He said to them 'When you pray, say: Father…'

8 In the Balance.

"The world is full of wonders but they become more wonderful, not less wonderful, when science looks at them." Sir David Attenborough[1]

"To find a balance on a very populated planet ... will require rethinking what we value ... to regain our balance as a species we need to re-connect to our human evolution and to our place in nature... [We also need] trust, community, shared values and reciprocity."
Emilio Moran[2]

John (mainly) and Graham write ...

8.1 Introduction.

One of the clear take-home messages from earlier chapters is that our planet Earth is a very special place. That is not to deny the possibility of similarly special planets '... in a galaxy far, far away', but Earth is the planet that we know about. The ancient scriptures of the Hebrew Bible/Old Testament are full of references to the wonder and beauty of both the physical world and the living world. Jesus himself acknowledged the beauty of wild flowers ("... not even Solomon in all his splendour was dressed like one of these."[3]). Further, the Old Testament writers were profoundly aware that what they saw in the 'heavens above and the Earth beneath' was the work of God the Creator, while Jesus acknowledged the care that his heavenly Father has for creation. And it will be apparent by now that both authors see the hand of God in the existence and workings of the Universe, from the most transient of elementary particles right out into the vastness of space. We are reminded of the words of author and Victorian minister, Charles Kingsley: "I believe ... in the whole universe as one infinite complexity of special providences."[4]

As we look from a scientist's standpoint at the 4.6 billion-year history of Earth, one clearly apparent feature is that the planet and the living organisms on it have evolved together. Not only have changing conditions on Earth elicited changes (by natural selection) in the living world but living organisms themselves have shaped the planet. Thus bacteria, the earliest of life-forms, mobilised minerals from the Earth's rocks as long ago as 3.8 billion years before present. Later, photosynthetic bacteria (blue-green bacteria or cyanobacteria) oxygenated the atmosphere and reduced its CO_2 content. Both these processes were continued by photosynthetic algae and by land plants. Land plants also brought about and continue to bring about changes in the landscape. Large forests, in addition to their role in locking up CO_2 (thereby reducing global warming), also affect weather patterns. In the tropics for example, large areas of forest experience a much higher rainfall than equivalent areas of savannah, and this difference becomes self-reinforcing: the rainfall promotes the continued growth of the forest. In death too, organisms may contribute to the Earth's structure; limestones for example, are largely formed from the exoskeletal remains of marine invertebrates.

In any one period in Earth's history, following the origin of life, the array of living organisms and the zone in which they live – the **biosphere** – is in a dynamic equilibrium with the structure of the planet itself. Some scientists have encouraged us to think of this synergistic biosphere-geosphere-atmosphere complex as being like a huge living organism, a concept to which James Lovelock gave the name **Gaia**[5]. If planetary conditions change, for example in warmer or cooler periods (as have occurred during the Earth's history), the balance is disturbed but eventually a new equilibrium is reached – or in Lovelock's words: Gaia is reset. The concept has been built on by current Earth-system scientists such as Tim Lenton who show that the self-regulating system, involving negative feedback, is not incompatible with natural selection (as had been claimed)[6]. In the words of bio-mathematician, Mark Staley, natural selection favours "... organisms that are best adapted to prevailing environmental conditions. However, the environment is not a static backdrop for evolution, but is heavily influenced by the presence of living organisms. The resulting co-evolving dynamical process eventually leads to ... equilibrium ..."[7]

8.2 Networks and connections in the natural world.

8.2.1 Major cycles.

I will now focus more specifically on the biological component of the biosphere-geosphere-atmosphere complex. It is here that we see some amazing examples of the interdependence of living organisms. Some are very general, affecting the whole biosphere, while others are very specific and affect only a few (sometimes as few as two) species. A major example of the more general kind is the **carbon cycle**. As previously noted, the advent of photosynthesis was a key event in the evolution of the planet. Firstly, photosynthetic organisms are the transducers of an energy source external to the Earth - the Sun's light energy. They are thus key **primary producers** in the overall food chain without which complex organisms, including ourselves, would not be here. But more than that, while photosynthesis uses light energy to drive the fixation of CO_2, it also releases oxygen into the atmosphere as a by-product. This allows aerobic (air-using) organisms to utilise oxygen in burning carbohydrate as fuel, in a process known as aerobic respiration, which in turn releases CO_2.

So, plants fix CO_2. By this I mean that in the process of photosynthesis, CO_2 is pulled out of the air and built into compounds that are useful to the plant. Much of the CO_2 is used to build the plant body but some of it is used in respiration: plants are themselves aerobic organisms (I use the word plants in its widest sense, from the largest trees down to microscopic algae and phytoplankton). And right across the globe, all other aerobic organisms are using plants as food and fuel either directly or indirectly. Thus CO_2 initially fixed by plants is returned to the atmosphere by aerobic respiration. Non-photosynthetic organisms and photosynthetic organisms need each other. In the absence of any except the most basic of human activities, there is actually an annual net gain of fixed carbon of about two to three percent over the amount that is produced by respiration. However, that is counteracted by the release to the atmosphere of CO_2 emitted during volcanic eruptions, by naturally occurring fires and to a lesser extent by the weathering and solubilisation of limestone rocks. Thus, given stability in the conditions on the planet, CO_2 concentrations remain more or less constant.

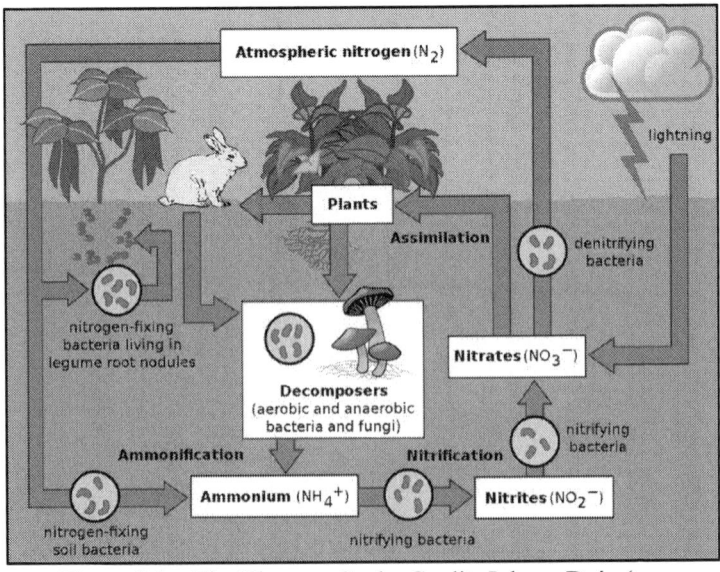

Figure 8.1. The Nitrogen Cycle. Credit: Johann Dréo (see frontispiece).

The second major cycle that illustrates the dynamic equilibrium of the Earth is the **nitrogen cycle** (see Figure 8.1). Nitrogen is another very important element for life. Although carbon provides the essential 'skeletons' for biological molecules, nitrogen is also a major component of DNA, RNA and proteins. The building blocks for DNA and RNA are nitrogenous bases while the building blocks for proteins are amino acids (acids which carry an amino or NH_2 group). Nitrogen is the most abundant element in the air, making up nearly 80% by volume of the atmospheric gases. Nitrogen also exists in the biosphere-geosphere in the form of ions such as nitrate and ammonium, as shown in Figure 8.1.

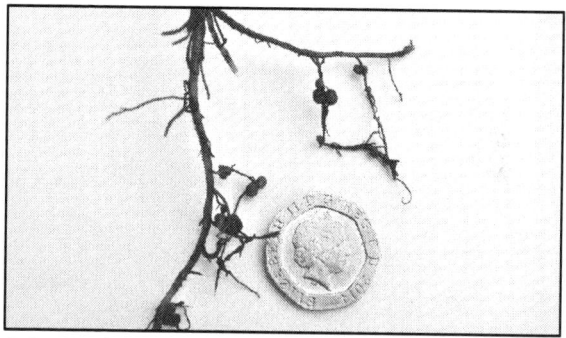

Figure 8.2. Nodules on roots of runner bean (*Phaseolus coccineus*) plants. The nodules are the sites of symbiotic *Rhizobium* bacteria which fix nitrogen. The scale marker is a UK twenty pence coin.
Credit: John Bryant.

Although the atmosphere is potentially a huge source of nitrogen, it does not readily join other elements in chemical linkage. It is here that the living world is dependent on **nitrogen-fixing bacteria** which are able to fix nitrogen; to drag it out of the atmosphere and to use it to build biological molecules. Many of the bacterial species that can do this are free-living but others (in the genus *Rhizobium*) exist in close symbiotic relationship with plants in the pea and bean family which thus make their own fertiliser (see Figure 8.2)[8]. In addition to nitrogen-fixation by bacteria, a small amount is fixed in lightning strikes which provide enough energy to overcome the chemical inertia of nitrogen. Thus, bacteria play a key role in the nitrogen economy of the biosphere. Figure 8.1 shows us that bacteria and fungi are also involved in keeping the nitrogen moving between different chemical forms, thus ensuring that it is recycled. There is also some loss of nitrogen back to the atmosphere because of the metabolic activity of de-nitrifying bacteria but this is replaced by the nitrogen fixed by other bacteria (as described above). The nitrogen cycle thus provides another excellent example of inter-dependencies in the biosphere, with micro-organisms playing key roles.

8.2.2 Local networks, connections and interdependencies.

The balance between biosphere, geosphere and atmosphere, termed Gaia by Lovelock, is very clear in our quick look at two of the major cycles involved in maintaining that balance. However, networks and connections are also involved at a more local level, which are nonetheless important in the ecosystems in which they occur[9]. There is effectively an internet of living things. The following list gives just six examples from a range of many thousands that I can choose from.

Figure 8.3. Pollination of Russian sage (*Perovskia atriplicifolia*).
Credit: John Bryant.

1. Plants and pollinators

The earliest angiosperms (flowering plants) were almost certainly pollinated by beetles, as is the most primitive species of angiosperm, *Amborella trichopoda*, still in existence today. Since those earliest examples, pollination mechanisms have evolved in amazing and diverse ways. The most advanced flowering plants such as grasses (including our cereal crops) are wind pollinated, as are some trees, but nearly all other species rely on animals to transfer pollen.[10] Animals involved in pollination include birds, bats and mice but the vast majority are insects, including bees, butterflies, moths and hoverflies (see Figure 8.3), providing an amazing example of the co-evolution of two completely separate groups of living organisms that have come to depend on each other, sometimes in very specific ways. Pollination goes on all around us whenever plants are in flower and yet we often do not notice or we take for granted this widespread and important example of plant-animal cooperation.

2. The world beneath our feet

As we look around at the vegetation on the Earth's surface we are often unaware of the world of living things beneath our feet. For example, 80 – 90% of the plants we see are able to form symbiotic relationships with underground fungi, thus forming **mycorrhizae** (and the majority actually do so). The term mycorrhizae actually means fungus-roots, emphasising the very close physical relationship between fungal and plant tissues. These symbiotic associations have evolved several times during the history of land plants and indeed symbiotic fungi are thought to have been important in aiding the original invasion of land by liverwort-like plants in the Ordovician period. In these associations, the fungus benefits by receiving sugars synthesised by the plant during photosynthesis and the plant benefits from greatly increased efficiency of nutrient uptake from the soil.

The most developed mycorrhizal associations occur in woodland and forest trees where huge networks of fungal threads (mycelia) provide linkages between the trees. These extensive branching networks enable trees to mutually support each other nutritionally and may also act as signalling channels, for example to mobilise defences against predation or environmental stresses. In the words of Robert Macfarlane, they are "... a forest of arborescent connections and profuse intercommunication".[11]

3. Walking ecosystems

How many cells are there in an average adult human body? This is a trick question. Does the questioner mean human cells or did the question include the cells of the micro-organisms that live on us and especially within us? A 70 kg human has about 30 trillion (3×10^{13}) human cells and is also home to about 38 trillion (3.8×10^{13}) micro-organisms, mainly bacteria but including some microfungi and **protists**. This assemblage of micro-organisms is termed the human **microbiota** and the overall genetic makeup of a person's microbiota is its **microbiome**. About 99% of these micro-organisms live in our gut, residing in the loose outer layer of mucus external to the gut lining (epithelium). They have co-evolved with us to live in harmony in a mutually beneficial way: for us, they help to digest dietary fibre and for the micro-organisms we provide a stable, nutrient rich environment.

The overall composition of this microbial community varies between people and is affected by the diet of the host human. As might be assumed from what I have just written, diets rich in fibre promote a flourishing microbiota, while diets rich in saturated fats and simple carbohydrates cause a reduction in microbial diversity. And this may have effects on our health. There is now considerable evidence that products of metabolism from a diverse microbiota can aid food digestion, boost the immune response to pathogenic bacteria and protect against inflammation of the gut lining. Further, current research suggests that microbial metabolites may interact with our brain biochemistry to affect our moods, raising the concept of 'feel-good bacteria'. If this is confirmed it would be a remarkable added dimension to what is already an amazing example of interplay between completely unrelated organisms. Even if it is not confirmed we can state that each of us is an individual ecosystem.

4. Light in the Darkness

Many of our readers will be familiar with bioluminescence, the emission of visible light by living organisms. We see it, for example, in glow-worms (which are not really worms but the larvae of a number of species of beetle) and fireflies, (known as lightning bugs in the USA) which are beetles. We also see bioluminescence in the many pinpoints of light emanating from luminescent marine micro-organisms, visible when we disturb a calm sea on a dark night. About 450 species of sea-fish are also luminescent, emitting light from a special light organ which may, as in angler fish, protrude from the upper back and over the head like a fishing rod. The functions of light-emission in sea-fish are varied and in different species may include illumination for finding food/prey, distraction or scaring of predators and location and/or attraction of mates. However, unlike glow-worms and fireflies, these fish cannot generate their own light. The light organs are inhabited by species of *Photobacterium*, light-emitting bacteria. Only three species of this large genus of bacteria enter these symbiotic relationships, with each of those species showing strong preference for particular families of fish. It is obvious that for a luminescent fish, this relationship is obligate. However, this is not actually so for the bacterium which can live successfully without its relationship with the fish. Nevertheless it is currently thought that those bacteria which do inhabit fish light organs benefit from the provision of oxygen, nutrients and a safe habitat.

5. *The Joshua Tree*

The Joshua Tree (*Yucca brevifolia*; Figure 8.4) is an iconic representative of the flora of semi-desert regions of the South-Western USA (as well as the title of an excellent album by U2!). It is also involved in a remarkable mutualistic relationship that ensures efficient pollination and seed set. All but one of the different species in the genus *Yucca* is pollinated by Yucca moths with each moth species showing a strong preference for a particular *Yucca* species. Adult moths emerge when the plants are in flower. When they visit their first flower, pollen sticks to the moths' bodies. Amazingly, the moth then collects the pollen together into a little ball which it carries on a special appendage on its neck. During its next visit to a *Yucca* flower, the female moth lays a very small number of eggs in the plant's ovaries. It then (and here the story becomes almost surreal) climbs onto the stigma – the site of pollen receptiveness – and places the pollen ball there. This ensures that the ova are fertilised and that seeds will form.

Meanwhile, the eggs that the moth has laid in the ovaries start to hatch and the caterpillars feed on the developing seeds. However, the small number of eggs that had been laid means that some seeds escape being eaten, grow to maturity and will be able to germinate. When the caterpillars are fully grown, they emerge from the plant's fruit (in which the seeds are contained), crawl down to the ground into which they burrow for pupation. The next generation of moths emerge from their pupae during the next *Yucca* flowering season and thus the cycle starts again. It is a beautiful example of a detailed interdependence of two totally unrelated living organisms which induces in me and many other biologists a sense of wonder, even as the story becomes familiar to us.

Figure 8.4. Joshua Trees (*Yucca brevifolia*) growing in the Nevada desert, USA. Mount Charleston in the background. Credit: John Bryant.

6. *Coming home to roost*

Many of us are familiar with pitcher plants – carnivorous plants that lure prey into slippery-sided pitchers where the bodies of the unfortunate victims are digested. These pitchers would seem to be the last place in which a small mammal would choose to roost – but that is just what a tiny bat, Hardwicke's Woolly Bat, does in South-East Asia. The pitcher plant in question is a particular sub-species of *Nepenthes rafflesiana* (*N. r. elongata*) that has longer pitchers and much less digestive fluid than the typical sub-species. Further it does not produce the scent that the typical sub-species produces. Inevitably then it attracts much less prey than the typical subspecies. This is where the bat comes in. The structure of the pitcher is such that it can accommodate a tiny bat (or even two) without any danger of the bat(s) coming into contact with the digestive fluid. The pitcher thus makes a very safe place for a bat to roost during the day[12]. But the plant benefits from this arrangement too. It is able to use the urine and faeces of the bats as a source of nutrients, thus supplementing the poor supply of normal prey (typically, large insects) – a remarkable example of mutualism.

8.3 Stewards of creation.

I am very conscious that in subsection 8.2.2, had both space and time permitted, I could have cited many more examples. In dealing with the underground fungal networks I did not talk more generally about forest and woodland ecosystems with their range of biodiversity, including other plants, birds, mammals, invertebrates and many more. I have not talked about food webs and food chains, including predator-prey interactions. I have not mentioned the complex multi-host life-cycles of many parasites. Nevertheless, it is clear that the balance of nature is relevant at all levels, from the major cycles that maintain a dynamic equilibrium in the biosphere-geosphere-atmosphere to the very detailed and equally balanced relationships between sometimes only two types of organism. Nature is truly a wonderful, intermeshed web of networks, or in the words of Robert Macfarlane, " ... an assemblage of entanglements of which we are messily part"[11]. It is those words 'of which we are messily part' that I now want to focus on.

There is currently a lot of emphasis on humankind as part of nature. We are indeed part of the animal kingdom, related to great apes and thus firmly embedded in the biosphere. According to the early 20th century American naturalist, Aldo Leopold, we are "plain members and citizens of the land community"[13]. Now, while that is a very nice thought, it is also, when pushed to its limits, unworkable. Only humans have the ability to make that sort of statement or decision and in that sense we can never be equal citizens with other members of the land community. But that does not mean that we are exempt from caring about the natural world.

We are by far the most intelligent animals on the planet and have by far the greatest ability to modify nature. In that sense we are separate from the rest of the biosphere. This tension is evident in much modern writing about environmental concerns. Several authors use the term 'Anthropocene'[14] to describe the present geological epoch in which the planet is being altered by humankind. Some go on to suggest that if we were able to see ourselves more as part of nature than apart from nature, we would be better able to take care of the planet rather than altering it so dramatically.

This brings us back to thinking about what it means to be human but looking at the question in wider terms than purely biological. It is a tenet of both Judaism and Christianity that humans carry the image of God, as mentioned at the end of Chapter 6. It is not an easy concept to understand and carries several implications, including the possibility of a spiritual interaction with God, the Creator. In the original Hebrew use of the term in the Genesis story, it implies that humans are God's representatives or agents; that agency includes exercising our dominion over nature in an attitude of stewardship and care, not of rapacious exploitation. And even if we do not have a religious faith, stewardship is still a very helpful concept, as discussed elsewhere[15]. It helps us to think about preservation and care of the natural world on behalf of others and especially on behalf of future generations[16].

All this sounds very good but we must also acknowledge that there is a tension between dealing with human need and protecting the planet. Thus, from the earliest days of humankind we have constructed places to live and to store food. Later in our history we started to need land for crops and pasture. As our population has grown, the need to clear land for human existence has grown and that growth has been further stimulated by technological development, especially since the Industrial Revolution. We cannot ignore this tension; the question is whether we can provide for human existence while exercising stewardship of the Earth and its resources [15].

Part of the discussion about how to resolve this question concerns the way in which we value the environment. Here we can see several different approaches. Firstly, there is the human-centred or **anthropocentric** approach. The environment is valued only or mainly according to what it provides for humankind. That value may be financial or material. There have, for example, been attempts to write equations to quantify the financial value of the environment and of environmental services such as the pollination of crops. This approach, which attempts to put a price on everything, has been strongly criticised by many commentators, including the environmental ethicist and theologian Christopher Southgate[17]. Nevertheless, attempts to do this continue.[18] There are others who, while adopting this human-centred approach, value the environment for reasons other than financial. These may include the health benefits, both mental and physical, of contact with nature and the sense of spirituality that people may experience in wild places. The environment is thus valued in the context of human flourishing.

Then there is the **biocentric** approach which holds that all living things have value for their own sake while in **ecocentrism**, it is the whole geosphere-biosphere-atmosphere complex, either local or global, that is valued for its own sake. Using an example close to my heart, mountains are valued because they are there, rather than (or perhaps in addition to) their value in relation to human flourishing. In the more rigid forms of these approaches, humans are no more special than any other living thing – we have no more rights than any other living organism. Indeed, **deep ecologists** believe that humans have become a nuisance species with a population size that far exceeds the capacity of our habitat to support us [15]. Use of biocentrism and/or ecocentrism in valuing the environment has led to several cases in which specified ecosystems were granted rights as if they were humans. Whether this is an appropriate route to environmental protection is open to question but in at least two of the cases, it prevented habitat loss and environmental degradation which would have been a likely outcome of unsympathetic exploitation (see section 8.4). In practice, it is often found that people who have some concern for the environment hold a combination of anthropocentric and soft bio/ecocentric views (and sadly, we have to admit that some people, including many in powerful positions, seem to have no concern at all). For example, they may ascribe rather less value to a mosquito which transmits malaria than to a rare butterfly or a polar bear. In the first instance, the welfare of humans is considered more important than the flourishing of an insect species while in the second instance, the welfare of an iconic and threatened species may over-ride human interests. This raises a further problem in that focus on these iconic species, while generating public interest, may result in a failure to address more general underlying problems.

Finally, there is the **theocentric** or God-centred approach to valuing the environment. In some Eastern religions and in some forms of paganism, nature itself is regarded as divine, thus generating an essentially respectful approach to all living things. In the Judaeo-Christian tradition, God is regarded as the Creator who has vested in humankind a responsibility for the world. However, the shortcomings of theocentrism are alluded to by several commentators, of which the most notable is the American historian Lynn White[19]. His thesis was that the 20th century ecological crisis was actually caused by a Judaeo-Christian approach, placing emphasis on that aspect of dominion over nature that leads to exploitation rather than the aspect that involves stewardship. I think he was at least partly right. However, it is good that in more recent years we have regained (or in some Christian cultures, started to regain) a sense of respect and care for creation and to exercise stewardship, working in acceptance of a thread that runs throughout the Bible – "The Earth is the LORD's"[20].

It is fair to ask which of these approaches best deals with the tension between the needs of human society and the needs of the environment. In my view, all three approaches have something to offer. A soft form of biocentrism focuses strongly on nature but recognises that humans have needs too. A soft form of anthropocentrism may motivate us to care for the environment so that it can continue to provide for human needs. Theocentrism also involves caring for both people and nature but with the added motivation of serving God. It thus seems to me that faith groups and secular groups have a great deal to offer each other in caring about the environment. We will return to this later in the chapter.

8.4 It's in the balance.

8.4.1 The general picture: it's a five-fold problem.

So, how are we doing? In recent months, huge areas of the Amazon rainforest have been burning in Brazil while the wildfire season in parts of Australia has been much longer, more widespread and more intense than usual. There have been wildfires north of the Arctic Circle in Siberia. The area of ice-free water in the Arctic is larger than has previously been recorded. Iceland held a memorial service for a major glacier. About 670,000 tonnes of plastic waste are dumped in the oceans every month. Species of living organisms are becoming extinct at a rate that is several hundred times greater (some experts say 1000 times greater) than the background rate estimated from the fossil record. There is much more that I could say, but I have said enough to show that we are not doing very well. The balance of nature is indeed in the balance.

What are the actual problems? It would be all too easy to present a litany of examples, adding to and/or expanding on what I presented in the previous paragraph. Instead, I will provide a more general summary, illustrated with a few examples with a longer look at climate change. Readers who wish to have more detail can find it in *Introduction to Bioethics*[15] and *Introduction to Environmental Ethics*[17]. There are actually five major interlinked problems in our relationship with the environment. These are pollution, environmental degradation, over-exploitation of resources, habitat loss (with associated decrease in biodiversity) and climate change.

I still have a well-thumbed and slightly battered copy of the first edition of Rachel Carson's seminal 1962 book *Silent Spring*[21] which is credited with kick-starting the environmental movement. It is a reminder that many instances of pollution are actually unintended consequences of actions which had been previously considered safe. We can cite the use of certain pesticides in agriculture (as in *Silent Spring*), the use of chlorofluorocarbons (CFCs) in refrigerants and the inclusion of microplastic beads in some cosmetics and toothpastes. Pollution may also be deliberate, as in the discharge of toxic wastes into rivers and into the atmosphere (in many places this was fortunately discontinued in the last century) and, as mentioned already, the dumping of eight million tonnes of plastic items into the ocean each year. Finally there is accidental pollution as typified by the nuclear accidents at Chernobyl (1986) and Fukushima (2011) and by the leakage of toxic gases from a chemical plant in Bhopal, India in 1984.

It is very clear that many types of pollution lead to a degradation of the environment, decreasing the range of living organisms that can live in a particular area. The accidents at Chernobyl and Bhopal provide major examples but actually much environmental degradation results from deliberate actions. Spoil tips from mines of many types provide clear examples of this, even at those mines where the waste material is not toxic. Something as simple as fly-tipping degrades the environment, while a smouldering cigarette butt, itself a minor form of pollution, can cause extensive environmental degradation if it starts a wildfire.

The third problem in our relationship with the environment is over-exploitation of natural resources; treating the Earth as if it had an inexhaustible supply of what humans need. Overfishing is one of the best-known examples of this, but the imposition of strict regulations in many parts of the world has led to at least a partial recovery of many fisheries. Another example is the clearance of forests, both in temperate regions and in the tropics (see below). My final example, from the many I could have chosen, is the use of scarce metals that are needed for many modern devices, including mobile phones. Overall, we are using the planet's resources at a rate that would require three Earths to sustain it.

Habitat loss and decreases in biodiversity again highlight the tension between human need and the natural world. There is clear evidence that loss of habitat is contributing to extinctions and to increased vulnerability of many of the surviving species. The built environment, which replaces natural habitats, mostly arises to satisfy the needs of human society. Coupled with this is the use of land for agriculture, replacing the original habitat with a different one which, according to how the land is managed, may or may not be as species-rich as the original. But whether or not it is, it will certainly host a different range of species; a new balance will be reached.

I want to look at one aspect of this, deforestation, in slightly more detail because it will lead directly into the discussion on climate change. We tend to focus on tropical forests but in fact deforestation in temperate regions has been even more dramatic in terms of percentage losses. For example, 3000 years ago much of mainland Britain was forested but as agriculture was introduced and human settlements became larger, so forest was cleared.[22] By the time of the Norman Conquest, forest cover in much of lowland Britain was between zero and 40%. Similar trends can be traced across northern Europe. The major clearances were thus pre-industrial, but clearance continued after the Industrial Revolution. Now (in 2020), 13% of the total land area in the UK is wooded with the lowest coverage in southern England and Northern Ireland, and the highest in several areas of Scotland, mostly in the Highlands. What we think of as the British countryside is largely the result of human activity. The removal of so much forest, albeit over many centuries, will have certainly changed the water cycle in these islands. It is likely that forested Britain was wetter than deforested Britain – another example of the interaction of the biological with the physical. And it certainly changed the range of animals and plants. But there is an irony here too. Birds like the skylark, corn bunting and the lapwing thrive in open countryside typified by areas of arable land. Changes in farming practices have led to declines in these species which were advantaged by the earlier deforestation. Nature conservation can be confusing sometimes.

In contrast to the cool temperate zone of northern Europe, loss of tropical rainforest did not get under way (except for small localised clearances) until the 1950s. In 1950, these forests covered about 14% of the planet's surface. By 2019 that had been reduced to just under 6%[15]. Even so, these forests are still home to about 50% of the Earth's known plant and animal species: they are rich in biodiversity. Because of the evaporation of water from the leaves of so many densely packed trees, the forests are very wet – hence their name. In addition to the effects on the water cycle, these forests also have locked up within them many tonnes of CO_2. As with the temperate forests, the clearances, often by burning, have been done for the sake of plant crops (mainly the growth of oil palm, sugar cane and soybeans) and ranching (mainly in South America). Taking all types of forest together, an area approximately equal to that of the UK is still being lost each year. The effects on biodiversity are almost too obvious to mention – a monoculture of oil palm is very different from a forest. But there are other effects; large-scale losses of forest lead to decreases in rainfall, de-stabilisation of soils and the release to the atmosphere of large amounts of CO_2. Loss of tropical rainforest contributes to global climate change.

8.4.2 Climate change.

Climate is the last of my list of five interlinked environmental problems but is arguably at present by far the most pressing. We need start our discussion of this by talking about carbon dioxide (CO_2). It is present in the atmosphere in very small amounts. Prior to the Industrial Revolution, it represented 0.029% (290 parts per million, ppm) of the gases in the atmosphere. For comparison, nitrogen represents about 78% and oxygen 20%. However, since the start of the Industrial Revolution, and especially since World War II, that concentration has increased; it peaks in May every year (because of the annual functioning of the carbon cycle, mentioned in section 8.2.1). In 2020 that peak was recorded as 0.0417% (417 ppm), an increase of 43.8% above the pre-industrial baseline.

How does the greenhouse effect warm the Earth?

This amount of CO_2 is still a tiny proportion of the gases in the atmosphere, so why does it matter? It matters because of a particular feature of CO_2 chemistry, namely that it absorbs radiation at the infrared end of the spectrum, the part of the spectrum that we refer to as heat radiation (as experienced if we sit by a well-stoked open fire). The Sun emits immense amounts of radiation across the electromagnetic spectrum, with the peak intensity in visible light. Of the solar energy arriving at the planet, about one third is reflected back into space by the atmosphere and by the Earth's surface (land, sea and ice). The remainder is absorbed and heats the planet, and as a warm body at about room temperature, the Earth re-radiates the absorbed energy as infrared radiation. Some atmospheric gases, the so-called greenhouse gases, namely CO_2, water vapour and methane (CH_4), allow visible light to escape to space, but trap certain forms of infrared radiation. These gases effectively form a partial blanket that helps keep Earth about 30°C warmer than it would be otherwise. If there were no greenhouse gases in the atmosphere to trap the infrared radiation, the Earth would be a snowball (and for periods in the deep past this was the case). Indeed, the presence of CO_2 has been essential for the evolution of life in that it ensured that Earth was warm enough for life to flourish.

The ability of CO_2 – and water vapour – to trap heat was demonstrated by Victorian naturalist and mountain climber, John Tyndall in 1860.[23] By the time of the Second World War, meteorologist Guy Callendar predicted that increased burning of fossil fuels would lead to increased atmospheric temperatures.[24] This prediction has been strongly borne out by subsequent research. The key factor is that much of the carbon which had been fixed by photosynthesis in previous geological periods, especially in the Carboniferous, became fossilised, for example as coal. By burning these fossil fuels we are returning that CO_2 to the atmosphere at rates many times faster than the rate at which it was fixed. Further, the loss of current sinks of fixed carbon, caused for example, by burning or clearance of forests, adds to the problem (see previous section).

Over a period of about 150 years, the mean global temperature has increased by nearly 1°C. This represents a rate 50 times greater than the warming that occurred after the last ice age. One degree may not seem much but the effects of this rise on weather patterns, on polar ice and on sea levels are already apparent[15]. Fourteen of the 15 hottest years on record have occurred this century. The balance that we described earlier is clearly being disturbed but what does this actually mean for the Earth itself?

Firstly, we need to say that there have been periods when Earth was much warmer than it is now, such as during the Carboniferous period when there was no ice in the polar regions and trees grew within the Arctic and Antarctic Circles. It is estimated that the mean global temperature was around 6°C higher than now. The Earth obviously carried a different balance of nature in these times, a balance that has been re-adjusted several times in subsequent periods of cooling and warming. As Lovelock would have put it (see section 8.1), Gaia can be reset.

How does global warming affect climate and increase sea level?

The fact that the Earth itself will not be destroyed by global warming (GW) does not mean that we can ignore it. To this end, the UN Intergovernmental Panel on Climate Change (IPCC) was formed in 1988 to monitor developments and provide the best science to inform global policy related to climatic change.

There is a diversity of effects that impact climate arising from human-caused GW. Perhaps the most obvious is that rising temperatures increase the intensity and frequency of heat waves and drought. Apart from the debilitating and often lethal effect this has on the human population, the drying out and heating up of the land drive worsening wildfires. The wildfire season is longer than it was a few decades ago and wildfire events are now larger and more destructive (as was apparent in Australia during the 2019-2020 Southern hemisphere summer). Such episodes also produce a dangerous feedback effect, by releasing further CO_2 into the atmosphere, which drives further warming. Furthermore, in semi-arid regions, the direct heating caused by GW has increased the incidence of dust-bowl formation, resulting in the loss of agricultural land.

In more temperate zones, wet areas of the world have become wetter, with more intense and more frequent precipitation. This occurs because air is able to hold more water vapour as the temperature rises. This increase in atmospheric water vapour is matched by increased rainfall, resulting in an escalation in flooding events. There is also good evidence that climate change is affecting the jet stream and weather systems in such a way as to cause storms to slow down or come to a standstill, giving them more time to dump heavy rain.

The increase in sea surface temperature associated with GW has a multiplicity of consequences. Warming raises sea levels because of the expansion of water and the melting of polar ice around the North Pole and particularly in Greenland and Antarctica. The frequency of large storm events is also enhanced, because hurricanes draw their source of energy from ocean warmth and increased sea surface temperatures serve to make such storms more intense and destructive. The resultant lowering of pressure at storm centres raises the local sea level, causing devastating storm surge events.

Returning to the issue of sea level rise, it is clear that the principal driver is polar ice loss. The current decline in Arctic ice began around 1900, in response to rising levels of CO_2. However, this trend has accelerated markedly in the last three decades or so and over the last decade it has been possible to monitor this accurately by spacecraft such as the European Space Agency environmental research satellite Cryosat 2. Measurements of polar ice thickness are possible to an accuracy of around 1 cm using space-borne radar instruments. Such measurements from orbit, combined with other techniques, indicate a current annual ice loss of the order of 250 billion tonnes in the Antarctic alone[25]. Furthermore, climate science shows that the Arctic is warming at a greater rate than the rest of the planet; an effect referred to as polar amplification. There are a number of factors that drive this; for example, as highly reflective ice melts, it is replaced by darker surfaces such as land or sea, which absorb more solar energy, so increasing warming. It is also the case that in cold conditions, more of the incident solar energy results in warming rather than evaporation.

In this brief account, we have attempted to outline the basic science that describes how global warming leads to climate change. But the real story is much more complex, with a mix of many inextricably-linked factors interacting with each other to form the whole picture. It should also be emphasised that no individual storm, flood or drought can be attributed directly to GW, but the frequency of occurrence and intensity of these events is increased (for a more detailed discussion, see endnote [26]).

In the autumn of 2019, Swedish teenager Greta Thunberg made a strong statement about use of fossil fuels and climate change by sailing across the Atlantic to address the UN Action Summit on Climate Change. Later that year, the 25th United Nations Climate Change Conference (COP 25) took place in Madrid, Spain. The talks continue, but is there sufficient action to counter the effects of climate change? From all that has already been said and written, it is apparent that we continue to supply much of our energy needs by the burning of fossil fuels, so that the rate at which the global average temperature is rising continues to increase. It is also clear, from developments over the last couple of decades, that it is the poorer nations that are affected most by this trend. Moreover, some ecosystems are already experiencing disruption of their balance, upsetting the dynamic equilibrium that has been discussed earlier in this chapter.

However, there are glimmers of hope globally that effort and resources are being expended to counter the effects of GW. For example, in the UK, there was a three-month period during the Summer of 2019 when 50% of the UK's energy needs were met from renewable sources – principally wind and solar farms. Further, in the Spring of 2020 there was a period of 68 days when the UK used no fossil fuels in the generation of electricity. These are encouraging portents but, more generally, are we doing enough to avert a climate disaster?

Do we face a climate emergency and what is at stake if we do not act?

Even in the relatively benign meteorological environment of the authors' home nation, the UK, it is apparent that things have changed over our lifetime. The frequency of potentially destructive or disruptive storms has increased, as has the occurrence of flooding events. Heatwaves seem to occur more often, especially since the turn of the millennium. Is this a just a subjective view, based on memories of the good times when we were growing up or is it borne out by the data? The one sure thing is that the global army of research scientists, reporting through the IPCC, tell us what the science is saying – that climate change will mean the UK will experience more extreme weather, along with the rest of the planet.

In response to this, the UK parliament declared a national environment and climate emergency in May 2019 and the timescale to achieve zero net carbon emissions is now a subject of debate. Although this helps raise awareness, it is not clear that there is a coherent plan to achieve zero net emissions in a timely fashion, since the situation requires urgent action. In parallel with these developments, a global environmental organisation called 'Extinction Rebellion' was formed in October 2018. The stated aim of this people's movement is to use nonviolent civil disobedience to force government action to stop climate change and the associated loss of biodiversity.

In December 2015, the Paris Climate Accord (Paris Agreement) was adopted by an almost unanimous consensus of 195 nations[15]. The Accord sets out limits to greenhouse gas emissions that will be needed to avoid dangerous climate impacts. Current predictions suggest that this requires limiting the temperature rise to less than 2°C which will in turn mean stabilising the level of atmospheric CO_2 to less than 450 ppm. Disappointingly, however, in June 2017 the USA withdrew from the agreement and another major emitter, Russia, failed to ratify. The output from these abstaining nations represents about a quarter of global emissions. Hopefully this will be a temporary setback. To achieve these critical limits on temperature and CO_2, we have to act rapidly and globally, establishing significant technological and social changes in the 2020 to 2040 timeframe.

If we fail in this and continue with business as usual, then we can expect a global average surface temperature rise of between 4° and 6°C, and an atmospheric CO_2 content in the region of 1000 ppm by the century's end. This would be accompanied by a sea level rise of between one and two metres, so the map of coastal nations will look very different. There will also be a decrease in agricultural land to feed a growing global population – estimated to be approaching 10 billion by 2050. If these things come to pass, then we are looking at the climate disaster that scientists talk about. Most environmental problems, such as a polluted river or an area of fly-tipping can be cleaned up, but climate change is different. If we adopt the business as usual approach, then 2100 will see the climate damaged and the timescale for its recovery will be centuries, if not millennia. These risks are unparalleled in human history, and it is possible that our grandchildren will see this unfold unless we take urgent action. As we said above, climatic change does not destroy the planet but it does threaten the continued existence for all currently extant creatures – including humans – and plants on planet Earth. We know that humans are very adaptable to change but this kind of threat probably means survival in a subterranean (or extra-terrestrial?) setting.

In November 2019, the urgency of the global situation was further emphasised by the publication of a warning endorsed by 11,000 scientists from 153 nations[27]. This warned of 'untold suffering due to the climate crisis' unless there are major transformations in global society. The report summarises the sort of radical social and political changes that are needed within a short timeframe to avoid a climate disaster. These changes include ending population growth, leaving fossil fuels in the ground, halting forest destruction and significantly reducing meat consumption. It goes on:

> "We declare clearly and unequivocally that planet Earth is facing a climate emergency ... To secure a sustainable future, we must change how we live. [This] entails major transformations in the ways our global society functions and interacts with natural ecosystems ... The climate crisis has arrived and is accelerating faster than most scientists expected. It is more severe than anticipated, threatening natural ecosystems and the fate of humanity."

What is to be done?

The document signed by those scientists lays out clearly the effects of climate change that are faced by the global community and raises questions about what should be done to ameliorate or mitigate these effects. In discussing possible courses of action, we make no apologies for emphasising again that the situation is serious. It is rightly called a climate emergency and thus demands urgent responses. Courses of action need to be taken nationally and internationally – which will involve wide ranging sociopolitical decisions – and more locally, which will involve groups and individuals. It is our view that Christians should be involved in taking action. Any idea of stewardship (section 8.3) and especially the sense of caring for God's creation both for God's sake and on the behalf of others, including future generations, should motivate us to do something. Working together, Christian and other faith communities can be a real force for change, as recognised by Ian Christie, senior lecturer in Sustainability at the University of Surrey, who says: "A sustainable future also depends on changes in values and behaviour. As this becomes ever more apparent, the need for a spiritual and ethical vision to bring policy to life will grow. ...Together, the faiths and secular organisations could indeed 'move mountains' "[28].

So, what should we do? First, it is plainly obvious that emissions of CO_2 must be reduced significantly, mainly by a drastic reduction in the use of fossil fuels. At the policy level this means extensive decarbonisation of both energy generation and transport.[29]

If we are to maintain our technological society in the developed nations, this must be underpinned by a growing supply of renewable energy such as solar, wind, tidal, wave, hydro, geothermal and nuclear. This creates a new economy, dragging the industrial infrastructure away from fossil fuel-based energy to sustainable and low/zero carbon sources. This offers a great opportunity for investment, research and development, but clearly there is significant inertia in the system, making this transition difficult. There are also clear vested interests in the fossil fuel-based economy which is currently creating resistance to change, posing a threat to future progress in overcoming climate change. Those representing these interests are nevertheless influential, prompting the question: Will capitalism kill the planet?

The use of nuclear energy, which is effectively zero carbon, seems at first sight to be an ideal solution. Nuclear fission energy power stations have been with us since the 1950s and these generate power by splitting the nucleus of heavy elements such as uranium. There are, however, environmental concerns about the disposal of the radioactive waste that it produces. Alternatively, the development of a viable nuclear fusion reactor has been the goal of scientists for many years. As discussed in section 4.3, this is the energy source that powers the stars and creating a mini-star on Earth has proved very challenging. If this could be accomplished, nuclear fusion energy would be the ideal solution to supply an energy-hungry planet, as it is a zero-carbon source with effectively an infinite fuel supply (sea water) and no radioactive waste issues. However, it has become (rather cynically) known as the energy of the future, because its realisation seems to remain firmly beyond the grasp of the present. Some scientists suggest that a working fusion reactor may be online around the 2040s but is this too late to contribute to combatting climate change?

The transportation sector has been a rapidly-growing source of CO_2 because of the rapid rise in car use and the huge growth in the use of air transportation in recent decades. For anyone travelling by air more than once a year, air transport is likely to be the largest contribution to that person's carbon footprint (although there are mitigation schemes, see below). For short-range personal transport, the goal is to replace petrol/diesel-powered cars with electric vehicles (EVs). To ensure that this is beneficial for the climate, the electrical charging system must, of course, use renewable energy sources. If the 43 million or so cars in use in the UK (alone) were electrified, the task of providing sufficient green grid energy is a major challenge. There is also the chicken and egg conundrum concerning the provision of charging stations for EVs. The purchase of EVs is inhibited by a perceived lack of charging stations but it is difficult to source the significant investment needed to develop a wide-spread charging infrastructure when there are few EVs in use. The electrification of personal transport is clearly a complex issue, involving questions about the overall cost of EVs as compared to petrol/diesel-powered vehicles and also the status, cost and recycling of battery technology.

Clearly, there must be more investment in environmental

energy sources and in the use of electric power for transport. Where it is impossible to avoid the use of fossil fuels, both corporate and individual usage needs to be critically evaluated. For individuals, this may mean questioning our choices in use of transport, for example in thinking about public transport versus private cars or train versus aeroplane.

Secondly, there needs to be extensive measures to mitigate the emissions of carbon dioxide caused by use of fossil fuels. One effective method for doing this is by planting trees. Trees fix CO_2 by photosynthesis and much of that CO_2 is used to make the tree itself, thereby locking it up until the tree dies and decays. Extensive re-afforestation is one way in which this can be achieved. At an individual level, those of us with gardens should plant trees and there are several mitigation schemes which encourage people to pay to offset their fossil fuel use by tree-planting, especially in tropical and sub-tropical zones of less developed countries.[30]

Thirdly, we must develop methods for carbon capture to both prevent emission of CO_2 in situations where burning of fossil fuels cannot be avoided and also to reduce the current high levels of CO_2 in the atmosphere. The latter will not be easy. Tree-planting will help but more direct methods are also needed. Although there are well-known chemical reactions that turn CO_2 into solid chemicals (such as calcium carbonate), scaling them up to a point at which they can make significant inroads into the amount of atmospheric CO_2 is a challenge. Nevertheless, it is a challenge that must be met.

8.5 Concluding remarks.

We live on a beautiful planet. There is a dynamic equilibrium between the biosphere and the physical elements of our environment, the geosphere and the atmosphere. There is an intricate balance of nature which is apparent at a variety of scales as we saw in section 8.2. We see this as an expression of the creative wisdom of God: He has indeed "made everything beautiful in its time"[31]. Humans have a place within this balanced system as part of the biosphere. However, they also have a distinctness from it. That is partly because humans have intellectual and technical abilities which enable them to affect the rest of the world in ways in which no other animal comes close. At the same time, they can at least partly isolate themselves from the rest of the biosphere. But there is another dimension: God has made us spiritual beings, able to respond to him; to paraphrase Ecclesiastes, Chapter 3, verse 11, He has put eternity in our hearts. Both these features give us immense responsibility in caring for God's world and for our fellow-humans as we act as God's representatives and exercise stewardship of the Earth's resources.

However, it is clear from sections 8.4.1 and 8.4.2 that all is not well with the way that humans have treated the Earth. We have not treated it with care and this has led to disruptions in the balance of nature, some local, some more widespread. Sadly, it is often the poorer citizens of the world who are negatively affected by the way that the Earth's resources have been spoiled and/or over-exploited. And now, by reason of its overall global effects, climate change is currently the worst of the whole range of effects of human activity. If climate change is unchecked, the whole balance of nature will be re-set as the overall temperature of the planet increases. Much of the Earth then will not be habitable by humans and there will be significantly less land on which terrestrial animals and plants may live. Although well outside the lifespan of our readers, a period of 5,000 years has been predicted for the total melting of all the polar ice. This is only 2.0 to 2.5% of the time that humans have been present. During this history of humans on the Earth, there have been two glacial periods (ice ages) and we are currently in an interglacial period. This is part of a much longer cycle of alternating glacial and inter-glacial periods, going back about 34 million years which was the last time that the planet was ice-free. The prediction of ice-free poles in only 5,000 years really does bring home the seriousness of the situation. This planet may then still be beautiful but it would not be as we know it today. With the positive attitude of thankfulness for what we have and a desire to serve God and our neighbour, let each one of us decide how we should respond.

Chapter 8 endnotes:

[1] Quotation widely attributed to David Attenborough. See, for example, https://www.youtube.com/watch?v=sjcpeHBFXGc.

[2] Quotation (slightly edited for clarity) is taken from People and Nature, Blackwell, 2006. Emilio Moran is the John A. Hannah Distinguished Professor of Global Change Science, Michigan State University, USA.

[3] The Holy Bible (NIV): Luke's Gospel, Chapter 12, verse 27.

[4] From Charles Kingsley: His Letters and Memories of his Life, edited by Frances Eliza Kingsley (his wife), 1877. Published by Cambridge University Press, 2011.

[5] J. E. Lovelock, Gaia as seen through the atmosphere, Atmospheric Environment (1972), Vol. 6, pp. 579-580. Gaia was actually the name in Greek mythology given to the Earth goddess. Lovelock claims somewhat insouciantly that his use of the term has no religious or mythological connotation. Nevertheless, it has been seized on enthusiastically by adherents of New Age philosophy and of nature-based religions. Some Christians have been unwilling to use the term but nevertheless it embodies a scientific concept for which there is growing evidential support.

[6] T. Lenton and A. Watson, Revolutions That Made the Earth, Oxford University Press, 2011.

[7] M. Staley, Darwinian selection leads to Gaia, Journal of Theoretical Biology (2002), Vol. 218, pp. 35-46.

[8] One of the current objectives in research on crop genetic modification is to see whether it is possible to build symbiotic relationships between N-fixing bacteria and cereal plants such as maize and wheat.

[9] See also https://scienceandbelief.org/2015/04/09/the-cooperation-of-living-things/.

[10] M.J. Hodson and J.A. Bryant, Functional Biology of Plants, Wiley-Blackwell, 2012.

[11] Robert Macfarlane, Underland, Penguin/Random House, London, 2019.

[12] See https://www.sciencephoto.com/media/659864/view.

[13] Aldo Leopold, A Sand County Almanac: and sketches here and there, Oxford University Press, 1949.

[14] Several different authors have been credited with inventing the term. Its informal use dates back at least as far as the mid-1970s but in this century it has been more widely used by environmental scientists and geologists. At the time of writing there has been a proposal that Anthropocene should be formally added to the 'top' of the geological time-scale, above the Holocene.

[15] J.A. Bryant and L.B. la Velle, Introduction to Bioethics (2nd edition), Wiley-Blackwell, 2018.
[16] A.C. Armstrong, Here for our Children's Children?, Imprint Academic, 2009.
[17] Christopher C.B. Southgate, Introduction to Environmental Ethics. A chapter in: Bioethics for Scientists (editors J.A. Bryant, L.B. la Velle, and J. Searle), Wiley, 2002, pp. 39-55.
[18] See for example: https://tinyurl.com/Price-of-Birdsong.
[19] Lynn White, The historical roots of our ecological crisis, Science (1967), Vol. 155, pp. 1203 - 1207.
[20] The Holy Bible (NIV): Psalm 24, verse 1.
[21] Rachel Carson, Silent Spring, Houghton Mifflin, 1962.
[22] J.O. Kaplan, J.M. Krumhardt and N. Zimmerman, The prehistoric and preindustrial deforestation of Europe, Quaternary Science Reviews (2009), Vol. 28, pp. 3016 - 3034.
[23] See Spencer Weart's website: The Discovery of Global Warming - https://history.aip.org/climate/index.htm.
[24] Guy Callendar, The Artificial Production of Carbon Dioxide and its Influence on Temperature, Quarterly Journal of the Royal Meteorological Society (1938), Vol. 64, pp. 223-240.
[25] Eric Rignot et al., Four decades of Antarctica Ice Sheet mass balance from 1979 to 2017, Proc. Natl. Acad. of Sciences of the USA (2019), Vol. 116, pp. 1095-1103.
[26] Joseph Romm, Climate Change – what everyone needs to know (2nd Edition), Oxford University Press, 2018.
[27] William J Ripple and Christopher Wolf et al., BioScience, Online Journal of the American Institute of Biological Sciences, November 2019, https://doi.org/10.1093/biosci/biz088.
[28] Ian Christie, Can religion steer the world towards a greener future?, Green Futures magazine, September 2011.
[29] As discussed for example in Biofuels and Bioenergy (Editors John Love and John Bryant, Wiley, 2017); see also end-note [13].
[30] For those of us who make an annual tax return, that can be a good time to also make an assessment of the year's carbon footprint. We suggest the use of a carbon offsetting organisation. One such is a Christian organisation, Climate Stewards, (www.climatestewards.org) whose mitigation activities include but go beyond community forestry.
[31] The Holy Bible (NIV): Ecclesiastes, Chapter 3, verse 11.

9 Epilogue.

"The more I study nature, the more I stand amazed at the work of the Creator. Science brings [people] nearer to God." Louis Pasteur

"For the Christian theologian, the facts of nature are the acts of God."
Aubrey Moore[1]

John and Graham write ...

9.1 Introduction.

The title of the book *From the Big Bang to Biology* ... intentionally covers a wide range of sciences. As Christian believers, we see the Universe – including of course our own home planet – as God's creation and science as God's revelation in that creation. Consequently, what current science tells us about the world speaks of just how awesome is our creator God. This in a nutshell is our philosophy of how it all fits together. It has been our intention to explore this viewpoint to see how it holds up in light of the evidence we see around us.

A further motivation for Graham was to put his testimony, his journey to faith, on record. As he explores in Chapter 4, his story was inextricably linked to the issues of the relationship between science and faith. He has attempted to weave this personal thread through some of the physics, which hopefully provided some relief to readers who do not share his degree of enthusiasm for the subject itself.

9.2 Science reveals God's creation.

At the beginning of this book, we made the claim that the idea of a conflict between science and religious belief is totally erroneous. We talked about what science actually does and what it does not – or cannot – do. As is evident from what we have written in previous chapters, science is very good at doing what it is supposed to do, namely telling us how the Universe, at all levels, works (we also noted that there are some genuinely scientific questions that science finds itself unable to answer). Much of that we find awesome. Each of us has our own favourite awe-inspiring facts, but here is one that we share. It is not only amazing but it has also inspired a well-known musician to write a song about it: humanity is linked to the stars (Joni Mitchell: 'We are stardust, we are golden, we are billion-year-old carbon …'). In a very real sense, we are stardust because the only places in which the element carbon (on which life is based) can be made are stars. We cannot understand our origins without this cosmic context. That is awesome.

We also noted that science actually does more than tell us how the Universe works. It is a side-effect of science that it points us to big questions that lie outside the purview of science itself. Science cannot fully satisfy our search for truth and, as we outlined Chapter 2, it is a delusion to think otherwise. One of those big questions has arisen several times as we have written about the science: is there a mind or a designer behind or involved in the origin and the working of the Universe at all levels? Data from across the range of sciences force us to consider that question. It is part of our search for truth about our existence. This leads us to say, as others have done, that science and religion are not only compatible but are actually embarked on the same quest, albeit using different approaches in that quest. As John Polkinghorne so aptly says "Science and theology have things to say to each other since both are concerned with the search for truth attained through motivated belief".[2]

Epilogue

But is what we have said about science and its limitations enough to fuel that belief? Some of the new atheists, or anti-theists, are fond of saying that scientific knowledge is based on evidence but that religious belief is based on blind faith. On that basis they insist that religious faith is entirely incompatible with science. This conviction is also propagated widely by popular media and is a widespread belief in the UK, as the short story at the beginning of Chapter 1 illustrates. However, looking further at faith it is apparent that it abounds throughout the world. Atheists have faith that God does not exist. Scientists, as we saw in Chapter 2, must have faith that the world [Universe] is governed by the laws of nature. Otherwise scientific method does not work and science cannot develop and progress. Everybody has faith in design engineers and maintenance workers each time they use a car, board an aircraft or use a bridge. Furthermore, that faith is based on evidence and experience. Everyone needs and uses faith, not just religious people.

It is at this point then that we challenge the concept that religious belief involves blind faith. As scientists, we look for evidence and that evidence has led to, or confirmed our faith; we share that standpoint with many eminent scientists who are overt Christians. This includes the physics Nobel laureates Arno Penzias and Abdus Salam, and prominent life scientists such as geneticist Francis Collins, Director of the National Institutes of Health in the USA, and ecologist Sir Ghillean Prance, former Director of the Royal Botanic Gardens at Kew. There are about 1,000 members of Christians in Science (and many more scientist-Christians who are not paid-up members), a UK organization concerned with the relationship between science and Christian faith. Also, in the UK, there is a Society for Ordained Scientists for science practitioners who have trained to become church ministers, either part-time while continuing with science, or full-time. They include John Polkinghorne (mentioned above) who gave up a successful career in quantum physics, David Wilkinson who was an astrophysicist and indeed Lee Rayfield, Bishop of Swindon, who provided our foreword.

It is also widely known that several of the 12 moon-walking

astronauts were Christians. During the first landing mission, Buzz Aldrin took communion prior to the first moon walk; and the last man on the moon, Eugene Cernan, reflected during a quiet moment soon after setting foot of the moon's surface. He described his experience as spiritual and dream-like – "I was witness to a small part of the Universe that I happen to believe a Creator up there put together ... to me it was sort of like sitting on God's front porch."[3] So how is it that these men on the moon's surface professed a religious faith? They were after all hard-headed scientists/engineers/test pilots.

So how does this work? We need to go back a few centuries to gain perspective. As scientist-believers down the centuries have stated, there are essentially two books of God's creation – scripture and scientific revelation. As career scientists and Christians, we regard both of these as precious, and consequently we have a personal need to integrate these complementary views of the world. This is an important point. We do not keep our science and our faith in separate boxes; these aspects are part of an integrated whole. Our appreciation of God's creation has been and is still enhanced through science and the more we learn about the world [Universe] and explore the frontiers of science, the more we discover things that are way beyond what we could have imagined. Furthermore, we can gain some understanding of God's nature through what science reveals about His creation.

For the Christian who is also a scientist, there are therefore effectively two entirely complementary worldviews which, as the words of John Polkinghorne quoted earlier indicate, actually enhance each other. So, as scientists and Christians, we must be able to achieve the important task of marrying the two viewpoints without compromising either. In this process of harmonisation, we must attempt to strike a balance between, on the one hand, binding scripture and scientific revelation too closely together, and on the other, ignoring what science tells us about the world and accepting the whole text of the Bible as literal truth. This is expressed very well by John Lennox:

"We Christians need to remind ourselves of the two dangers ... .
Firstly, we must beware of tying our exposition of scripture so close

Epilogue

to science that [scripture] falls if the [science] changes. On the other hand, we would be very unwise to ignore science through obscurantism or fear, and present to the world an image of Christianity that is anti-intellectual. No Christian has anything to fear from true science. Many Christians have made, and continue to make, first rate contributions to science." [4]

This process can be very challenging – we each have personal views about how science and scripture fit together and hopefully this has come out in what we have written. In our experience, there are some Christians who are afraid that scientific knowledge will threaten their faith, and so won't approach it with an open mind (as discussed for example in Chapter 7). Our own view is that God gave us a brain and an inquisitive nature, with which to attempt to uncover the secrets of His Universe, and through this process to learn more about Him, even if we can never completely understand Him[5]. There is something humbling, especially for a scientist, about a God that is essentially incomprehensible.

In summary, we have seen from Chapter 2 that many pioneering scientists were Christians with faith in a Creator God who fashioned an ordered world [Universe]. That is, one in which creation was governed by rules (the laws of nature). This was the firm foundation upon which the pioneering scientists built a scientific worldview, to attempt to "think God's thoughts after Him" (Kepler). The discoverer of genes was a Christian monk, Gregor Mendel, while the first proposer of what became the Big Bang theory was a professor of physics who was also an ordained priest, Georges Lemaître. Christian faith was a powerful and natural philosophical framework within which to nurture the development of science. And, coming right up to modern times, even Stephen Hawking said that the development of a 'Theory of Everything' would enable us "to know the mind of God". It was almost as if he was hoping that science would help him answer life's bigger questions. But, as we have noted before, although science reminds us of these questions, it cannot answer them. So why do we – John and Graham – believe?

9.3 Why believe?

Evidence for design
We have written several times throughout this book about the evidence for design in the structure and functioning of the Universe; the Universe appears to be imbued with purposeful design and this becomes ever more apparent as science progresses – revealing that the cosmos is an ordered system governed by laws. For example, who would have thought before 1915 that science would reveal that the Universe came into being in a moment of creation about 14 billion years ago? Or indeed that the information specifying life itself is encoded on large molecules using an elegant quaternary (0123, or actually ATGC) genetic language? Why the Universe has the appearance of purposeful design remains unresolved, unless, of course there is a designer.

Further, even if you are not a scientist, hopefully you are now aware that the physical laws of nature that we have discovered are usually expressed in terms of the mathematical laws of science (see section 2.4). Einstein found it miraculous that we can understand the Universe in this way, given that mathematics is purely a product of the human mind – what does maths have to do with what goes on outside our head – out in the real world? However, this observation of the intelligibility of the Universe rests well within a theistic framework. If we are God's creation and we bear His image, then we too should expect to share in His creativity. We should expect God to appeal to our rational faculties and for there to be some connection between the workings of His mind and ours.

These aspects of the material world were very much part of Graham's journey to faith, although, as he describes in Chapter 4 there had to be more than that. John on the other hand learned about these aspects of science some time after deciding to follow Jesus. For him, the start of the journey was imitation of the faith of his parents but that was followed up later by satisfying himself of the reliability of the Biblical accounts of the life, death and resurrection of Jesus, i.e., that Jesus is God and that He is now

Epilogue

present with us through the Holy Spirit. These facets of our faith became real to Graham in quite a dramatic way during an Alpha course (Chapter 4). Graham says:

> "The very surprising and, at the time, quite alarming encounter with God on the Alpha Course in November 2001 was the first tremor which heralded the revelation that there was more to the world than the bits described by the physicists. The shockwaves that radiated from this tremor were to change my life in many significant ways subsequently. I have no idea why God chose this instant in my life to reveal Himself, or why He decided to do it at all."

We thus came to faith at very different stages of our scientific careers. In contrast to Graham, John's development as a scientist was from the start interlocked with his development as a Christian. In his own words:

> "I never saw a conflict between science and faith, nor did I ever see evolution as problematic. I knew in my teens that I wanted to be a scientist and was especially encouraged when the assistant minister of the church that our family attended said that we needed more Christians to go into science. And as I progressed in my science career, so these aspects of science which are consistent with the Universe being designed became more apparent. Indeed, even when writing Chapter 5, in describing the mechanisms involved in the actions of genes, a topic on which I worked throughout my career, I became even more amazed at the wonder and beauty of those mechanisms."

It is obvious that the appearance of design described above is totally compatible with and perhaps points to the idea of a creator God but of course it does not itself provide direct evidence for the existence of God. So here is a question: if the limitations of science plus the appearance of design were all we had, would that be enough to lead anyone to a faith in God? Graham testifies that they can be a spur to start a journey towards faith, but there needs to be more than that. And indeed there is.

Spiritual experiences

We both, alongside many other Christians, experience phenomena that defy a purely materialistic explanation. These include persistent inner voices that direct us towards particular courses of action. We could dismiss these episodes as just our brains playing tricks, except that many of us have found that taking the action indicated by the inner voice turned out to be very important. John has friends whose obedience to an inner voice urging actions that seemed irrational, led in one case to someone being helped and supported through a state of despair and in another, to the prevention of suicide (the person saved from suicide was completely unknown to the person who heard the inner voice). For John, one example of several led to his very early diagnosis of a skin cancer (melanoma), so early in fact that it had had no chance to spread and only required minimal treatment. In another example, a friend who in her late teens rejected Christianity, had the experience in her early 30's of God speaking to her. This led her on a journey to faith and she has gone on to be a nationally influential 'Christian voice'.

Similarly, some people have experienced visual phenomena, such as visions of Jesus. Again, it would be all too easy to dismiss these as 'brain stuff', as Richard Dawkins would say. Someone immersed in the Christian faith ('indoctrinated', as new atheists say) might experience a vision as a symptom of brain disturbance or even something like a migraine. However, further examination suggests that we cannot explain such phenomena so easily. For example, John once talked with a sales engineer who worked for a company that made complex equipment for molecular biology, who was not a Christian – indeed he thought religion was a comforting 'fairy tale for women and children' – until he had a vision of Jesus sitting in his car while he drove to an appointment. After several weeks of discussion and questioning with the minister of the church attended by his wife and children, he came to faith. It is a beautiful story which he willingly shares with anyone who comments on the fish badge (known as an 'ichthus' – Greek for fish – a stylised image used as a symbol of Christianity) that he wears on his jacket[6]. Another example comes from David Hay's book *Religious Experiences Today*[7] – a person in hospital was in a state of real and deep panic about a forthcoming treatment when 'Jesus stood by my ordinary hospital bed. It seemed quite natural. He was calm and serene and his whole presence filled me. His calmness and sereneness had a tremendous sense of power and love.'

A good friend, Jack (not his real name) recounts another very personal experience of an encounter with God which merits us presenting it in detail. He was a medical consultant who in the later stages of his career was ordained as a priest. He emphasises that his medical practice was very evidence-based and he took the same approach to his Christian faith which, in Jack's own words "rarely had much emotional content and certainly I had never had the sort of deep experience of God which some Christians have and which have been recorded by believers over the centuries. I am just not that sort of person." However, a major crisis occurred in his ministry which left him spiritually and emotionally deeply hurt, ready to give up, with his "faith dwindled ... to a barely glowing ember". But, while in literally a desert place, high on an African mountainside, Jack heard God speak to him: "to my utter astonishment, I heard a voice, deep within me, 'You do not want to leave too, do you?' ". Jack recognised instantly that it was a verse from John's Gospel[8]. Jesus had been deserted by large numbers of erstwhile followers and he posed that question to his disciples. Peter replied on behalf of all of them "Lord, to whom shall we go? You have the words of eternal life." [9]As Jack puts it: "Jesus was asking me the same question he had asked his disciples 2000 years before. So I replied as Peter had done ... . After some time pondering what had happened ... the embers of faith began to glow brightly, becoming a gentle but inextinguishable flame."

We could give many more examples but instead, in scientific style will pose questions: are these events 'epiphenomena' related to brain activity which one day will be understood in purely physical terms or do they indicate another dimension of our existence beyond the physical? And how do they relate to those feelings (which we have both experienced) that we are in the presence of something greater than ourselves, experiences of the numinous? Graham has described a particularly vivid experience of this on his journey to faith[10], while our friend Jack had a different but equally vivid experience during a spiritual crisis.

However, as we saw in Chapter 6, even people without any inkling of religious faith have such experiences (see also books by Hay[7] and astrophysicist and priest Rodney Holder[11]). Indeed, if we take these three types of phenomena together (inner voice, visions and experiences of the numinous), surveys undertaken in the later years of the 20th century indicate that about half the UK population has had such an experience at least once in their life-time.[7,11] Furthermore, very similar events are described in the Bible.

Healing
Are we seeing what our friend John Samways would call God's Fingerprints?[12] If they are indications of the presence of God, how else might that presence be revealed? Here are three examples. First, the girlfriend of a former colleague of John's had an untreatable brain tumour. The colleague had a dormant Christian faith and it was suggested to him that his girlfriend should be prayed for. She agreed and during the prayer time, with those praying also laying hands on her head, she had an experience which she described as what she imagined it was like to be struck by lightning. From that time on the tumour started to shrink away. It was a miraculous healing. Further, the event re-awakened the colleague's faith and he became a much more overt Christian in his professional life and work. In our second example, a very senior scientist in a position of responsibility in a major organisation was asked, in a panel discussion, whether he had ever experienced anything miraculous. His reply was interesting: yes, in his younger days he had experienced a healing miracle, "much against his will" as he put it. After a severe leg injury which was likely to permanently affect his mobility, a friend offered to pray for healing. Although our scientist was a Christian he expected nothing to happen but as he was prayed for, the injured leg warmed up and full mobility was restored.

Similarly, some years ago, Graham's wife Marion was experiencing some issues with mobility, and was subsequently diagnosed with arthritis in her hips. Clearly hip replacement surgery would be necessary, and in the interim life was getting more and more difficult, with increasing pain and with issues

Epilogue

concerning her ability to do things like climbing stairs. However, after receiving healing prayer in her own church family, over time things improved. Ultimately, she completely regained her mobility and over the many years since, Graham and Marion have enjoyed mountain walking holidays together. Clearly, she has had no need of surgery, which is something that can be confirmed by her doctor.

Graham too is grateful to have received healing through prayer. He suffered a depressive illness in the winter months called seasonal affective disorder, brought on by a deficit of light due to the shortening of daylight hours. This went on for many years, and as such he could not imagine life without it – it had become part of him. Rather than using drugs, fortunately he was able to reduce its severity using light therapy each day. This was provided by a 'light box' which produced a source of very bright daylight spectrum light. One day a close friend felt she was being prompted to take him to a local church where they offered healing prayer sessions each week. After receiving prayer, the depression lifted and ultimately Graham's light box was no longer required, and was retired to the attic.

For us – Graham and John – all these events are particularly powerful pointers to the existence of supernatural healing which in turn points us towards God. Added to this, many branches of the Christian church are involved in healing ministries of various types, including healing services, activities such as Healing on the Streets, regular prayer for healing and, as in the cases above, recognising that some people are especially gifted as healers. Further, both of us, with our wives, Marje and Marion, are involved in prayer ministry at our respective churches and at Lee Abbey, Devon. In both situations it is appropriate to pray for healing which may be spiritual, emotional or physical. We will return to the topic of healing in a little while. Meanwhile, it is here that we should formally 'introduce' the Holy Spirit whom we have mentioned from time to time throughout the text.

The Holy Spirit

It is our conviction that the phenomena discussed above indicate that God is in the world, fulfilling the words of Jesus that He would be present in the form of the Holy Spirit. The Holy Spirit of God, in Christian theology the third member of the Trinity, is God's interface with the physical world. He was sent by God to the members of the early Christian church as a helper and counsellor after the resurrection and ascension of Jesus. The coming of the Holy Spirit in a new way occurred at the Jewish festival of Pentecost and was marked by supernatural events, including the auto-translation of the apostles' Aramaic speech into languages understood by people from other countries (Acts, Chapter 2). This type of action of the Holy Spirit still happens today. A close friend of John told of an occasion in an eastern European country where he was explaining the Christian faith, speaking in English. His listener was astounded to hear the words in his own language. Similarly, a very 'contained' Scottish minister told John about his son, who was working in an isolated region of Uganda and woke up one morning to find that he could speak the local tribal language. "Do you not think that was remarkable?" asked the minister. John did indeed think so and added that it showed that the Holy Spirit was active in the world today. Further, in addition to this type of linguistic gift, many Christians experience the gift of tongues in which they are enabled to pray and worship in what, for want of a better phrase, we describe as a special spiritual language.

But whether or not a person speaks in tongues, it is true for all Christians that when they decide to follow Jesus, the Holy Spirit enters their life and starts to change them. For some, those changes may be subtle but for others, for example if they have previously been involved in crime, the changes may be quite dramatic. In John's church it has been a privilege to see ex-offenders change and to exhibit the 'fruit of the Spirit' (Galatians, Chapter 5, verses 22, 23). Even for those who have led a more conventional life, there may be clear changes of attitude and motivation.

For Graham, this aspect of encountering the Holy Spirit was very much part of his starting to follow Jesus. He says:

Epilogue

"...before my coming to faith I had no idea who or what the Holy Spirit was, and furthermore He was not a part of my experience or even vocabulary. However, in retrospect I now believe that the new insights into the physical laws that occurred to me by the pool in Guernsey all those years ago were orchestrated by Him".

The Spirit had already started His transforming work in Graham and this book is one of the products of that transformation.

In New Testament times, the early church was described as turning the world up-side down as Christians challenged the conventional views of success and power. In the Roman Empire, Christians were thought of as subversive and at times their faith was regarded as criminal (although later, Emperor Constantine became a Christian and made Christianity the official religion). Their attitudes to other people were driven by the Holy Spirit and are neatly summed up by the words of Emperor Julian: "These impious Galileans are very strange; not only do they care for their own poor, they care for ours too" ('impious' because they would not worship Roman gods). Christians still have this role today; they run foodbanks and debt-counselling services, they work in prisons, they work with ex-offenders and the homeless and with refugees. They still challenge the conventional values of success and power. Like the early Christians in Rome, we are driven by the Holy Spirit.

At this point let's return to the topic of healing. We are not in any way demeaning the work of the medical profession but it is our experience that, through the work of the Holy Spirit, some people experience a direct healing which in some cases was not possible medically. When we pray for people to be healed, we are in effect opening up the situation to God's Holy Spirit. However, we need to emphasise that God regards healing in many ways. When we think of healing, we usually think in terms of physical healing but it is often the case that it is emotional and/or spiritual healing that is required. Further, we have to accept that sometimes prayers for physical healing apparently fail. We say 'apparently' because our prayers may have effects other than physical healing. Graham and a prayer partner prayed some years ago for a dear friend who had cancer – essentially, a melanoma that had spread through his body. Despite our weekly prayer sessions, he did not recover, and it was heart-breaking. Clearly, our prayer for physical healing had not been answered, but our prayers for peace, and relief from anxiety and pain manifestly had been. It is only God who has the big picture; for us mortals, this is a very hard lesson to learn and we will never understand why God chooses to heal some people physically and not others. However, the point is that we have seen miracles today – as scientists we have seen the evidence with our own eyes and evaluated that evidence in our own minds. These things are part of our reality: we cannot ignore or deny them.

This brings us back to our individual lives. Both of us continue to experience from time to time those encounters with the numinous that may occur during prayer but can also come out of the blue. John has such experiences sometimes when he is out in wild places, but not exclusively – once he felt the intense presence of God on a rather mundane flight from Manchester to Exeter. The details differ between us – for John, there is often an intensification and whitening of the ambient light accompanied by the feeling of powerful serenity (completely different from the visual effects that he gets in migraines) – but the key thing is the experience of something/someone other than ourselves at a different level of existence. Graham frequently is able to tangibly sense the presence of the Spirit which has proved helpful in prayer ministry and pastoral work and through which he can bless others. Similarly, John often receives vivid insights and/or pictures that help other people both in prayer ministry and in more general situations. So, although God is unseen, His power, love, healing and direction can be made apparent through the agency of His Holy Spirit!

9.4 Conclusion.

In this book, we have been motivated to share how we view a satisfying synthesis between science and faith. We are, of course, not the first to attempt to do this, as witnessed by the numerous texts we have referenced throughout. We hope that what we have said reveals the outlines of a fulfilling harmony between these two ways of looking at the world. Also, although we have shared a view that we find rewarding, we are aware that it is a view that you may not share. However, if you have got this far in the text, then you have given it a fair hearing. Having discussed our view of the synthesis of science and faith, we must leave the process with each of you of integrating (or otherwise) what we have said with your own beliefs. If we find disagreement, hopefully we can still sit and eat together – in other words, remain friends and talk it through.

Although this harmonisation is particularly important to us as 'Christians in science', it also needs to be said that the issues we have discussed do not in the least bit affect our salvation, or your salvation, in what Jesus Christ has done for us all on the cross.

The 'science explains everything' creed

This has been a preoccupation in the text – we referred to it as the Science Delusion in Chapter 2 – and is widespread in popular culture. However, science in its current materialistic form provides no explanation of our own personal experiences described above and so we are left with the inevitable conclusion that science gives an incomplete account of reality. In this text, we have proposed a narrative where the themes of science and faith are interwoven. Clearly science can tell us a great deal about the world, but in our experience there is more. To paraphrase Alister McGrath: "[people] end up believing rather a lot of things that lie beyond the scope of scientific method ... the things that really matter to us – not the shallow truths of reason, but the deep existential truths about who we are and why we are here."[13] Recognising the complementarity of science and faith allows a more profound grasp of the things that really matter in life.

God's revelation in nature

Our experience as career scientists has led us to the insight that science affirms the faith view of the natural world more strongly than the secular/atheistic view that it all happened by blind chance. Science is God's gift to humanity and is simply His revelation in nature. The impression of purposeful design in the world [Universe] is remarkable and is a strong pointer to the hand of a creator. We have both found that having a Christian faith has added a new dimension to our work as scientists. It has allowed a greater sense of awe at the majesty and grandeur of God's creation.

Glimpsing God's character

We can gain some understanding of God's character through what science reveals about His creation. Two thousand years ago the apostle Paul sent a letter to the Christian church in Rome in which he wrote "For since the creation of the world God's invisible qualities – his eternal power and divine nature – have been clearly seen, being understood from what has been made, so that people are without excuse."[14] In other words, we see God's fingerprints all around us – all we need to do is look and there He is. God has placed us in a Universe, the attributes of which speak of His existence, and also something of what He is like. He has given us an intellectual capacity to seek an understanding of His creation, but also a yearning for something beyond the physical world. In the words of Augustine of Hippo around 1,600 years ago: "You have made us for yourself, O Lord, and our hearts are restless until they find their rest in you." The need to fill a God-shaped hole, that many of us feel at some time in our lives, probably accounts for why over 80% of humanity profess some kind of religious faith.

Stewardship of God's creation

In scripture, God assigns the responsibility to look after and take care of this world to humans. However, as we saw in Chapter 8, this aspect of human activity is not going at all well. At this moment in history, humanity has arrived at a crossroads where responsible stewardship of God's creation has become a critical issue, one of survival of all living things on the planet. The deterioration of the environment, and the accompanying extinction of many species, has been driven by many decades of financial vested interest in fossil-fuel based industries. Another way, involving renewable energy sources and clean industrial practices and transportation, is possible but requires radical political and social changes within a short time scale. The challenge is hard but must be met.

At the time of writing, it appears that a new era of space exploration is underway, with current plans to return humans to the moon, and then to venture to Mars. Several of the Apollo era moon-walking astronauts were captivated by the beauty of the blue orb in the sky, our home planet, and that they could lift an arm and cover it with a gloved thumb. If we can summon the technology to once again reach for the moon, then surely our ingenuity and resources can be harnessed to preserve God's Good Earth and all its beautiful diversity of life.

Where is God?

In the title of the book we posed this question. Our experience of life and reality provides, for us, an answer in clear and certain terms. He is here in our lives and in our science; He initiated the Universe and is still actively sustaining it. For us who see God in science, it is almost as if we can use the words of John's Gospel[15] – "we have seen His glory". The God of the genome and of the Universe is the same as the God of the Bible. He can be worshipped in the cathedral and in the laboratory.

Chapter 9 endnotes:

[1] Quoted by Denis Alexander in Rebuilding the Matrix: Science and Faith in the 21st Century, Lion Hudson, 2001, p. 177.
[2] John Polkinghorne, Faraday paper No.1, The Science and Religion Debate – an Introduction, Faraday Institute for Science and Religion, Cambridge University, 2007.
[3] Last person to walk on the moon dies, Miami Herald Archives, January, 2017, https://www.miamiherald.com/news/state/florida/article222707590.html.
[4] John Lennox, Seven Days that Divide the World – the beginning according to Genesis and Science, Zondervan Books, 2011, p. 86.
[5] The Holy Bible (NIV): Isaiah, Chapter 55, verses 8,9. "For my thoughts are not your thoughts, neither are your ways my ways,"

declares the Lord. "As the heavens are higher than the earth, so are my ways higher than your ways and my thoughts than your thoughts. ..."

[6] Very recent and very dramatic examples which have received much attention in the media are the visions that the then atheist, now Christian, Nadim Ednan-Laperouse experienced during and after the death of his daughter Natasha:
https://www.bbc.co.uk/programmes/articles/1c575Zkjg7RDmy3Hgd0l KrP/a-bright-yellow-light ;
https://www.bbc.co.uk/programmes/m000cmsf.

[7] David Hay, Religious Experience Today: Studying the Facts, Mowbray, 1990.

[8] The Holy Bible (NIV): John's Gospel, Chapter 6, verse 67.

[9] The Holy Bible (NIV): John's Gospel, Chapter 6, verse 68.

[10] An American biochemist, Sy Garte who, like Graham, came to faith later in life, describes a journey which also involved a vivid spiritual experience: https://www.christianitytoday.com/ct/2020/march/sy-garte-science-answers-inconvenient-questions.html.

[11] Rodney Holder, Nothing but Atoms and Molecules?, Monarch, 1993.

[12] John Samways, God's Fingerprints: the evidence is everywhere, Matador, 2015.

[13] Alister McGrath, Inventing the Universe: why we can't stop talking about science, faith and God, Hodder & Stoughton, 2015, p.143.

[14] The Holy Bible (NIV): Romans, Chapter 1, verse 20.

[15] The Holy Bible (NIV): John's Gospel, Chapter 1, verse 14.

Glossary.

Agnosticism/Agnostic: one who would say that knowledge of God's existence cannot be achieved.

Allele: alternative version of a gene, for example a version carrying a mutation.

Amino acid: An organic molecule that carries both a carboxyl (COOH) group and an amino (NH2) group. 20 different amino acids are the building blocks of proteins.

Anthropic: of or relating to humans, or the era of human life.

Anthropocentric: describes an approach to environmental ethics that is mainly focused on humans.

Anti-codon: a sequence of three bases in the adaptor molecule, transfer RNA that recognises, by specific base-pairing, a codon in messenger RNA (see also codon).

Antiparticle: a subatomic particle of matter having the same mass as a specific particle, but an opposite electric charge. Their existence was confirmed in 1932.

Apologist: one who speaks or writes in defense of someone or something.

Archaea: bacteria-like organisms that split from the bacterial lineage early in the evolution of life on Earth.

ATP/Adenosine triphosphate: the main energy-carrying molecule in living cells.

ATP synthase: the enzyme that carries out the last step in the synthesis of the cell's energy-carrying molecule, ATP. See also chemi-osmotic coupling.

Billion: the definition of billion throughout is taken as one thousand million – that is, 1,000,000,000.

Biocentric: describes an approach to environmental ethics that is mainly focused on the biosphere.

Biosphere: the zone on the surface of the Earth in which living organisms occur; often used more loosely as a collective noun for all living organisms on the Earth.

Black hole: an exotic celestial object that results when the core of a massive star undergoes gravitational collapse at the end of its life. If the core is massive enough, the force of gravity can overcome all other forces and crush the stellar matter into tiny region of space-time called a singularity. The resulting black hole has a gravity field so intense that not even light can escape – hence the name.

Bonobo: one of the two species in the Pan (chimpanzee) genus; the other is the common chimpanzee.

Carbon cycle: biogeochemical cycle in which carbon in various forms is circulated through the geosphere-biosphere-atmosphere complex.

Cetacean: a member of the group of aquatic (mainly marine) mammals comprising whales, dolphins and porpoises.

Chemi-osmotic coupling: the mechanism that uses the energy of a positive electrical gradient to make the cell's energy-carrying molecule, ATP.

Chromosome: structures within cells in which the genes are carried; each contains one DNA molecule and many genes are arranged along the length of each DNA molecule. Humans have 46 chromosomes – two sets of 23.

Codon: a sequence of three bases in messenger RNA that specifies a particular amino acid (also see anti-codon).

Cytoplasm: this is the part of the cell contained within the cell's bounding membrane except for the nucleus. Its consistency is of a viscous fluid or even jelly-like. Organelles and particles such as mitochondria, chloroplasts, ribosomes and the cell's endomembrane system are located in the cytoplasm.

Deep ecology: a philosophical movement that ascribes equal moral value to all living things; humans are not regarded as having special moral rights but are held to be equal with all other living things. In more extreme forms of deep ecology, Homo sapiens is regarded as a 'nuisance' species with a population that greatly exceeds the capacity of the Earth to sustain it.

Deism: belief in the existence of a supreme being, specifically of a creator, who does not subsequently intervene in the Universe.

Diploid: containing two sets of chromosomes; in most multicellular organisms all cells except the sex cells (gametes) are diploid.

Ecocentrism: describes an approach to environmental ethics that is focussed on the whole geosphere-biosphere-atmosphere complex.

Empirical: based on, or verifiable by observation, experiment or experience, rather than theory or pure logic.

Glossary

Endo-symbiont: an organism that lives inside the cells (or cell) of another organism in a mutually beneficial manner.

Enlightenment: a mainly 18th-century European philosophical movement characterized by a reliance on reason and experience rather than dogma and tradition, with an emphasis on humanitarian political goals and social progress.

Enzyme: a protein that carries out a biochemical reaction. A large majority of different proteins are enzymes.

Eukaryotic: eukaryotic cells are cells with true compartmentation, including a nucleus in which the genes are located. All organisms except for bacteria and archaea consist of eukaryotic cells and are thus known as eukaryotes.

Exon: the parts of the gene, spaced out by the introns (see below) that actually code for proteins.

Gaia: the hypothesis that the geosphere-biosphere-atmosphere form a self-balancing complex giving a dynamic equilibrium. When the balance is badly upset by a major change of conditions, the equilibrium is reset. The term comes from the name of the mother-Earth goddess in Greek mythology.

Gene: a defined part of a DNA molecule with a specific coding function, for example, to direct the synthesis of a protein.

Genome: the total of all the genes and the non-coding DNA in an individual or a species. In relation to 'sequencing', the genome of a species is the consensus sequence of several or many individuals.

Genotype: the trait or traits encoded in a gene or genes (see also phenotype).

God of the Gaps: this refers to a belief that 'God did it' when there is a lack of scientific understanding of a physical phenomenon. In other words, God is used to fill the gaps in our scientific knowledge. Of course, as science progresses God is squeezed out of the gaps.

Haploid: containing one set of chromosomes; in most multicellular organisms, this is the state of the sex cells (gametes) that are produced by meiosis (see also meiosis).

Heliocentrism: the theory that places the sun at the centre of the Solar System with the planets revolving round it.

Higgs Boson: a subatomic particle predicted theoretically by Peter Higgs in 1964, and subsequently discovered at the Large

Hadron Collider in 2012. The Higgs boson's role is to attribute mass to other species of particles, and its discovery strengthens confidence in the so-called standard model of particle physics.

Hominin: a member of a biological group consisting of extant and extinct humans and their immediate closely related ancestors.

Intron: a tract of DNA within a gene that interrupts the coding sequence; they are edited (spliced) out from messenger RNA to give the uninterrupted coding sequence.

Isotope: an isotope of a particular element has the same number of protons, but a different number of neutrons as the element. For example, hydrogen has one proton, and no neutrons in the nucleus. Isotopes of hydrogen include deuterium (one proton and one neutron) and tritium (one proton and 2 neutrons).

Joule (J): a unit of energy, named after British physicist James Prescott Joule (1818-1889). An informal definition of 10 Joules is roughly the amount of energy expended in raising a one kilogram mass through a height of one metre.

Logical positivism: a systematic reduction of all human knowledge to logical or scientific foundations.

Meiosis: a type of cell division in which the number of chromosomes is halved; it is made necessary by the fusion of two cells in sexual reproduction.

Messenger RNA: genes are copied into messenger RNA and it is the messenger RNA that is actually decoded to make proteins.

Microbiome: the overall genetic diversity of a community of micro-organisms, especially those that live in the human body.

Microbiota: a community of micro-organisms, especially that which lives in the human body.

Mitosis: the process of 'normal' cell division in which each 'daughter' cell receives a full complement of chromosomes.

Mutation: a change in a gene.

Mycorrhizae: literally 'fungus-roots'; structures that are formed in intimate symbiotic relationships between fungi and plant roots.

Neutron star: an exotic celestial object that results when the core of a massive star undergoes gravitational collapse at the end of its life. If the core is massive enough – between 1.3 and 2.5 times the mass of the Sun – then gravity is strong enough to scrunch the protons and electrons together to form a 'star' composed of neutrons. A sphere around 20 km in diameter results with a density of more than a billion tonnes per cubic centimetre.

Nitrogen cycle: biogeochemical cycle that circulates various forms of nitrogen around the biosphere and atmosphere.

Nitrogen-fixing bacteria: bacteria that are able to 'pull' nitrogen out of the atmosphere into chemical linkage with carbon-based molecules.

Numinous: having a strong religious or spiritual quality, indicating or suggesting the presence of a divinity.

Paradigm: a well-established framework for viewing/understanding a particular aspect of reality (Note – definitions vary according to the context in which the word is used. This definition is the one that best fits the use of the word in science).

Pantheism: a doctrine which identifies God with the Universe, or regards the Universe as a manifestation of God.

Phenotype: the traits exhibited by an organism, most of which are encoded in the genotype (see also genotype).

Post-modernism: a philosophy, based in sociology and the arts that started in the second half of the 20th century but which can be traced back to the work of Nietzsche. It essentially rejects the possibility of objective truth in any area of human endeavour, including science. Its 'motto' is/was 'all things are relative'. It is clear then that the claims of both science and religious faith are rejected in the 'stronger' versions of post-modernism.

Primary producer: in the context of Chapter 8, the initiators of the overall food chain on which all or nearly all other organisms are dependent. The term refers to photosynthetic organisms which are able to use an external energy source (the Sun) to empower growth and food production.

Primate: a member of a group of advanced mammals that includes monkeys, apes and humans.

Protein: proteins are made of amino acids; they come in many shapes and sizes, according to the number and type of the amino acids of which they are made. There are thousands of different sorts in each cell.

Protists: single-celled eukaryotic organisms that cannot be classified as plants, animals or fungi (see also eukaryotic).

Quantum: a discrete amount of a physical quantity, such as energy or electric charge.

Quantum gravity: the theory that unifies quantum mechanics with Einstein's theory of gravity (the general theory of relativity). This is sometimes referred to as the 'Theory of Everything'.

Quantum mechanics: the theory, developed primarily in the 1920s, that describes the physics of the very small – molecules, atoms and subatomic particles. It overturned the deterministic character of Newton's laws, and introduced the notion that reality at the microscale is probabilistic.

Quark: an elementary particle with a fractional electric charge that 'feels' the strong force. They exist in 6 types (up, down, charm, strange, top and bottom). Protons and neutrons each comprise three quarks.

Quasar (or Quasi-Stellar Object)**:** An extremely distant celestial object which shines so brightly that it eclipses the ancient galaxy that hosts it. These extremely luminous and compact galactic nuclei are probably powered by super-massive black holes, and typically have a star-like appearance – hence the name.

Radioactive decay: the spontaneous breakdown of one type of unstable atomic nucleus into another, accompanied by the emission of harmful radiation.

Ribosome: particles in the cell that hold the messenger RNA so that it can be decoded in order to make proteins.

Scientism: an exaggerated trust in the efficacy of the methods of natural science applied to all areas of investigation (as in, for example, philosophy, the social sciences, and the humanities).

Sentient (or sentient beings)**:** able to experience and respond to sensations and to external stimuli. As used in science, the term implies possession of a complex nervous system – thus the ability of plants to respond to environmental factors is not sentience.

Serendipity: discovery made by accident or chance.

String theory: the theory that proposes that elementary particles are tiny, vibrating loops of 'string', rather than the tradition view that they are point particles. It is a prominent research avenue in the search for a theory of quantum gravity.

Superluminal: exceeding the speed of light.

Synthetic biology: the redesign of existing biological systems for a useful purpose; the design and engineering of biologically based parts, novel designs and systems.

Tectonic plate: the rocky outer layer of the Earth (the crust plus upper mantle) is not continuous but consists of huge 'slabs' of rock that can move in relation to each other; these are the tectonic plates.

Theism: belief in the existence of one God viewed as the creative source of the world and the human race, who transcends but nevertheless intervenes within, or operates within the world.

Theocentric: describes an approach to environmental ethics that is mainly focused on God.

Transfer RNA: the adaptor molecule that recognises a particular codon, binds to and brings the appropriate amino acid to the ribosome.

From the Big Bang to Biology – where is God?

Index.

abiogenesis, 111, 162
A Brief History of Time (book), 37
Adam/ *a-dam/ha·'a·dam*, 170, 171
Adams, Douglas, xii, 75
aerobic, 136, 137, 177, 178
afterglow of Big Bang, 60, 61, 65, 73
Aldrin, Buzz, 208
Alexander, Denis, 140
Alpha course, 100-106, 211
altruism, 153, 156, 157
Amazon rainforest, 189
Amborella trichopoda, 180
amino acid(s), 115-120, 122, 124, 164, 168, 178
Anders, William, 45
Andromeda galaxy, 48, 58
angiosperm, 180
angler fish, 182, 183
animal and plant breeding, 133
Anning, Mary, 126
Antarctic, 166, 194, 195
anthropic principle, 86, 91, 92, 99
Anthropocene, 185
anthropocentric
  approach to environment 186-188
anti-codon, 117
antiparticle, 51, 68
Apollo program, xii, 36, 45, 221
archaea, 116, 121, 125, 136
Arctic, 189, 194, 195
Aristarchus of Samos, 169
asteroid collision, 141
astronauts, xii, 208, 221
Atacama Desert, Chile, 93
atmosphere, 78, 93, 94, 136, 141, 176-180, 185, 187, 190, 192-194, 201

ATP/adenosine triphosphate, 114, 115, 124
ATP synthase, 114, 124
Augustine, 171
Australia
  wildfires, 189, 194
awareness of self, 151, 152, 156, 157

Babylon, 168, 171
Bacon, Francis, 5, 6
Baconian/scientific revolution, 5
bacteria, 115, 116, 121, 122, 124, 125, 133, 136, 137, 140, 164, 176, 179, 181-183
Ball, Andy, 102, 104-105
base-pairing, 113, 117, 119, 120
bases in DNA and RNA, 111-113, 116-120, 129, 130, 168, 178
BBC, 1, 2, 167
beetles, 139, 180, 182
Bell Telephone labs, 61
Bentley Hart, David, 2, 3
Bhopal, 190
Bible, x, xi, 3, 30, 46, 162, 164, 168-172, 175, 188, 208, 214, 221
Big Bang (theory), 3, 9, 29, 37, 43-99, 109, 111, 123, 156, 164,165, 168, 209
  evidence for, 60-62, 65, 73
'big brain gene', 149
Bishop Ussher, 126
biocentric
  approach to environment, 187, 188
biodiversity, 170, 185, 191
  decrease/loss, 189, 190, 192, 197
bioethics, x, xi, 189

bioluminescence, 182,183
biosphere, vi, 176-180, 185, 187, 201, 202
black hole, 27, 32, 37, 48, 99
blue-green/cyanobacteria, 136, 137, 176
Bondi, Hermann, 60
bonobo, 147, 150, 152
Borman, Frank, 45
Boyle, Robert, 6, 17
Brahe, Tycho, 23, 24
Brazil
    wildfires, 189
British Aerospace, xii
Brno, Czechoslovakia, 128
Bryson, Bill, 71

Cain, 171
calculus, 20
Callendar, Guy, 193
Calvin, John, 169, 171
Cambrian, 125
Cambridge, ix, x, 1, 19, 25, 63, 128
Cape Town, University of, 38
carbon, 86, 98-100, 109, 110, 178, 193, 197, 199-201, 206
carbon cycle, 177, 178, 192
carbon dioxide/CO_2, 136, 176-178, 192-195, 197, 199-201
Carboniferous, 125, 193, 194
    forests, 139
Carson, Rachel, 189
CERN, 51
Cernan, Eugene, 208
cetaceans, 152
Chapman, Allan, 2
chemi-osmotic coupling, 114, 124
Chernobyl, 190
chimpanzee, 147, 150, 152
China, 95, 126
chloroplast, 137

Christians in Science, 207
Christie, Ian, 199
chromosome, 111, 137, 138
church-going, decline in, 6-9
climate change, 189, 191, 192, 194-200, 202
climate emergency/crisis, 196-199
coal, 139, 193
codon, 116, 117, 119
co-evolution, 139, 181
Collins, Francis, 9, 207
compassion, 153, 156, 157
conscience, 153, 157
consciousness, 9, 11, 27, 151, 152, 156, 157
Copernicus, Nicolaus, 3, 4, 17, 169
Cornell University, 67
cosmic fine-tuning, 91-92
    examples of, 95-100
cosmic microwave background radiation/CMB, 50, 60-63, 65, 73, 92
counter-culture, 1960s, 7
Cox, Brian, 8
creationism, creationist, 162-169, 171
Cretaceous, 125
    extinction event, 139, 140
    forests, 139
    reptiles, 139
Crick, Francis, 112
crop(s), 133, 139, 180, 186, 187, 192
Cryosat 2 satellite, 195
cytoplasm, 116

dark energy, 44, 66, 73, 75, 76, 94
dark matter, 44, 66, 67, 74-76, 94
Darwin, Charles, 6, 84, 111, 126-129, 134, 163, 165
Darwin, Erasmus, 127

Index

Darwin's Finches, 127, 128, 134-135
Davies, Paul, 34, 91, 110, 111, 117, 121-123
Dawkins, Richard, 9, 16, 17, 153, 212
deep ecologists, 187
deforestation, 191, 192
Denisova cave, Siberia, 147, 148
Denisovans, 147-150
De revolutionibus orbium coelestium (book), 4
Descartes, René, 17
design, impression of, 82, 87, 91, 100, 117, 123, 156, 206, 210, 211, 220
Devonian, 125
diploid, 138
DNA, 129, 138, 153, 178
   a very clever molecule, 111
   and genetic code, 115-117, 168
   and origin of life, 120-122
   double helical structure, 26, 112
   from fossils, 148
   genes made of, vi, 111
   information carrier, 111-113, 115-119, 124, 129
   replication, 11, 112, 113
   John's research focus, x
dogs, 133, 152
dolphins, 152
Doppler effect, 57
double helix, vi, 10, 112, 113, 138
Dyson, Freeman, 91

early-Modern period, 6
Earth, vi, xii, 3, 10, 45, 46, 47, 66, 73, 74, 87, 92, 93, 96, 99, 106, 111, 162, 166, 167, 177, 178, 181, 191, 221
   a very special planet, 109-110, 175
   and climate change, 192-194, 198, 202
   and evolution, 176
   and fine-tuning, 82, 84, 85
   and gravity, 20-23, 28, 85
   and heliocentrism, 3
   axis, 110
   in Genesis, 162, 164, 168-172
   life on Earth, 66, 84, 96, 99-141, 156, 162
   orbit, 85, 110
   resources, 190, 202
   stewardship of, 186, 188, 202
East Africa, cradle of humankind, 145, 149
ecocentrism, 187
ecosystems, 139, 180, 181, 185, 187, 196, 198
Ecuador, 127
Eddington, Arthur, 53, 92
Egypt, 10, 172
Einstein, Albert, v, xii, 17, 19, 26, 27, 30-37, 48-59, 66, 70, 72, 75, 83, 84, 96, 162, 210
electric vehicles/EV, 200
electromagnetic force, 28
electron, 33-35, 51, 60, 69, 74, 96
elephants, 152, 153
Ellis, George, 38, 89
empathy, 153, 157
Emperor Constantine, 217
Emperor Julian, 217
empirical methods, 10
endo-symbiont/endo-symbiosis, 137
Enlightenment, 2-6
environmental degradation, 187, 189, 190
enzyme(s), 116, 118-120, 122, 131, 155
Eratosthenes of Cyrene, 10
eukaryote/eukaryotic, 121, 136-138

From the Big Bang to Biology – where is God?

European Southern
  Observatory/ESO, 93, 94
European Space Agency, xiii, 195
evolution, 11, 46, 63, 75, 84, 99,
  117-120, 123, 125-141, 146,
  147, 153, 158, 164, 165, 172,
  177, 181, 193, 211
  and the Bible, x, 161-163,
    166-168
  of Earth, 176, 177
  of life on Earth, 135-141
  of religion, 157
  of Universe, 63-67, 161, 164
Exmoor Dark Sky Reserve, 76
exon, 121
expertise, death of, 8
extinction, 139, 189, 190, 220
  of dinosaurs, 139-141
Extinction Rebellion, 197
Extremely Large Telescope/ELT,
  94

false vacuum, 69-71, 74
Faraday Institute, 157
Faraday, Michael, 17, 28
'feel-good bacteria', 182
fine-tuning, 81-100, 110, 156
fireflies/lightning bugs, 182, 183
flowering plants, 111, 139, 180
  see also angiosperms
fossil, 124, 126, 128, 133-135,
  146-149, 189
fossil fuel, 193, 196, 198, 199,
  201, 220
French Revolution, 5
Friedmann, Alexander, 6, 67, 95
Fukushima, 190
fundamental forces, 20, 22, 27, 65,
  86
fungi, 137-139, 179, 181, 182

Gaia, 176, 180, 194
Galapagos Islands, 127-130, 132

Galileo, 3-5, 17, 46, 169
gamete, 138
gene(s), 116, 120, 121, 129-132,
  134, 135, 149, 153-155, 211
  and evolutionary history, 147
  and genomes, 111
  and lactose tolerance, 131
  and speech, 150
  'big brain', 149
  cystic fibrosis, 9
  definition of, 111
  discovery of, vi, 128, 129, 209
  expression of, 11
  in mammals, 146
  manipulation/modification of,
    x, 115
  monoamine oxidase A, 155
  regulation of, 14, 146
gene-environment-interactions,
  154, 155
general theory of relativity, xii, 26,
  37, 52, 98
Genesis, 126, 186
  creation accounts, vii, 45, 46,
    139, 162, 168-172
genetic code, 84, 111, 115-118,
  129
genetic determinism/essentialism,
  153-155
genetic variation, 129-132, 154
genome, 111, 122, 123, 130, 131,
  134, 135, 137, 146, 147, 154,
  221
genotype, 131, 132
geosphere, 176, 177, 179, 180,
  185, 187 201
giant tortoise, 127, 130
Gingko tree, 134
glacial & interglacial periods, 202
Glastonbury, 1
global cooling, 141
global warming/GW, 176, 192-
  196
glow-worms, 182, 183

Index

glycine, 117-119
God, reference to the word 'God' is numerous, and consequently we have not listed each occurrence
God hypothesis, 86, 89, 90
God of the gaps, x, 39, 123
Gold, Thomas, 60
Goldilocks
   Enigma, 82
   Zone, 110
Goldingay, John, 171
Goodrich, Samuel, 126
Graham, Linda, 139
gram-positive bacteria, 125
gram-negative bacteria, 125
gravitational force, 21-23, 28, 85, 99
gravitational waves, 92
gravity, xii, 19-32, 34, 36-38, 45, 46, 50, 52, 53, 55, 56, 64-68, 70-72, 74, 97-99, 106, 110
   Einstein's, 52-55
   Newton's, 19-25
great apes, 140, 146, 147, 185
great oxidation event, 136
Greene, Brian, 67
greenhouse effect/gas, 136, 192, 193, 197
Greenland, 195
Gribbin, John, 100
Grosseteste, Robert, 3, 17
grouse, 132
Guth, Alan, 67, 69, 96

habitat, 110, 132, 139, 140, 183, 187, 190
   loss of, 187, 189, 190
hadron, 51
Hales, Stephen, 6
Halley, Edmund, 25
Hannam, James, 2

haploid, 138
Hardwicke's Woolly Bat, 184
Hawking, Stephen, 30, 36, 37, 209
Hay, David, 212, 214
healing, 106, 214, 215, 217, 218
Heisenberg, Werner, 33, 34, 68
heliocentric/heliocentrism, 3, 4
helium, 96, 97
Henry VIII, 5
heritability of non-physical traits, 154
Higgs Boson, 51, 68, 95
Higgs field, 68
HMS Beagle, 127
hoatzin, 134
Holder, Rodney, 214
Holy Spirit, 85, 103-105, 211, 214-218
Hominidae, 147
hominins, 140, 146, 147, 149
Homo erectus, 147-149
Homo heidelbergensis, 147-150
Homo neanderthalensis, 147
   see also Neanderthals
Homo sapiens, 145-150
   see also humankind
Hooke, Robert, 24
Hoyle, Fred, 60, 63, 98-100, 109, 123
Hubble, Edwin, 57-59, 92, 93
Hubble-Lemaître Law, 57-59
Hubble Space Telescope/HST, 93
human cells, 114, 181
Human Genome Project, 9
humankind, 9, 46, 146, 161, 162, 168, 170-172, 185, 186, 188
Hume, David, 6

identical twins, 154
image of God, 157, 170, 172, 186, 210

Industrial Revolution, 186, 191, 192
inflation, cosmic, 65, 67, 69-71, 74, 75, 88, 96
inner voice, 212-214
intelligence, 91, 153-156
intelligent design/ID, 123, 162-164, 167
Interstellar (film), 48
Introduction to Bioethics (book), 189
intron, 121
invasion of land by plants, 138, 139
inverse square law, 22, 85
IPCC, 194, 197
irreducible complexity, 163, 164, 167

James Webb Space Telescope /JWST, 93
Jesus (Christ), 10, 102, 106, 158, 173, 175, 210, 212, 213, 216, 219
Joshua tree/*Yucca brevifolia*, 183, 184
journey to faith, 88-90, 100-106, 210, 211, 213, 216
Jurassic, 125
Just Six Numbers (book), 95

Kant, Immanuel, 153
Kepler, Johannes, 6, 17, 23, 24, 53, 169, 209
Kingsley, Charles, 176
Krauss, Lawrence, 68

lactose tolerance, 131
Lane, Nick, 114, 115, 123, 124
Large Hadron Collider/LHC, 51, 95
Last Common Ancestor/LCA, 115

Lavoisier, Antoine, 6
laws of nature, vi, 11, 18, 27-31, 39, 84, 85, 91, 92, 123, 161, 167, 207
laws of science, 28, 29, 37, 87, 210
Lee Abbey, vii, 76, 215
Lemaître, Georges, 9, 57, 58, 67, 95, 209
Lennox, John, 46, 146, 208
Lenton, Tim, 177
Leopold, Aldo, 185
Le Verrier, Urbain, 26
Lewis, C.S., 18
life and energy, 113-115
life and information, 111-113
light year, definition of, 47, 48
Linnaeus, Carl, 6
logical positivism, 15, 16
London Planetarium, xii
Lord Kelvin, 44
Lovell, Jim, 45
Lovelock, James, 176, 180, 194
lungfish, 134
Luther, Martin, 5

macaques, 153
Macfarlane, Robert, 181, 185
magpies, 152
mammals/ Mammalia, 121, 131, 134, 137, 139, 146, 147, 185
diversification of, 140, 141
learning in, 151
Mangan, Lucy, 8
manta rays, 152
Mars, 221
mass and energy, equivalence, 49-51, 95, 96
McGrath, Alister, 14, 219
McLeish, Tom, 3
McVittie, George, 92
meiosis, 138

Index

melanoma, 212, 218
Mendel, Gregor, vi, 128-132, 209
Mercury, 26, 66
methane, 193
microbiome, 182
microbiota, 182
micro-evolution, 133, 164
microfungi, 182
Milky Way galaxy, 48, 58, 71, 76, 167
mind, 27, 38, 151, 152, 156, 157
mind-body duality, 152
miracle, 19, 110, 111, 214, 218
Mitchell, Joni, 206
Mitchell, Peter, 114
mitigation of CO_2 emissions, 201
mitochondria, 114, 137
mitosis, 137
mocking bird, 127, 130
modern humans, 145, 149, 150, 153, 156, 170
   brain, 149-152, 154, 155
   distinctiveness, 150, 151
   evolution of, 146-150
   general characteristics, 146, 147
Molecular Aspects of Gene Expression in Plants (book), 113
molecular phylogeny, 134
monoamine oxidase A (MAOA) gene, 155
moon
   and gravity, 85, 110
   importance of, 110
   in Genesis, 46, 169
Moses, 45, 63
Mount Palomar telescope, 92
Mount Wilson telescope, 57, 92, 93
mudskipper, 134
multiverse, 86-90
mycorrhizae, 181

National Institutes of Health, 9, 207
natural philosophy, 5
natural selection, vi, 84, 115, 125-127, 129, 132, 140, 153, 161, 163, 164, 176, 177
Neanderthals, 148-151
nepenthes rafflesiana, 184
Neptune, 26
neutron, 27, 28, 51, 60, 74, 96
neutron stars, 27, 37
new atheists, 16, 17, 27, 207, 212
Newton, Isaac, 3, 6, 17, 19-27, 33, 36, 49, 50-53, 68, 85
Newton's laws, 21, 33
Nichols, Tom, 8
nitrogen, 93, 178, 179, 192
nitrogen cycle, 178, 179
nitrogen fixation, 179
Nobel Prize/Nobel laureate, 33, 62, 88, 114, 207
Norman Conquest, 191
North Pole, 195
nuclear energy, 199, 200
nuclear fusion, 28, 92, 96, 97, 200
nucleosynthesis, 62, 98
nucleus, atomic, 28, 33, 200
nucleus of cell, 116, 121, 136, 137
numinous, 105, 158, 213, 214, 218

Occam's razor, 89
O'Hair, Madalyn Murray, 45
On Human Nature (book),152
On the Origin of Species by Means of Natural Selection (book), 126, 134, 163, 165
orang-utan, 147, 152
Ordovician, 125, 181
Origen, 171

origin of life, 91, 111, 120, 123-126, 135, 156, 161, 162, 176
see also abiogenesis
over-exploitation, 189, 190
oxygen, 62, 98, 99, 136, 137, 139, 177, 183, 192
ozone/ozone layer, 136, 139

Paine, Thomas, 6
pantheism, 91
Paris Agreement, 197
particle physics, v, 94
Paul, apostle, 220
Pentateuch, 45
Penzias, Arno, 61-63, 207
Permian, 125
phenotype, 131, 132
photobacterium, 183
photosynthesis/photosynthetic, 135-137, 139, 170, 176-178, 181, 193, 201
pitcher plants, 184
planetary motion, 19, 23-25
polar ice, 193, 195, 202
Polkinghorne, John, 26, 39, 87, 99, 206-208
pollination/pollinators, 139, 180, 181, 183, 187
pollution, 189, 190
Pope Urban VIII, 169
post-modernism, 7, 8
Prance, Ghillean, 9, 207
Pre-Cambrian, 124, 125
pre-mRNA, 121
primary producers, 177
primate, 147, 150
primeval atom, 57
Princeton University, 91
Principia (book), 19, 25
promoter, 121
protein, 114-122, 124, 164, 167, 168, 178

unlikelihood of correct synthesis, 121
proton, 28, 51, 60, 74, 96, 114, 123, 124
pyramids, 10

quantum
gravity, 37, 38, 64
mechanics/QM, 33-37, 44
physics, 24, 76, 207
world, 14, 51
quark, 28
Quaternary, 125

radioactive/radioactivity, 28, 110, 200
rainforest, 150, 189, 191, 192
Ray, John, 6
Rayfield, Lee, 207
Rees, Martin, 86, 88, 95, 100
Reformation, 5
Religion and Science (book), 14
Religious Experiences Today (book), 212
renewable energy, 196, 199, 200, 221
rhizobium, 179
ribosome, 116, 117, 119
River Nile, 10
RNA, 111, 115, 117, 178
messenger RNA/mRNA, 116, 118, 119, 121
pre-mRNA, 121
ribosomal RNA, 116
transfer RNA/tRNA, 117-119
Romanian orphans
brain development of, 155
Rome, 5
early Christians in, 217, 220
Royal Botanic Gardens, Kew, 9, 207
Royal Institution, London, 44
Russell, Bertrand, 14

Index

Sagittarius A*/Sag A*, 32
Saint Hildegard, 3
Salam, Abdus, 207
Samways, John, 214
Scargill House, vii
Schrödinger, Erwin, 33
science
  and the Bible, 161-173
  definition of, 9
  early history, 9, 10
  limitations of, vi, 9-12, 13-39, 206, 219
  scientific method/methodology, vi, 10, 11, 14, 19, 20, 25, 26, 31, 35, 36, 38, 88, 125, 165, 167, 219
scientism, 2, 14
Scopes monkey trial, 163
Scottish crossbill, 132
Scruton, Roger, 152
sea level, 193-195, 197
seed, 131, 132, 139, 183,
serendipity, 10
sex, 137, 138
Sheldrake, Rupert, 13, 27
Siberia, 147, 189
Silent Spring (book), 189
Silurian, 125
Smolin, Lee, 29, 34, 86, 88
Snyder, Michael, 146
Society for Ordained Scientists, 207
Solar System, 25, 26, 29, 53, 65, 66, 164, 169
Solvay Conference (1927), 57
Southgate, Christopher, 187
space-time, 49, 52-56, 60, 64, 65, 67, 69-71, 73, 74
speciation, 128, 133, 139
specified complexity, 164, 167, 168
speech, 150, 151
  FOXP2 gene, 150

spiritual/spirituality, xiii, 9, 15, 76, 101, 102, 104, 106, 156, 157, 172, 186, 187, 199, 202, 208, 211, 213, 215-217
spiritual experiences, 76, 211-214
Staley, Mark, 177
standard model,
  of cosmology, v, 63-65
  of particle physics, v, 226
Stanford University, 146
St Augustine of Hippo, 104, 220
Steady State/SS theory, 59, 60, 63, 98
Steinhardt, Paul, 96
stewards/stewardship
  of creation, 185, 186, 188, 199, 202, 220
Stonehenge, 10
string theory, 38
strong nuclear force, 28, 96, 97
Sumerian myths/texts, 171
Sun
  and fine-tuning, 85
  and heliocentrism, 3, 169
  and planetary motion, 19, 20, 23-25, 28, 52, 66
  and strong nuclear force, 96, 97
  curvature of space-time, 52, 53, 55
  distance from Earth, 48, 110, 167
  Earth's orbit of, 110
  energy output, 50, 66, 68, 92, 96, 98, 113, 135, 177, 192
  formation, 99
  in Genesis, 46, 169-171
  knowledge of, 10
  mass of, 32
  origin of, 65, 99
  stability of, 98
  perihelion, 26
supernova, 99
synthetic biology, 122

tectonic plates, 110
Tertiary, 125, 140, 146
testimony, Graham's, 82-90, 100-106
The God Delusion (book), 16, 17
The Goldilocks Enigma (book), 110
theocentric approach to environment, 188
Theory of Everything, vi, 15, 30, 34-36, 39, 85, 87, 209
The Science Delusion (book), 13, 27
The Theory of Everything (film), 36
The Vital Question (book), 114
Thunberg, Greta, 196
time travel, 48, 63
transitional forms, 134
Triassic, 125
Tyndall, John, 193

ultra-violet radiation, 136
UN Action Summit, 196
UN Climate Change Conference/COP25, 196
uncertainty/uncertainty principle, 33, 34, 68
Universe, v, vi, xii, 4, 9, 11, 15, 22, 26, 27, 31, 32, 36-38, 47, 50, 51, 65, 93-96, 123, 151, 156, 161, 165, 167
  'an unlikely place', 82, 86
  current state, 48, 71-77
  evolution of, 63-67, 161, 164
  finely tuned, 81-100, 109, 110
  ideal for life, vii, 84-86, 91-92, 100
  impression of design, 80, 86, 87, 91, 206, 210, 211, 220
  in Genesis, 45, 46, 168, 169
  non-capricious, 3
  number of galaxies, 14
  order in, 18, 19
  origin of, 3, 28, 43-77
  regulated by laws, 18, 19, 27, 28, 29, 161, 210
  rational, 18, 19
  spiritual dimension, 15
  size of, v, xii, 10, 14
  work of Creator 7, 18, 29, 31, 76, 77, 86, 89, 90, 105, 176, 205-209, 210, 220, 221
Uranus, 26

Venter, Craig, 122
Very Large Telescope/VLT, 93, 94
viruses, 111, 115, 130
visions, 212, 214

Wallace, Alfred Russell, 84, 127
Wall-Schleffler, Cara, 157
warped/curved space, 52-54, 68, 72
warrior gene, 155
water vapour, 193, 194
Watson, James, 112
wave-particle duality, 33, 34
Ways With Words festival, 152
weak nuclear force, 28
Weinberg, Steven, 88
White, Lynn, 188
Wilde, Jane, 36
wildfires, 189, 190, 194
Wilkinson, David, 207
Williams, Julian, 100, 105
Wilson, Harold, 6
Wilson, Robert, 61, 62
WIMPS, 67
Winn, Raynor, 156, 157
Wittgenstein, Ludwig, vi
Woese, Carl, 118
Woolsthorpe, Lincs, 19, 20
World War(s), 6, 192, 193

Index

worship, x, xi, 3, 4, 157, 216, 217, 221
wren, sub-species, 132, 133

Yucatan Peninsula, Mexico, 141
Yucca, 183, 184
Yucca moths, 183, 184

Printed in Great Britain
by Amazon